A
Birdseye View of
MONTICELLO
Designed by Jefferson
Completed in 1805
Drawn by Harrie Wood

THOMAS
JEFFERSON

The jacket,
endpapers, and illustrations
for this volume have been drawn by
HARRIE WOOD

THOMAS JEFFERSON

BY GENE LISITZKY

NEW YORK   MCMXLIX
THE VIKING PRESS

FIRST PUBLISHED OCTOBER 1933

SECOND PRINTING JULY 1934

THIRD PRINTING MARCH 1935

FOURTH PRINTING AUGUST 1937

FIFTH PRINTING JULY 1942

SIXTH PRINTING FEBRUARY 1945

SEVENTH PRINTING MARCH 1947

EIGHTH PRINTING NOVEMBER 1949

TO
ANNA DAUER MANN

THOMAS
JEFFERSON

CONTENTS

I

TWO WORLDS

THE colony of Virginia was divided into two parts so different from each other that they did not seem to belong to the same country. These two parts were right next to each other, had the same governor, were settled by the same people speaking the same language, and yet they might have been on two entirely different continents as far as the life of the two peoples was concerned. These two worlds were known as Tidewater Virginia and Up Country Virginia. The chief reason for their great difference was geography.

If you glance at a map of Virginia, you will see that the

whole western end of it looks as if a great cat had drawn his
paw through the sand, scratching up a long line of parallel
ridges with his claws. This is the Appalachian Mountain
Range, of which the easternmost ridge is in fact called the
Blue Ridge Mountains. From here Virginia's rivers start on
their passage to the sea.

For half the distance to the ocean the rivers are just ordinary streams, not very wide, with here and there rapids and
little waterfalls. The country they flow through is somewhat
hilly, and is called the Piedmont, which means simply "foothills."

Midway to the sea the land becomes a flat plain. Ages ago
this whole eastern half of Virginia sank down so low that
the sea came in and filled the river valleys to the brim. So
now the tides sweep their salt water up the James, the York,
the Potomac, and the Rappahannock, and when the tide is
high these large rivers actually flow backwards! Hence this
part is called the Tidewater country.

The first settlers in this land built their homes on the
eastern plain. They dotted the banks of the "drowned river
valleys" with their great slaveholding plantations. The small
ocean-going ships of those days could ride up with the tide
to the planters' very doorsteps. The ships brought the Tidewater planters the latest books and newspapers from England, the latest styles and gossip from London, the newest
comforts and inventions from Liverpool. They took from the
plantations great cargoes of tobacco, letters to friends in England, and young sons going "home" for an education. In
short, Tidewater planters were first of all Englishmen, who
kept in closer touch with the mother country three thousand
miles away than they did with New York or Boston on the
same seacoast.

When all the eastern plain of Tidewater Virginia had been taken up for plantations, the colonists began to push westward, "up country" into the foothills of the Piedmont. Here the rivers were too narrow, too shallow, and too rapid for ocean-going vessels. Here the news from England was never fresh and scarcely ever personal or important. Here manufactured goods had often to be transported over tiresome overland roads and dangerous trails. Instead of English manor houses there were log cabins; instead of ruffles and lace there were coonskin caps and buckskin shirts; instead of great plantations there were small farm clearings in the forests. A Tidewater planter would go calling on a neighbor in his imported coach, but a Piedmonter went visiting only with a rifle. In short, here you had pioneers, men who were already Americans before they were Englishmen, people to whom "home" might mean the thirteen colonies on the seacoast but never the British Isles.

Thus there were two worlds in Virginia when Thomas Jefferson's father was a young man. To the east were the Tidewater Virginians who were called "Tuckahoes," to the west the Up Country settlers who were known as "Cohees." Geography had made them different. The Jeffersons, father and son, were to be among those who brought them together again. Peter Jefferson helped bring the east to the west by opening up plantations in the Piedmont like those in the Tidewater. He was among the many who carried civilization from the seacoast to the mountains. Thomas Jefferson, on the other hand, brought the west to the east. He carried Americanism from the mountains to the seacoast. He brought back to his father's home country the democratic ideas, the sturdy independence from England, which had grown up among the pioneers.

The father of the third president of the United States was
born in 1707 in Chesterfield County midway between the
aristocratic Tidewater and the primitive Piedmont. The Jeffersons had already been American for some generations, but
had not become large estate owners. Peter grew up to be a
fine example of the typical American colonists of his time.
In a country of strong men he was noted for his physique.
The story is often told how he could take hold of a thousand-
pound hogshead of tobacco in each hand and with one motion up-end them from a lying position. Once when he was
directing three able-bodied slaves while they vainly tried to
pull down an old shack with the aid of a rope tied about it,
he impatiently waved them aside and dragged it down single-
handed.

Peter Jefferson was a self-made man in a self-made land.
Like most of his neighbors he had received no regular school
education, but he managed to read a great deal not only of
the best literature of the time but also of scientific and
technical works. He taught himself mathematics, in which he
became quite proficient, and even passed the examinations
which made him county surveyor. This was also Washington's early profession.

At the age of twenty-four Peter Jefferson was appointed a
magistrate of Goochland County where he then lived. He
was also sheriff of the county, but he continued his surveying
work all this time. This work took him over the whole county, and it was thus that he met William Randolph who became his best friend.

The Randolphs are to this day known as one of the oldest,
most aristocratic families of Tidewater Virginia. William
was therefore a real "Tuckahoe." Indeed, though only by
accident, the estate he had inherited from his father was

called Tuckahoe. The mansion just happened to be built on Tuckahoe Creek very close to the James River. This was pretty far west for a Tidewater plantation, but tobacco raising has a way of quickly wearing out the soil, and the big planters were forever reaching farther and farther into the interior after more fertile land. Even William was beginning to feel crowded on his land though you would have had to travel miles to find the next plantation.

In 1737, when Peter Jefferson was thirty years old, there was started one of those land rushes which have swept America like a fever many times since. The Indians had again been pushed farther inland, this time beyond the Blue Ridge Mountains, and fertile farmlands awaited the first comers who would stake them off and clear them of timber. It was not likely that a young man as active and ambitious as Jefferson would escape the tremendous land hunger that suddenly seized everyone about him. Soon Jefferson and Randolph were following the James River westward in search of new plantations.

A few miles below where the Rivanna empties into the James River, the two pioneers came to Dungeness, the plantation of Isham Randolph, uncle of William. Kept here for a while by the open-handed hospitality for which these estates were so famous, the young men had time to admire the plantation with its hundred slaves and the scientific ideas of its master, for Isham Randolph was fairly well known as a naturalist and botanist. But especially, as far as Peter was concerned, there was Jane Randolph, the oldest daughter of the house, to admire.

Finally the young men continued up the Rivanna until they came to some likely-looking land that had not been taken up. Determined to be neighbors they laid out their claims on opposite sides of the river, not far from where it descended from the mountains. The Rivanna is not a very deep or wide stream at this point, but William still considered it a barrier between them. He therefore made Peter accept four hundred acres of land, suitable for a building site, on his side of the river. To make the transaction legal something had to be given in exchange, so Peter was to pay William with the largest bowl of arrack punch to be had at the Raleigh Tavern in Williamsburg.

Peter Jefferson and William Randolph were the third and fourth settlers in this territory. Their purpose was, of course, the raising of wheat and tobacco. They would have to put their produce on rafts, or on canoes lashed together, and float it downstream to the private dock of some Tidewater plantation where the water was deep enough to float ocean-going ships.

Their first task was to prepare the land for farming. Brushwood had to be cleared, workmen and slaves transported, farm tools bought or borrowed. On his several trips back and forth between Goochland and the Rivanna, Jefferson became a frequent visitor at Dungeness. Isham Randolph's scientific hobbies continued to attract him, and so did Isham Randolph's daughter. In 1739 Peter Jefferson married Jane Randolph, then nineteen years old. The self-educated county surveyor was now the owner of a large plantation and had married into one of the most aristocratic families in Virginia. Now William Randolph and Peter Jefferson were cousins as well as friends.

On the site allotted him for that purpose by Randolph, Jefferson erected the new home for his bride. It was then the custom to name your plantation after some place dear to you in England. So Peter called the plain weatherboarded house on the north bank of the Rivanna "Shadwell" after the London parish in which Jane Randolph had been born. Here, while the wilderness was being conquered, were born Jane, Mary, Thomas, and Elizabeth Jefferson.

Shadwell was a story and a half high. Downstairs were four large rooms and a hall. The half-story above consisted of garret chambers. There were huge chimneys at each end of the house, rising from the ground outside as if they held the house up between them. The farm remained wild country for a long time. Peter could step out any morning and shoot a deer from his porch.

To plant tobacco and wheat, Peter had to remove large tracts of thick forests. The easiest way to do this was simply to start a fire, burn down all the trees at once, and hope that you could control it so that it did not become a raging forest fire. This may sound like a rather wasteful method. But in those days men could afford to waste forests. Even before the coming of the white men, the Indians had used forest fires as a hunting method. They sometimes fired dry leaves in a ring five miles around, fanned the flames toward the center of the burning circle, and thus easily killed all the terrified game that had been driven inward. A lazy frontiersman, rather than have to climb a tree several times to gather its nuts, would sometimes chop it down so that he could do his picking from the ground.

Since tobacco quickly saps the soil of its fertility, an Up Country farmer had to hold some cleared fields in reserve, so that he might continue planting while his old fields were resting up. Jefferson, however, could not very well afford to put his farmhands at the long, heavy task of chopping down trees and pulling stumps on his reserve fields. There was a simpler, easier way if you had lots of land to spare. You

picked a particular plot of ground some winter day before
the sap was rising, and you cut the throat of every tree on that
plot. You cut a deep ring through the bark into the wood all
around the trunk. When spring came, the sap could not rise
above this ring. The tree would never bear leaves. It would
die of starvation; it would rot standing. In a few years, during some wind, it would crash to the ground and become
ready-made firewood. And when you needed it, the plot
would have become ground almost cleared for planting. But
at dusk a forest of these tall trees with their barren limbs
must have been a fearsome sight. When a branch crashed,
it would sound like thunder.

The different fields were separated by fences four feet
tall. Instead of being planted in the ground, the posts of these
fences leaned zigzag against each other. Such a fence could
be lifted in one whole piece and transferred from a worn-
out field to a new clearing. This type of staggering fence gave
rise to the New England expression for a man who tried to
walk while he was drunk. People said: "He is making Virginia fences."

By the year 1744 the region around Shadwell had become
so fairly well populated with new plantations that it was
made into the county of Albemarle. A county needs a government. A government needs officers. Peter Jefferson was
now an old settler, and it is not surprising that he was made
one of the justices of the peace. William Randolph, too, was
honored with the position of sheriff. The ambitious settlers
were now intent on having all the things that go with civilized communities. Peter Jefferson was one of four men chosen
to view and survey the upper James River for a site on which
to build a courthouse as good as the one in Goochland
County which had cost 10,000 pounds of tobacco. There were

plans to follow the courthouse with a prison and, of course, stocks and pillory. These were very soon put to use, for Albemarle was not long to remain a backward Up Country region. A woman named Eleanor Crawley was sentenced to receive fifteen lashes on her bare back for stealing some linen worth about twenty cents; and a Negro slave belonging to a Mr. Cabell, for stealing about a quarter, was branded in the hand and given thirty-nine lashes at the whipping post.

Every frontier colony had military as well as civil duties. The redskins had not ceased entirely to be a menace, and now the French in the Ohio territory were getting too close for comfort. Jefferson was therefore made lieutenant-colonel of the militia under the command of the surveyor, Professor Joshua Fry of William and Mary College.

From these strivings after a civilized mode of life, it may be gathered that living conditions were still rather crude in Albemarle County. Little Tom Jefferson, who had been born on April 13, 1743, did not seem to be in the best position to receive the kind of broad education that his father had in mind for him. But at this time an event took place which, though in itself sad, put an entirely different kind of life within the reach of the Jefferson family.

Even after they were both married, Peter Jefferson and Randolph had continued to see each other as in the old days. Peter would go to see William, dine, spend the night, dine with him again on the second day, and return to Shadwell in the evening. William in the course of a day or two returned his visit, and spent the same length of time in his house. This occurred once every week; and thus they were often together four days out of the seven. But when Tom Jefferson was two years old, William Randolph died. William's dying request to his best friend and cousin was that Peter

should take care of the three children he left behind. He
asked especially that Peter should look out for the education
of his small son, Thomas Mann Randolph, and that, the better to do this, Peter should move to Tuckahoe, Randolph's
estate in Goochland County, with his whole family. All these
last wishes of his dying friend Peter faithfully fulfilled.

The Jefferson family moved into Tuckahoe on horseback.
Though Tom was then only two years old, he could later
look back to this trip as his first memory, a memory of himself lying on a pillow across a horse's back. Thus the Up
Country child was introduced to life on a Tidewater plantation.

How full Mrs. Jefferson's heart must have been as they
approached Tuckahoe through the avenue of beautiful elms!
It was six years now since she had last lived in a lovely old
house like this, surrounded by English gardens with rose
bushes, lilies, and bridal wreath. Once in the house they
found themselves on the brow of a wooded hill with a magnificent view of the James River and of the plantation
around. Here it would be cool in the hottest summers.

Tuckahoe was a typical Virginian manor house built of
wood and brick in the form of an H. It really looked like
two separate but similar houses connected by a long saloon
or drawing room. Each of the two houses, or, more properly
speaking, wings, was two stories high, and the saloon unit-
ing them had a very lofty ceiling. It was an ideal arrangement for guests, for they could have practically a whole house
to themselves. And Virginia planters were always entertaining visitors.

In the ceiling of the saloon was an immense chandelier
which could be brightly lit with candles whenever there was

held one of the frequent neighborhood balls. Balls and dances
gave the young Virginians who lived so far apart a chance to
meet each other, and so dancing was considered a very important part of every girl's and every boy's education. Sometimes teachers were brought into a neighborhood to organize
dancing schools. The young people would meet each week
in the saloon of a different plantation and there be taught the
steps of the minuets, the reels, and the country dances.

Now there were seven children in Tuckahoe, enough for
plenty of fun, as well as enough to make up a school. Besides
Tom, there were his two older sisters Jane and Mary, his baby
sister Elizabeth, and the three Randolph children: Judith,
Mary, and Thomas Mann. There was a little schoolhouse
right on the grounds of the estate. It is standing to this day.
Here at the age of five Tom began to learn reading, writing,
and ciphering.

Writing was the most important of the children's studies.
A man was not considered really educated unless he wrote a
clear, beautiful hand. One schoolmaster in Virginia was
thought to be an excellent teacher until it was discovered
that a pupil of his wrote a better hand than he did. Whereupon the poor man, his reputation for scholarship ruined,
was compelled to resign. Tom made rapid progress in this
art, and his handwriting always remained fine and legible.

After school and on holidays the estate made a glorious
playground. The children's games sometimes had queer
names, like Thread and Needle, Scotch Hoppers, Stone
Poison Tag. Tom's sisters and cousins played house and imi-
tated their mothers and servants at work. They tied a string
to a chair and then ran buzzing back and forth to imitate the
colored women spinning. They got straws and pretended
they were knitting. They took rags and washed them without

water. They got sticks and splintered one end of them for brushes, or, as they called them then, clamps, and scrubbed the floor.

Marbles and kites were boys' favorites even then. Not far from Tuckahoe was a mill pond where Tom skated in winter. In summer there was, of course, swimming, in which the boys might practice the overhand stroke learned from the Indians; white men had used only the breast stroke.

Back of the big house were apple and peach orchards and a grape arbor. But the most exciting of all were the many outhouses, far enough away from the big house to leave it an unobstructed view on all sides.

Scattered over the estate were several of these small buildings. There was the soap house, where all the fat was saved during the year, to be boiled down into home-made soap in great copper vessels. There was the smokehouse where the famous Virginia hams might be curing. There were the different tobacco houses where the leaves were stripped and stacked and dried. There were the stables and the barns. And still farther back were the slave quarters.

On Sundays the roads would be full of horseback riders and coaches on the way to church and the rivers alive with boats on the same errand. The Jeffersons sometimes went to church in Richmond, which could be reached by boat. Church-going in Virginia was not like church-going in Puritan New England. Here it was a festive affair, a chance to meet all one's neighbors as much as to worship. The planters could exchange business news and the latest English newspapers, so that the church steps became a combined stock exchange and circulating library. A Virginian was always ready to discuss tobacco prices and fine horses, and this was his best opportunity. The women had English styles to talk about. They came with silk scarves wrapped about their faces, only their eyes showing, looking as if all the girls in the world had suddenly got the same toothache. But it was only their milk-white complexions they were protecting.

The sermons were usually not very long, and there was time afterwards for gay, chattering groups of planters and their wives to gather outside and invite each other home for Sunday dinner.

For seven years Tom Jefferson lived in Tuckahoe, in this sort of society, learning to be a gentleman, although, from his father's example, never ceasing to be a frontier boy. Here began his love for a life lived among beautiful surroundings.

A Tidewater boy, like the son of an English squire, began to be a gentleman at about the age of six. As soon as he started going to school, Tom would be given his first dress suit, exactly like his father's, velvet or silk breeches, and coat with a flowered waistcoat, silk stockings, silver buckles, lace stock and ruffles, and a cocked hat. Some boys had their heads shaved so that they could wear powdered wigs with a long pigtail tied with a black silk bow. Most girls and boys wore corsets from the age of five, real instruments of torture made of steel and canvas. Of course the children did not play or go to school in such regalia, but they were expected to wear them at their frequent formal parties.

The heart of Tidewater existence was tobacco. This weed, which the Indians had taught the white settlers to smoke, was now in great demand all over Europe. There were fortunes to be made in growing and selling it. The Virginians lived almost entirely on tobacco exports to England. Tobacco even became a sort of money with which a preacher's salary could be paid or a crinoline skirt be bought.

It was tobacco, too, that brought the English ships riding

up to the planter's doorstep to collect his year's crop. Then
the whole plantation—grownups, children, and slaves—would
stream down to the wharf in the greatest excitement, for the
captain usually came laden with gifts and messages from
friends and relatives in England. He might bring gooseberry
and currant shrubs for the homesick Virginians who wished
to plant them and make their American homes seem more
like England. Gifts like these were called "tokens" and were
sent free of charge.

Instead of fashion books, Paris dress designers in those
days used little jointed dolls which they dressed completely
in the latest fashions. Every ship that arrived from London
would be sure to bring one of these Paris dolls—not for
the children, but for the colonial dames. There might even
be a spinet on board, or a coach, or new clothes for the children. Sometimes when a pair of slippers came for a little
seven-year-old girl it would be so long since they had been
ordered that they no longer fitted the growing child. Even a
grown man might have become much fatter or thinner after
the several months since he had sent his measurements to a
London tailor.

In return for English tokens, the Virginians would send,
along with their tobacco, American plants—hickory nuts for
tulips, and pawpaws for anemones. For English claret they
would return American cider. A favorite token to send was
money, which your friend across the ocean was to spend in
drinking your health.

A great Tidewater plantation required many field hands,
but working men were hard to find in the colonies where any
man might become a plantation owner like Peter Jefferson.
Thus, on account of tobacco, many Negro slaves were kidnaped from their African homes and sold in Virginia. There

were times when the Negroes outnumbered the white people in this colony. Once started, it seemed impossible to do without Negro slavery; it was so much cheaper than free labor and so much easier to get. A common laborer would have to be paid twenty-five to thirty cents a day with board and lodging. In those days a quarter was a lot of money. For thirty-five or forty dollars you could buy a slave for life, and all his children would also be your slaves.

Many Virginians did not feel entirely happy at having to own slaves. Such men were more likely to treat their slaves with some kindness, but even the kindest masters were far from pampering their field workers. Slave labor was cheaper because you could save as much as you pleased on the clothing and food of the Negroes, many of whom were still frightened savages barely able to speak English.

At Tuckahoe the Jefferson family had been increased by two more sisters, Martha and Lucy. Now Peter Jefferson was ready to go back to his own estate at Shadwell, having carried out his friend Randolph's wishes. Tom was nine years old now and fit to go on with more advanced schooling. In 1752 Peter sent his son to live with the Reverend William Douglas, a Scotch clergyman in Louisa County, who taught Greek, Latin, and French. The rest of his family he took back to his Up Country home in Albemarle County.

When Peter Jefferson came back to Shadwell, he was already a man of some prominence in Virginia. In 1749 he had been commissioned to assist Professor Joshua Fry in surveying the boundary line between Virginia and North Carolina. These two men had then drawn up the first complete and reliable map of Virginia. So it is not surprising that, when Fry died during the French and Indian Wars, leaving his sur-

veying instruments to Jefferson in his will, Peter was sent in
his stead as representative of Albemarle County to the House
of Burgesses. Fry's command was taken over by the twenty-
two-year-old Colonel George Washington. In 1755 Peter Jefferson was also made County Lieutenant, or governor, of
Albemarle, a position of great responsibility during the
border wars.

Good scholar though he was, Tom looked forward to the
vacations he spent in Shadwell with keen eagerness. He was
growing up into a tall, strong youngster, loving exercise and
the out-of-doors. This trait his father encouraged to the ut-
most, first by his own example and exploits, and secondly by
giving his son a gun, a horse, and much instruction in wood-
craft. Tom's summers became one long series of excursions,
on foot through the forest, on horse, or on the river in a
boat.

It was no hardship for Tom to give up the stately mansion
of Tuckahoe for the clapboard house at Shadwell, for Shadwell was set in the midst of a boy's paradise. Without leaving
the estate Tom could roam through virgin forest and hunt
small game, such as gray squirrels. Even in the old abandoned
clearings there were sure to be wild turkeys scratching for
worms. Tom never went walking without his gun. It was always possible for an Up Country boy to meet up with an
otter, a panther, a bear, or a wolf. There was a bounty of
140 pounds of tobacco for the scalp of an old wolf. And it
was every boy's ambition some day to shoot a buffalo, for
this huge animal had not yet entirely disappeared from the
Virginia woods. Some of the early settlers had knitted stockings from buffalo hair, and from its horns the Indians still
made spoons.

Next to their ability to ride, Virginia boys would pride themselves on being good shots. In their shooting matches one brave boy might hold the piece of wood which was the target at arm's length or between his legs while another boy potted at it. Or they would organize moonlight expeditions, accompanied by servants and dogs, to hunt possum and coon. The boy who went fishing never had to return home with empty hands. The waters were stored with trout, bass, and perch.

The oak and hickory forests were the homes of many small birds—cardinals, goldfinch, wood-thrush, and mocking birds. Sometimes wild pigeons would fly past in such enormous flocks that they darkened the skies and made people indoors think there was a thunderstorm coming. They would perch on the trees in such numbers that the limbs would break under their weight. The Virginians did not waste powder on them then, but struck them down with poles. In autumn came the wild ducks. From their hoarse call the Indians named them Cohunks, and the Indian year began with the moon of the Coming of the Cohunks, which was in October.

An old woodsman like Peter Jefferson would surely know how to make his son's boyhood a happy one, and how to make Shadwell the most interesting place in the world. Besides hunting and riding and boating and Indian lore, he taught his son to appreciate the beauties of the country around him. In spring you could hear the sapsucker working away at a sugar tree or the great crested woodpecker drumming on the yellow poplars deep in the forest. Brilliant butterflies and no less brilliant humming birds flitted among the red flowering maples, sassafras, dogwood, locusts, redbuds, chestnuts, fringe trees, tulip poplars, cucumber trees. wild

lilies, May apples, and the pawpaw trees, from whose wood
when dried the Indians made fire sticks. At night the fireflies
became so bright that they sometimes caused the late traveler
to run into a tree by dazzling his sight. The pompous bull-
frogs and dainty treefrogs also did their best to turn night into
day.

Peter Jefferson had made many Indian friends on his surveying trips. Ontassetie, the great Cherokee warrior and orator, was always Peter's guest on his trips to and from Williamsburg, where he made treaties with the whites. On one
occasion when Ontassetie made a farewell oration to his people because he was about to leave for England, Tom was
present at the campfire. The moonlit scene made a lasting
impression on the boy, and the oratory which he did not
understand moved him none the less with awe and admiration. Not far from Shadwell were the deserted remains of
an Indian town from which the boys dug up many an arrow
point, stone hatchet, and stone tobacco pipe. There was also
one of those mysterious Indian mounds, which are supposed
to be ancient burial grounds; at the age of ten Tom had seen
many Indians make a pilgrimage there.

Now in spite of the wild surroundings Tom did not suffer
the hardships of real pioneer life; unlike Lincoln, for instance,
he knew only its pleasures. After all there were a great many
slaves on the plantation to carry on all the work, to do all the
chores, the cleaning and washing and cooking, the soap and
candle making, the butchering and farming. Tom did not
have to fill the wood box, or milk the cows, or groom the horses.
And although Shadwell was not a real Tidewater mansion,
Peter had by this time added two wings to the clapboard
house, so that there was plenty of room for the constant
stream of visitors.

In August 1757, Peter Jefferson died. Fourteen-year-old Tom became head of the family, consisting of his widowed mother, his six sisters, and his baby brother Randolph. To the latter Peter in his will had bequeathed a smaller estate he owned on the James River known as Snowden; to his oldest son he left Shadwell. Tom was now a large landed proprietor. Of course, until he was a little older, he would be under the guardianship of one of his father's friends, John Harvie.

One of Peter Jefferson's last requests was that Tom should have a classical education. The self-taught pioneer was determined that the son, whom he had himself taught so much, should not lack for what the father had always craved. So Tom's guardian sent him off to live and study with the Reverend James Maury, "a correct classical scholar," who had a log-cabin school only fourteen miles from Shadwell in Louisa County. Dr. Maury was to become a teacher of Presidents indeed, for he later had as pupils James Madison and James Monroe. He was a man of broad mind; for instance, though himself an Episcopal minister and living in an age of intolerance, there was nothing he detested so much as religious persecution. In Parson Maury's log schoolhouse Tom studied Latin for the next two years.

The schoolboy continued to come home for his vacations. He no longer had his father's companionship, but he still had the habits his father had encouraged—roaming through the woods with a gun, riding over the plantation on horseback. He grew into even closer comradeship with his older sister Jane. Their favorite evening entertainment was the playing of duets, she at the harpsichord, the eighteenth-century piano, and he on his violin, while they both sang psalms. Psalms were then nearly all the songs that youngsters knew.

The loneliness of his days was now relieved by the friendship he struck up with Dabney Carr, a neighboring boy of his own age and with similar tastes. The most exciting book for boys in the Shadwell library was undoubtedly Anson's *Voyages around the World,* the tale of an English captain who had made one of the most adventurous trips around the world in the whole history of seafaring. Now Tom had someone to tell his great desire to travel; someone to share a passion for foreign lands that was never to leave him all his life. Tom also brought Dabney to his secret retreat. Across the river from Shadwell, on the land that Peter had first staked out, there was a hill about six hundred feet high. In Italian you would call a little mountain like that a *monticello.*

The boys would climb its side and build a campfire under a particular oak tree. While Dabney roasted the pigeons or partridges they had shot, Tom would be mixing some cornmeal into cakes, which he would then bake like the hoecakes the Negroes made. Then they would both sit under the tree before the fire telling each other their dreams and ambitions. Tom knew what he wanted most after traveling. When he grew up he would build a grand house on the peak of this "little mountain." It was to be *their* little mountain. They solemnly pledged each other that whoever died first would be buried by the other under their favorite oak.

II

WILLIAM AND MARY

January 14, 1760

To John Harvie.
Sir:

I was at Colo. Peter Randolph's about a fortnight ago, and my schooling falling into Discourse, he said he thought it would be to my Advantage to go to the College, and was desirous I should go, as indeed I am myself for several Reasons. In the first place, as long as I stay at the Mountain, the loss of one-fourth of my Time is inevitable, by Company's coming here and detaining me from School. And likewise my Absence will in a great measure, put a Stop to so much Company, and by that Means lessen the

Expenses of the Estate in Housekeeping. And on the other Hand
by going to College, I shall get a more universal Acquaintance,
which may hereafter be serviceable to me: and I suppose I can
pursue my Studies in the Greek and Latin as well there as here,
and likewise learn something of the Mathematics. I shall be glad
of your Opinion, And remain, Sir, your most humble servant,

THOMAS JEFFERSON.

THESE must have been just the right arguments to use
with Mr. Harvie, for that same month, when he was
not yet seventeen years old, found Tom Jefferson riding to
Williamsburg to enter College. The college was, of course,
William and Mary. There were two other colleges in the
colonies, Harvard in Massachusetts and Yale in Connecticut,
but Southern boys were more likely to go to England for
their education than to New England.

Tom rode through the woods on horseback. The newspapers were full of daring robberies committed on lonely
roads, of forests swarming with highwaymen, but in England,
not America. There were not enough wretchedly poor people
in the colonies to make criminals of this type, and so hold-ups
in the American wilderness had never been heard of.

But Tom had other dangers and inconveniences to fear.
There were great numbers of dead pines in the woods, and in
windy weather one might crash down on the road and cause
a nasty accident to horse or rider. Huge trunks lay strewn over
the trail, and sometimes travelers had to turn half a dozen
times in a single mile because the horses could not jump
them. Tom need not expect to find bridges across the streams.
If he were lucky, he might find a ford to wade over; if not,
he would have to swim his horse across.

Otherwise, there was very little in the way of adventure to
meet on the road to Williamsburg, for all that it was a fairly

lonely road. A heavy trampling in the underbrush might be a deer or a bear, but usually it meant only a runaway cow with her calf. If it was a cow run wild, Tom must report it in his next letter home, for each of the neighboring planters was entitled to a certain share of all such animals. When he was near a plantation, Tom might meet an occasional team of oxen going into the forest for a supply of firewood. And later, nearer the town, he would pass ladies and gentlemen riding in their carriages.

But most of the time Tom was riding through the unbroken gloom and winter solitude of a forest. The black burnt forests were the worst. They were caused by travelers and squatters not troubling to see whether their great campfires were put out when they reharnessed their teams in the early morning. When such fires spread to the trees from the dead leaves, whole mountains might sometimes blaze for three or four months.

Fortunately for Tom, all along the road to Williamsburg the Jeffersons had planter friends with whom he could stay the night. For the few inns, or "ordinaries," as they were called, were unpleasant places to sleep in. In the middle of the night a belated traveler and a perfect stranger to you might walk into your room, undress, and without a by-your-leave, crawl into bed beside you.

Williamsburg was the largest community Tom had ever seen. It was then the capital of Virginia and boasted two hundred wooden houses; brick and stone houses were considered unhealthy to live in. Through the center of town ran the very wide main street, about three quarters of a mile long. At one end stood the college and at the other the capitol building. Midway between the two was a square on which

was situated a church and some public buildings. This street,
or rather road, for of course there was no pavement, was dusty
by day and unlighted by night.

At last Tom Jefferson had reached the goal of his travels
and of his ambitions. As he rode up to William and Mary
College, the place was not entirely strange to him. An uncle
of his had once been its president, and Tom knew something
of its romantic history.

After the visit of the Indian princess Pocahontas, King
James had become interested in the education of her people
and he had founded a school for Indian children here. But
the people the king had sent over to found the school were
all massacred by the Indians, who seem to have been extremely unwilling pupils.

However, seventy years later the school was again established, part of the money then raised for it coming from
pirates. The first president of the college, while still in England raising funds, persuaded the government to release from
prison two notorious pirates on condition that they gave
part of their ill-gotten wealth to his school. The Cherokee
Indians were finally prevailed upon to allow one of their
children to be taught reading, writing, and sums. They sent
the chief's small son to Williamsburg. The overjoyed teachers
did all they could to make him happy, but the little Cherokee
grew more and more sullen and refused to learn any of the
white man's teaching. Then one day he was gone. The town
was terrified. If the Cherokees learned of the disappearance
of their chieftain's son, they would surely go on the warpath.
But the Indians never came, though they had heard of the
runaway. They had heard about it from the truant himself.
The small boy had found his way unerringly through the
forests to the faraway wigwam of his parents.

At the time Jefferson came to William and Mary, it had grown into three schools. There was first of all the original Indian school which now had two teachers and eight redskin pupils, and to which the children of Williamsburg also went during the day as an elementary school. Then there was the Latin school, or high school, which the boys attended until they were about fifteen, learning Latin and Greek from two teachers. And finally there was the college proper, like our modern college, with two professors besides the president of the entire college. All three schools had classrooms in the same building.

To enter the college Tom had to take a public examination. In the public assembly hall of the building, young Jefferson faced his future masters and the school president and answered aloud the questions that were put to him to prove what education he had already had. A minister in the town who was skilled in the ancient languages also examined him. According to the entrance rules, Tom must here show himself "not to be a blockhead or a lazy fellow." But as a result of this test Tom showed himself to be a brilliant scholar, and so the masters decided to admit him at once into the third or Junior year. Tom could now proudly don the cap and gown of the advanced students.

Tom installed himself in the dormitory building. The professors, who were not allowed to be married, also lived here. The rest of the household consisted of the bursar—who kept the college money in a strongbox in his room, for there were no banks—a housekeeper, a cook, a nurse, and a stocking-mender who was kept busy all day with the long hose of the men and boys. Tom's board cost him $65 a year, which he could pay in money or tobacco. The food was plain but plentiful: fresh and salt meat every day, and pies and puddings three times a week. There was a strict rule against serving salt butter, for as in many countries of Europe today only sweet butter was considered decent food.

Like any college Freshman nowadays Tom had to learn the campus rules. Some of our colleges forbid the students to keep automobiles, and for the same reasons William and Mary forbade its scholars from keeping race-horses, which was a difficult rule for a Virginia gentleman to abide by. Besides the ban on race-horses in college or town the students were warned "to be in no way concerned in making races, or in betting or abetting or making others play, or betting at ye billiard or other gaming tables, or keeping cards or dice, or fighting cocks, on pain of ye severe animadversion or punishment." In spite of which there was secretly a considerable amount of betting and keeping of game cocks, and boys had occasionally to be expelled from college.

Going to ordinaries was also forbidden, except at the invitation of parents or friends for a treat of pancakes and cider. But at the Raleigh Tavern, where Peter Jefferson had made a bargain with his friend Randolph over the biggest bowl of arrack punch, the town's big dances were held, and to these the boys might go.

Truth to tell, Tom found that most of the boys had not come to college to do a great deal of studying. As a whole the students were a boisterous crew. They kept dogs and guns in their rooms. Their minds were pretty constantly on cock fights, stables, dances, and fights with the town boys. These last were a regular occurrence, especially on Sundays, when the professors, who were all ministers, had gone about their various church duties.

Eight of the college students kept, besides their dogs and guns, slaves as valets to brush their silk and velvet suits, to polish their buttons, and to keep their rooms in some order. Tom at once decided to keep his own clothes in order. There was something he disliked about having a servant to help him put on his waistcoat.

Tom differed from most of the students of his class and rank in other ways, too. For one thing he took a passionate interest in his studies. For him college was an adventure, in which his mind did exciting things instead of his body. Whatever he learned was like an exploration into the great unknown world from which he had been shut off in his backwoods plantation. He found that the discovery of new ideas, great thoughts, scientific problems and solutions could be more thrilling than bear tracks in the forest, more exhilarating than a race on horseback.

But the course of studies the students were required to take was not made to be interesting, and Tom might very soon have lost his fresh excitement if one of his two professors had not then chanced to be Dr. William Small. Jefferson in after life never forgot the debt he owed to Dr. Small. All of Tom's courses—and it must be remembered that he was only seventeen years old—came under the head of philosophy. One of his two professors taught him "moral philosophy," which included rhetoric (grammar, composition, and elocution), logic (the rules of correct thinking), and ethics (the principles of morality and conduct). Dr. Small, the other professor, taught him "natural philosophy," by which was meant mathematics and science (chiefly physics and astronomy).

Professor Small, when he came over from Scotland, had introduced a new method of conducting classes in the colonies. Before his time the students in colleges were taught in just the same way they were in grade school, that is, they

memorized their lessons and then recited them in class.
Dr. Small brought in the lecture system. He did all the talking himself and let the students ask *him* questions. In this
way the bright boys were not held back by the less bright, and
each learned as much as he was capable of.

It was not long before Dr. Small noticed that a certain pair
of intelligent gray eyes were fixed most intently upon him
while he lectured. They belonged to the red-haired lad who
now and then asked him a keen question. Dr. Small sought
this boy out after class. He took him out for walks. Soon Tom
was his daily companion, and a new world was opened to the
boy.

Tom's father had had, for a planter in Piedmont, a fairly
good library. From it Tom had learned most of what he knew
of English history, of the Bible, of English literature, and of
travel. But there had been no books on science. Professor
Small was a friend of Erasmus Darwin, the eminent scientist
and grandfather of the great Charles Darwin. James Watt,
who was to invent the steam engine, was also his friend.
From Small's conversation Tom got his first glimpse of the
mighty labors of science in its attempt to draw a complete
picture of the world in which we live.

Not far from the college was a beautiful mansion known
as the "Palace." It was the residence of Francis Fauquier,
Lieutenant-Governor of Virginia. When Professor Small offered to introduce his pupil to the Governor, Tom was enchanted, not only because Fauquier was renowned for his brilliance, nor merely because of the social rank the Governor
held, but also because of the romantic history of the man,
with which Tom had some acquaintance.

For this Fauquier had actually been a friend of Admiral

Anson, the author of *Voyages around the World!* It was enough to make any man glamorous to boys like Tom Jefferson and Dabney Carr. Shortly after returning to England from his circumnavigation of the globe, Anson had met a young man named Fauquier. They played cards together, and in one night Fauquier lost to Anson the entire fortune he had inherited from his father. Much later Anson recommended Fauquier for the governorship of Virginia.

The story went that this was not the last fortune Fauquier had dropped at the gaming tables. He was even accused by some of having brought the passion for cards and dice to Virginia. But it did not need Fauquier to tell the colonists that in every coffee house in England nothing could be heard above the shuffle of cards and the rattle of the dice-box, and what was known to be the fashion in England was soon sure to become the fad of the Southern colony.

Fauquier was one of those typically clever men of the eighteenth century who wanted to know everything and to enjoy everything. He had been a director of the Bank of England and had written an important work on taxation. He was interested in physics and was a Fellow, or member, of the Royal Society, England's famous scientific academy; he sent this society notes about Virginia, including one account of a peculiar hailstorm. He was an accomplished musician. In short, he was everything that young Tom admired and wanted to be.

To top all, Fauquier, when Tom was finally introduced to him, proved to be one of the most charming of men. He seemed to be as genuinely delighted to meet the boy as was Tom to meet him. Evidently Small had already spoken to him of the lad with the exceptionally fine mind. When he heard that Tom played the violin, Fauquier asked him to come and take part in the musicales which were held once a week at the Palace.

After a few meetings Fauquier found the young man's intelligence to be all that Professor Small had claimed, and soon he made him one of his intimate friends. That part of Tom's education which Professor Small, or any school for that matter, could not give him he owed to Governor Fauquier. Not only did Fauquier lend the boy French and English books from his library; he also acted as Tom's model for a man of the world. A bright boy can learn much by watching. Tom observed the Governor's unfailing courtesy, the innumerable little politenesses that marked the trained gentleman of that day. The drawing room was a serious business in the eighteenth century; it was the battle-ground of wit and the showplace of manners. Probably without knowing it, Tom could not help but pick up a considerable polish on his frequent visits to the Palace, for as his model he had one of the most polished gentlemen in Virginia.

Professor Small introduced Tom to still another important friend of his college days. George Wythe was a brilliant young lawyer of about thirty, self-educated, but probably the finest Latin and Greek scholar in Virginia. These four—Fauquier, Small, Wythe, and Jefferson—made up a sort of informal little club that met once a week for dinner at the Governor's Palace. Surely there must have been something unusual about a boy seventeen years old to make three such learned and witty men accept him as an equal.

What discussions they had when the table was cleared and the wine served! Fauquier spoke as beautifully as he wrote. He spoke of London, of Paris, of the theaters, of concerts, of beautiful buildings, paintings, statues. He told stories he had heard from Anson of adventures on land and sea, of strange peoples, strange customs and places. And the others, too, talked of classical wisdom, of the latest scientific discoveries, of politics, and of the writing of books. The backwoods boy from Shadwell had indeed plunged into the great world of his dreams. But now Williamsburg could no longer satisfy him. He must now see with his own eyes these foreign countries, these great cities, attend concerts where there were over twenty musicians, look at ancient buildings that housed famous beautiful pictures.

Of course, Tom made friends of his own age in college. Dabney Carr, his old chum from back home, came to Williamsburg, and some of his mother's relatives lived in the college town. But chief among his new friends was John Page, who, like Jefferson, was later to become one of the first governors of the State of Virginia. The two future governors became very intimate, and Tom confided in John all the heartaches that were being caused in him by Rebecca Burwell, the girl with whom he had fallen in love.

Rebecca and her equally beautiful cousin Fanny Burwell lived at Carter's Grove, the most beautiful estate near Williamsburg. Tom paid as many visits as he dared to this mansion of blue and red glazed brick on the top of a hill overlooking the James River. There he might hope to find Rebecca alone of an afternoon and get her to walk and chat with him on the beautifully laid terraces of the lawn. But on the whole these meetings did not seem to bring Tom much happiness, for his belle was a bit of a flirt, and he never knew from one day to the next how much of a favorite of hers he was. Once in despair he told Page: "As for admiration I am sure the man who powders most, perfumes most, embroiders most" (he meant, of course, the one who had the most embroidery on his coat), "and talks the most nonsense is admired."

It may have been because Tom was showing off as the fine gentleman before Rebecca, or because he was keeping up with his other fine friends; whatever the cause, Tom overran his allowance in his first college year. Certainly he was a dandy at this time, with his powdered hair and the immaculate lace of his ruffles. When a horse was brought him to ride, he would pass his handkerchief over its coat, and, if the fine cambric showed a speck of dust, he would loftily send the groom after another mount. Books, too, took as much of Tom's money as clothes and horses.

He had to write his guardian that, if he had spent more of the income from his father's estate than was his share, the amount should be deducted from his portion of the property. He had no desire to make his family pay for his good times. But his guardian wrote back: "No, not if you have sowed your wild oats in this manner, Tom; the estate can well afford to pay your expenses."

Twice a year Williamsburg was crowded with people and very gay. These were the times when the general assemblies were held to make the laws for the colony and when the law courts were in progress. The wives and daughters of the lawmakers and lawyers accompanied them to the capital decked out in new clothes and prepared for a brilliant social season. Then studies were all but entirely neglected at the college. The laundresses were kept busy starching ruffles, and Mrs. Foster, the stocking-mender, was nearly out of her mind repairing all the boys' hose at the same time. The Apollo Room of the Raleigh Tavern blazed with candles nearly every night while the gentlefolk held their balls and card parties.

Tom could often be found in the thick of this gay assemblage dancing the minuet. The minuet was a graceful dance requiring much more than merely nimble feet, for during the pauses the paying of pretty compliments to your lady partner and the gallant kissing of her hand were both important to a successful evening.

That winter a troupe of English players came to Williamsburg—real actors and actresses, who gave plays by Shakespeare, Marlowe, Fielding, Addison, and Steele. The program was changed every night, and after each play there always came a short comic skit, so that the theater-starved Virginians could within a week fill up with drama to their heart's content.

Performances began at seven. There were no box-offices and no reserved seats. Tickets were to be had at the Raleigh Tavern, and ladies were advised to send their maids early in the afternoon to hold their seats for them. For hours the servants sat tight in the box chairs until they were relieved by their mistresses and maybe allowed to go into the gallery. The boxes in which sat the ladies and gentlemen hung directly over the stage on each side of the auditorium. They sat on velvet cushions and leaned over velvet railings. What is now the orchestra was then called the pit, and it was jammed with movable seats bought by the middle classes. The gallery, where servants and poor people went, had no seats at all.

But the place to be was on the stage itself. Here Tom and the other young bloods sat or stood in the wings, and probably got in the actors' way. Occasionally, a youth who knew what was what in the London world of fashion would try to engage an actress in conversation between her speeches. But this sort of interruption did not appeal to the Virginians who had mostly come actually to hear the play. The brash young gallant would receive black looks from the boxes and hisses from the gallery. Among the most brilliant of the visitors to the theater, Tom would note the handsome Colonel George Washington, already famous at twenty-nine as a veteran hero of the French and Indian Wars.

Another period of gayety was the Christmas vacation. On his way home to spend the holidays Tom stopped at the plantation of Colonel Nathan Dandridge. Among the host of young people Tom's attention was caught by a man who seemed to enjoy a great deal of popularity, though by his country speech and his awkward appearance he would seem to be a little out of place in the crowd of young dandies. This man was telling a story that the group around him met with shouts of admiring laughter. Tom was immediately attracted by the tall, thin figure, slightly stooped, the pale face and homely features; only the deep-set gray eyes were beautiful.

Tom learned by asking that this man's name was Patrick Henry, a near neighbor of Colonel Dandridge's. With the little money he had inherited from his father Mr. Henry had bought a country store, which had just failed. Tom noticed that Mr. Henry talked like a backwoodsman, saying "naiteral" for natural and "larnin" for learning.

In the fortnight that Tom stayed at Colonel Dandridge's he and Patrick Henry became good friends. Henry was intending to make a fresh start of some sort in Williamsburg and promised to call on Tom when he came there.

The second college year passed much as the first with Tom perhaps studying even harder. The more he knew the more he wanted to know. He began to regret that there were only twenty-four hours in the day. Dr. Small continued to encourage this thirst for knowledge in him, and was forever opening new doors to learning. But at last the time came when the college had no more to offer him.

Tom graduated from William and Mary on April 25, 1762, when he was just nineteen years of age. His Latin and Greek were now excellent and he could read the most difficult authors in these languages with ease. Though he could not yet speak French very well, he read it extensively. He promised himself to learn, besides, the Spanish, Italian, German, and the American Indian languages.

He was six feet tall now—he was still to grow two more inches—and very slim. His freckles were disappearing, but his skin, the thin skin of the redhead, peeled when exposed to the wind and burned easily in the sun. His nose had a turned-up bump on the end of it and his face was too angular to be handsome but it immediately impressed everyone with its intelligence.

III

BELINDA AND THE LAW

TOM was beginning to believe he might have some success with Rebecca after all, for he had received from her a beautifully cut watch paper. What was his dismay when this token was destroyed during the first Christmas holidays after his graduation! He had stopped at Fairfield on his way home to Shadwell. He tells of the accident in a letter to John Page, the style of which is very grand.

Dear Page:

This very day, to others the day of greatest mirth and jollity, sees me overwhelmed with more and greater misfortunes than

have befallen a descendant of Adam for these thousand years
past, I am sure; and perhaps, after excepting Job, since the creation of the world. I am sure if there is such a thing as a Devil
in this world, he must have been here last night, and have had
some hand in contriving what happened to me. Do you think
the cursed rats (at his instigation, I suppose) did not eat up my
pocketbook, which was in my pocket, within a foot of my head?
And not contented with plenty for the present, they carried away
my jemmy-worked silk garters and half a dozen new minuets I
had just got, to serve, I suppose, as provision for the winter. But
of this I should not have accused the Devil (because, you know,
rats will be rats) if something worse had not happened. You know
it rained last night. When I went to bed, I laid my watch in the
usual place, and going to take her up after I arose this morning,
I found her in the same place, it's true, but all afloat in water,
let in at a leak in the roof of the house, and as silent and still as
the rats that had eat my pocketbook. It's my opinion that the
Devil came and bored the hole over it on purpose. Well, as I was
saying, my poor watch had lost her speech. I should not have
cared much for this, but something worse attended it; the subtle
particles of the water with which the case was filled, had, by
their penetration, so overcome the cohesion of the particles of the
paper, of which my dear picture and watch paper were composed,
that, in attempting to take them out to dry them, good God!
my cursed fingers gave them such a rent, as I fear I never shall
get over. And now, although the picture may be defaced, there
is so lively an image of her imprinted in my mind, that I shall
think of her too oft, I fear, for my peace of mind; and too often,
I am sure, to get through old Coke [the writer of a famous textbook on the law] this winter; for God knows, I have not seen
him since I packed him up in my trunk in Williamsburg. Well,
Page, I do wish the Devil had old Coke, for I am sure I was never
so tired of an old dull scoundrel in my life. . . .

And the long chatty letter goes on in this vein for many
more pages, until Tom finally comes to the point. He wants
John to ask Rebecca for a new watch paper for him.

Tell her that I should esteem it much more though it were a plain round one, than the nicest in the world cut by other hands.

Watches in those days were often bought in two parts: the works or insides from a watchmaker and the outer case separately from a goldsmith. Sometimes these two parts would not fit exactly, and the watch would rattle loosely in its case. To prevent this, an inside watch case of paper was made, and the cutting out and decorating of these watch papers was one of the accomplishments of the ladies, like embroidery and playing the spinet. It was at any rate one of Rebecca Burwell's accomplishments; and, as was sometimes the custom, she had cut her own silhouette on the paper she had given Tom Jefferson. You can imagine Tom's chagrin at having let this gift be destroyed, and his sheepishness at having to ask for another, "even a plain round one."

All of Tom's letters to John Page were at this time full of girls' names. He was evidently a popular young man and hated to leave all the friends he had made in Williamsburg. "Tell—tell—in short, tell them all ten thousand things," he writes to John of these girls and wants to know ten thousand things about them and mentions a bet with Miss Alice Corbin for a pair of garters.

After writing this letter, Tom stayed on at Fairfield for a few more days and then left for Shadwell, where he soon was bored without his Becky. Again he wrote to John: "We rise in the morning that we may eat breakfast, dinner, and supper and go to bed again that we may get up the next morning to do the same; so that you never saw two peas more alike than our yesterdays and todays."

This is the last letter to John in which Tom calls his Rebecca by name. From now on she becomes the mysterious "R. B." But, of course, other friends might recognize these

initials, and soon the lady appears in his letters as ";Belinda."
And he loved to play other mysterious tricks even with this
made-up name. For instance, he broke Belinda up into three
words, "bell in day," and translated them into dog Latin,
"campana in die." Let the inquisitive into whose hands his
letters might fall imagine that he loved some foreign lady
with the queer name of Campanaindie. Other times he wrote
Belinda backwards, but of course not in English letters. That
would be much too simple; he used Greek characters for his
darling Adnileb. And to make assurance doubly sure, the
letters always referred to Rebecca-Belinda-Campanaindie-
Adnileb as "he."

But even all these precautions did not seem quite safe to
Tom, and he wrote John that he must find some scheme of
writing to him that should be totally ununderstandable to
everyone but themselves. He planned to send him Shelton's
Tachygraphical Alphabet (a system of shorthand) with directions for use.

No young man just graduated from college likes to have
the gossips know about the affairs of his heart, especially when
he is by no means sure of the girl. And a restless young mind
like Tom's would be more than usually busy inventing dis-
guises for his feelings. Be sure that if he had by then achieved
his ambition to learn the Indian languages, and could have
made Page do the same, he would have written all these con-
fessions to his friend in pure Choctaw. But Tom also had
behind him centuries of romantic tradition. In the Middle
Ages the troubadors or minstrels *never* revealed their true
loves' names in their songs. The knight played exactly the
same tricks with his lady's name and gender as did Tom Jefferson.

But there was an even better reason, a commonsense one,

for being careful. The mail service was not very good. People who handled letters had no scruples about opening and reading them. Sealed envelopes gave no more privacy than post cards. One man about this time even fought a duel with another because the second man had sent him a letter through the common post where anyone might read it!

Now it is possible that love interfered with Tom's appetite that summer in Shadwell though he seems to have remained consistently healthy. It may be that Rebecca caused him to waste days in daydreaming as she certainly did cause him to spend hours in pouring out long letters to John Page. But whatever her disturbing influence she never kept Tom from engaging in the hardest work of his whole life. For he had just embarked on a plan which, though he did not know it, would make him one of the best-educated men in America.

With his diploma and scholarly honors behind him, Tom's next business was to set about preparing himself for his chosen profession of the law. There were no law schools in those days; legal training was acquired by working and reading under the direction of some member of the bar. The young apprentice would attend all the sessions of the court; he would help prepare his master's cases; and in his spare time he was supposed to read the law, and have the older man answer any difficult problems that came up. After clerking and studying in this manner until he had thoroughly absorbed the principles of law and acquired some practical experience, the young student appeared before a special board of Virginia lawyers and, if he won his license, could then hang out a shingle bearing his own name. Tom's friend, George Wythe, offered him a place in his office, after his first vacation.

For a student as brilliant as young Jefferson, who had completed his four years' college course in two, it would not have been very difficult to pass his lawyer's examination in a year or two. His friend Patrick Henry had done it in six months. But then Henry did not have this boy's enormous thirst for knowledge, or his grand ideas of what made an educated man and well-trained lawyer. In fact, if everyone had shared Tom's conception of the profession, there would never have been more than a small handful of lawyers in all Virginia.

For instance, Tom would not be satisfied with knowing a particular law. He would want to know its history; whether it came from the Romans, or the French, or the early Anglo-Saxons; whether it was still a good law or ought now to be changed; whether it helped people more or hindered them more.

To get this all-around picture of his chosen calling, this nineteen-year-old promised himself not to apply for a license for at least five years. Long before Tom felt himself ready, his old boyhood chum, Dabney Carr, had become a lawyer; but Tom stuck by his books, swallowing huge drafts of knowledge, becoming almost drunk on what he learned, and his thirst growing on what he put away.

For, of course, what Tom was doing was getting a university education. It was a one-man university in which Tom was all the students, but the professors were all the great men who had written books from the time of the ancient Greeks and Romans down to his own day. These professors taught him more than law (Tom never got over his distaste for law books and he often repeated his wish that "the devil had old Coke").

A friend once asked Jefferson for a good program of studies for a law student. Jefferson gave him the program he had made out for himself. It is really staggering, and we may well doubt whether the friend used it for very long.

"Latin and French," Jefferson told him, "are absolutely necessary. Mathematics and natural philosophy [science] are so useful in most familiar occurrences of life and so enjoyable and delightful as would induce everyone to wish an acquaintance with them. Besides this, the faculties of the mind, like the members of the body, are strengthened and improved by exercise."

Then Jefferson recommends a list of books on mathematics, astronomy, geography, physics, and chemistry. Having read the different books on these subjects, he says, "you may enter regularly into the study of law," taking with it such studies as will help to make one not only a lawyer but a learned man as well. These studies should be in physics, ethics, religion, natural law, literature, criticism, rhetoric, and oratory.

Then follows a simple suggestion for a day's work:

Till eight o'clock in the morning employ yourself in physical studies:

Agriculture	*Botany*
Chemistry	*Ethics and Natural Religion*
Anatomy	*Religion (Sectarian)*
Zoology	*Natural Law*

From eight to twelve, read Law.
Twelve to one, read Politics.
In the afternoon, read History:

Ancient
Modern
English
American

From dark to bedtime:

> *Belles-Lettres,* the poets, especially Shakespeare
> *Criticism*
> *Rhetoric*
> *Oratory.*

Where, in all this program, which is as full of work as an egg is of meat, did Jefferson find time for playing and practicing his violin? For, when he was at college and for a dozen years thereafter, Tom gave three hours of each day to his fiddle. He never traveled without one, even having a very small violin made which he could slip into his baggage when away from home. If, when visiting friends, he got up before the rest of the household, out would come the toy instrument. The thickness of the walls and the tininess of the violin, it is to be hoped, prevented the rest of the house from being awakened at ungodly hours.

Nor must it be forgotten that all this while Jefferson somehow helped run his plantation, kept numerous notebooks, took a daily ride on horseback, continued to see his friends, especially Fauquier's circle, and even attended balls.

Some years later, Jefferson's young friend James Madison took this course of self-education with him to Princeton. In a short time, it is said, his health broke down so badly under the strain of it that he did not recover for some years. Not everyone could have such a combination of iron mind and iron body as the enthusiastic young Jefferson.

The law never has been a study that allowed for a great deal of time for other things. Reading "old Coke" you had practically to learn a new language. Here, according to one writer, is the proper way in which you would have had to record the simple fact that John Doe committed suicide (which was a punishable crime in those days):

John Doe, not having the fear of God before his eyes, but being moved and seduced by the instigation of the Devil, at Williamsburg, in a certain wood as aforesaid, standing and being, the said John Doe, being then and there alone, with a certain hempen cord, of the value of threepence, which he then and there had and held in his hands, and one end thereof then and there put about his neck, and the other end thereof tied about a bough of a certain oak tree, himself then and there, with the cord aforesaid, voluntarily and feloniously, and of his malice aforethought, hanged and suffocated.

To digest a single chapter of Coke with its liberal sprinklings of law Latin and old-fashioned French would ordinarily take a bright student a month. Yet, when Tom had finished this famous book, he was far from satisfied with his information and went on, delving back among the old laws of England before the Norman Conquest, back into the age of King Alfred the Great.

Did Tom have to drive himself to keep up this strenuous pace? Perhaps he did at first, but you must remember that knowledge was to him what gold is to a miser. His program required of him fifteen hours a day of labor and, including his two at college, seven years of study in all. He gave them gladly. Of course, if he were not financially independent, he could not have done all this, but neither did he use his time and independence as most of the youth about him did, chiefly for racing and fox-hunting. Though he was always fond of attending the races, in all his life he entered a horse of his own in the meet only once.

The five years during which young Jefferson thus prepared himself for what he thought was to be his profession he spent mostly at Shadwell. Here he installed a clock in his bedroom. As soon as he could make out its hands in the gray of the summer morning, he rose and commenced his labors. In the winter he got up at five and went to bed at ten. Usually his only recreation was a gallop around the estate, or he would cross the river and take a walk at twilight to the top of Monticello. In the evenings he spent an hour or two talking with his family or playing the violin to his sister Jane's accompaniment.

On Tom's twenty-first birthday, he celebrated an old English custom that the gentlemen colonists had brought over with them. He had an avenue of trees planted near Shadwell which is standing to this day. Thomas Jefferson was of age.

His first act to celebrate his new manhood was to have the Rivanna, which flowed past his land, turned into a useful stream. Though deep enough, the Rivanna was too full of obstructions to allow the farmers to use it for transporting their produce down country. Jefferson got up a petition, sent it to the House of Burgesses, and finally had the satisfaction of seeing the stream cleared for navigation. It was his first act of public service, and he was extremely proud of it.

During the winter he had been coming often into Williamsburg, to consult with his master Mr. Wythe, to attend court and assembly sessions, and to stock his library. He would then visit old friends, though his teacher Dr. Small had by now returned to England. Tom was also one of the first members of the Flat Hat Club, founded by a small group of friendly students at William and Mary. This little college fraternity had no useful purpose, according to Jefferson, and met only for fun and talk. But in 1776, the year of Independence, Jefferson's club was to become the first chapter of Phi Beta Kappa, America's great honorary society of scholars. In Williamsburg Tom might also meet Patrick Henry and have a rousing political discussion; for the young hermit of Shadwell would come into town bursting with the ideas he had dug out of his year's reading. These would be the seasons when the most brilliant balls were held, and there was a particular lure which drew Tom to every one of these functions.

For now that young Thomas Jefferson, Esquire, was of age, there was one serious grown-up question he had to have settled. Would Rebecca Burwell marry him? He wanted to raise a small building on the summit of Monticello; how big should it be? That might depend on Rebecca Burwell. He was afire to go to Europe and visit the many marvels Fauquier had described, but dare he go without getting Rebecca's promise that she would wait for him? When he was in Williamsburg, he was miserable enough to write Page that it should be called Devilsburg. When he was at Shadwell, he was tormented by the thought that it would be best to speak to Rebecca and end his suspense.

He wrote Page that he was building a flat-bottomed sailboat. "Have you an inclination to travel, Page? For you must know that as soon as the *Rebecca* (the name I intend to give the vessel) is completely finished, I intend to hoist sail and away. I shall visit particularly England, Holland, Spain, Italy (where I would buy me a good fiddle), and Egypt and return through the British provinces to the northward home. This to be sure would take us two or three years and, if we should not both be cured of love in that time, I think the Devil would be in it."

But Tom did not hoist sail and he was not cured of his love. For, three months after he had written this to his patient friend, we find him going with a pounding heart to attend a dance in the Apollo Room of the Raleigh Tavern. Perhaps he hesitated before the leaden statue of Raleigh which stood over the main doorway of the inn. Maybe he gazed distractedly at the huge punch bowl over which Shadwell had been pledged to his father. He was weak and trembling, for he had resolved to ask Belinda for her hand that very night. He had thought the whole scene out very carefully in his mind. He knew just what he was going to say.

Things began well for Tom. Rebecca graciously accepted him as a partner for one of the minuets. His great moment came. And then—alas for Tom and his well-thought-out speech! All he could murmur was a few broken sentences uttered in great disorder, interrupted by long, painful pauses. Rebecca smiled her most charming smile at the stammerings of the dry-mouthed youth.

Through the rest of that night Tom knew what misery was. "I am in the most melancholy fit ever any poor soul was," he told John Page the next morning. This was the end, he thought. He could never face his Belinda again.

But, little as he thought he deserved it, he had one more chance. He approached Rebecca again. He kept himself firmly in hand. He spoke more calmly, more distinctly. He told her of his great esteem for her, that he was going to take a trip to England. Would she wait for him? It would make him so happy. Belinda neither accepted nor refused.

And then one fine day very soon after, Mr. Thomas Jefferson received an announcement of the approaching marriage of Miss Rebecca Burwell to Mr. Jacquelin Ambler.

This was a rival Tom had had no reason to suspect. What his emotions were on receiving this news we do not know. But he might have become more reconciled to his ill luck if he had known that another future great American had suffered the same fate at the hands of the Ambler family. For

Jacquelin Ambler's brother Edward had married Miss Cary, the lady who rejected George Washington's suit. Jacquelin Ambler later became State Treasurer and was known as "the Aristides of Virginia," after the ancient Greek who has come down in history as Aristides the Just.

John Page had better luck with the Burwell family, for he afterwards courted and won Rebecca's cousin Fanny.

So in his twenty-second year Jefferson was a disillusioned young man and a soberer student. He spent more time at Shadwell, following his program of studies and playing the violin. This year, 1765, was an important one for the Jefferson family. First came a happy event. Tom's most constant visitor at Shadwell had always been Dabney Carr, with whom he had hunted as a boy. By this time Tom knew that, much as his friend liked him, there was one at Shadwell he loved better, Martha Jefferson. And now when the two young men climbed the "little mountain" and sat under their favorite oak, it was Dabney who did most of the talking, and his main topic was Tom's sister. That July, Dabney and Martha were married.

But Tom's happiness was not for long. Two months after the wedding, his older sister Jane died. Tom had loved Jane above all the rest. She was the cleverest girl in the family, and it was to her that he had told all his plans and thoughts. Their shared love of music had drawn them even closer together. Now Tom was indeed lonesome at Shadwell.

John Page later said he had never known anyone who could work and study like Thomas Jefferson. At last Jefferson's five years were up. He knew himself now to be a well-rounded lawyer, a credit to his profession. He took his examination. He passed. In 1767, at the age of twenty-four, he was admitted to the bar.

IV

THE BURGESS OF VIRGINIA

WHEN Thomas Jefferson was first introduced to Patrick
Henry, he had been told that Henry was on his way to
Williamsburg to learn the law business. Tom, of course, imag-
ined his new friend to be at the beginning of several years of
study. They promised to see each other often in the city, where
Tom still had a year of college to complete.

But Henry had no intention of wasting his youth on books.
Once arrived at Williamsburg, he thumbed through several
volumes on law—when he could spare the time—for six

months, and then boldly asked for an examination. He had the right, of course, to do this at any time that he could collect together three established members of the bar willing to examine him.

The three lawyers that Henry got together were George Wythe, Jefferson's brilliant friend and later master, and Peyton Randolph and John Randolph, both kinsmen of Jefferson. These men questioned Henry about the law and—they found him very ignorant of it. Wythe was shocked and indignant. His ideals of the learned professions were the same as Jefferson's. He would never, never sign his name to the license of a man whose only substitute for knowledge was colossal nerve! He walked out of the affair in a huff. But the other two were won over. They saw something in Henry that they considered more important than a lot of memorized cases and rules. They saw genius in the young man, and the sort of persuasive tongue that they knew would be as effective with juries as it was with themselves. If Patrick Henry would promise to go home and study and catch up on his reading, they would sign. More, they would get a third lawyer to sign with them. Henry promised.

Peyton Randolph told Tom of the whole incident. At first he must have shaken his head over his own kindness, for, sad to relate, Henry did not keep his promise very well. He meant to, of course, but what could he do against the habits of a lifetime? He would conscientiously borrow law books from Tom, then go off on a hunting trip, and return the books unread.

Henry had always been like that about studies. His father had taught grammar school, and Patrick had, in spite of himself, to learn a little Latin and some mathematics. History, on the other hand, he devoured. But usually, when the school hour came around, the master's son was nowhere to be found, unless, of course, they were willing to search the Virginia forests for him. There he was sure to be for days on end, with no companionship but that of his gun. And Henry never got over his feeling that a fishing-rod was more important than "old Coke" or that a good day's hunting was more satisfactory than weeks in a stuffy little office. For Henry was one of those happy souls whom Tom could never hope to understand, those who loved idleness for its own sake.

In the end, however, Peyton Randolph's confidence in Henry was justified. If Henry did not get much out of books, he did finally learn the law very well from practice. In Hanover County, to which he had moved because the hunting was better, he began to make a name for himself as the kind of lawyer whom juries could not resist. His speeches could stir the passions of the most cold-blooded and indifferent of audiences. He had a way of making you feel you were on a glorious crusade if you did what he asked you.

Henry's cases began gradually to attract audiences, and he always gave them a picturesque show. Sometimes when the court was opened Henry's clients looked around for him in vain. Then suddenly he would appear, fresh from several days' camping in the woods, his saddlebags slung over one shoulder. His coarse cloth coat would be stained with the blood and grease of his hunt, his leather breeches and leggings with the mud and smoke of his campfires. He would pick up the first case, and the fireworks of oratory would be on.

In 1765 Henry moved to Louisa County, where Tom Jefferson had attended Dr. Maury's Latin school. Here Henry's brilliance as a lawyer won him the election to the House of Burgesses. These were exciting times and Henry felt that the most exciting place to be in was the Virginia legislature. Here his talents would show at their best. It was the time of the agitation over the Stamp Act.

The French and Indian Wars had been won by England and her colonies in 1763, but they had left the British Empire exhausted and burdened with taxes. It was felt by the English that the American colonies should shoulder a share of these expenses since, they said, the colonies had benefited by these conquests. Unfortunately the Parliament in London chose the worst possible way of collecting money from the colonies. And the worst possible time, for America was then suffering from a depression; business was bad and there was much unemployment.

The English Parliament, among other irritating measures, passed a law by which a tax was collected on all papers and documents, whether legal, commercial, or periodical. That is, no will was good unless it bore a stamp showing that a tax had been paid; no promissory note, no newspaper could appear without a tax unless the writers of them wished to go to jail.

In all the colonies there was a growing feeling of resentment. Moreover, the people who were most directly hit by the Stamp Act were just those who could best express their complaints. They were the most eloquent and influential of the people, namely the lawyers and editors. And in these hard times the rest of the country, which had already been subjected to other onerous taxes, was with them.

When Patrick Henry rode his lean nag into Williamsburg, to take his seat in the House of Burgesses, the colony was seething with protest but did not know what to do about it. Before the Act was passed, Virginia had begged the English Parliament not to permit it. Now that it was passed, what could loyal Englishmen do but pay up and shut up?

For days Henry sat in his new seat and waited for the exciting times that he had come expecting. Of grumbling there was plenty but of action none. A brand-new member, he waited for the older men, the leaders, to take charge and lead. Nothing happened. The dignified old aristocrats, to whom all the other Burgesses looked up, deplored old England's attitude, but *they* were not looking for excitement.

At last, two days before the close of the session, when nothing had been done, Patrick Henry tore a blank page out of "old Coke"—at last he had some use for it—and wrote down a set of resolutions he wished the Burgesses to pass upon. He stood up and read the resolutions, and then began to speak.

Among the visitors who were crowded about the doorway in the lobby (for there was no gallery for outsiders) was the young law student, Thomas Jefferson. He may have had some hint that this day there was to be a rebellion against the old guard in the House, the wealthy planters and aristocratic lawyers. With intense interest he saw his friend Henry rise in his place and introduce a set of resolutions condemning the English laws. He saw him begin to speak, faltering at first and conscious of his awkward clothes. Then he saw him gradually draw himself up erect as he launched into the full tide of his oration. With all the other onlookers Tom felt himself lifted up and carried away, felt the blood rush to his head as Henry denounced the tyranny of the obnoxious Stamp Act. He said afterwards that Patrick Henry had spoken as Homer wrote.

In the midst of this thrilling, magnificent speech, Henry thundered, while his eyes flashed lightning: "Cæsar had his Brutus, Charles the First his Cromwell, and George the Third——"

"Treason!" cried the chairman. "Treason, treason!" echoed from several parts of the House. Jefferson held his breath. But Henry did not waver for an instant. Tossing his head still higher, he finished his sentence distinctly:

"—may profit by their example. If *this* be treason, make the most of it!"

In the midst of a terrific uproar, the resolutions were passed. Henry had his excitement. The resolutions reminded the King that the colonists had certain inalienable rights as Englishmen, that the colonists had never given up these rights, that among them was the right to be taxed only by their own representatives, and that the colonists intended to pay only such taxes as they had levied upon themselves.

This last resolution was so defiant that, in spite of Henry's eloquence, it was passed by only one vote. After the vote had been counted, Peyton Randolph, who was then Attorney General, rushed out of the chamber. Tom in the doorway heard his cousin mutter as he passed him: "By God, I would have given five hundred guineas for one more vote." For Randolph was one of those conservative leaders who was by no means prepared to go so far as Patrick Henry. Again he had cause to shake his head at the thought of having signed Henry's license.

As for Patrick Henry, always impatient of mere details, he had mounted his skinny horse and, thinking his work done, cantered off for home. But the next morning several other members had come around to Randolph's opinion. These timid men had been enchanted into doing a braver thing than they could bear. With Henry and his accursedly spellbinding tongue out of the way, they wished the whole thing undone.

When Tom wandered into the House the next day before the bell had rung for the hour of meeting, he found his uncle Colonel Peter Randolph and one of the Tory members busily thumbing over the volumes on the clerk's table. They were searching for a previous case several years ago in which the House had stricken out of the minutes the record of its own vote on a certain measure. Whether they found the old case or not, Tom could not later remember, but that day the House, with Henry absent, voted to cross out from the record its own vote on Henry's last resolution.

But all their striking out, all their timidity and alarm, did the Burgesses no good. Like it or not, history had been made under their noses. The House itself had been thrilled by a new, revolutionary emotion. A large audience had heard the "treason speech" and had already begun to make it famous. Soon its message was being repeated in all Virginia and in all the colonies. And Tom Jefferson had heard it.

Many years later Jefferson was to say that it was Patrick Henry who started the ball of the Revolution rolling. This may not be quite so, but Henry certainly did start something rolling in Jefferson's mind, something that was to roll far beyond Patrick Henry's defiance of the King. In Jefferson's mind the thought grew, why just George the Third, why not defy all kings? Why resist just the tyranny of unjust taxation, why not all tyranny? Why stop merely with the rights of Englishmen; did they not have even greater rights to freedom as Americans, as men?

But it was to take more years of work and reading before Jefferson would see these ideas clearly. It was not until two years after the Stamp Act speech that he took his examination and became a lawyer, and it was only two years after that, in 1769, that he entered politics himself.

The same year that Jefferson won his right to practice at the bar, the royal Governor of Virginia died. Up to the last years of his life Governor Fauquier continued to give the little dinners that had introduced Jefferson into the world of men with ideas, and Tom had continued to attend them. In his will Fauquier left his body to medical science.

It was not until the second year after Fauquier's death that Lord Botetourt, who had been appointed Governor by the King, came to Virginia. He arrived in Williamsburg with a great train of servants and baggage, in a magnificent coach drawn by seven milk-white horses, which was said to be a personal gift from George III.

In England, when a new King ascended the throne, Parliament was dissolved and new elections were held. So in Virginia, upon the arrival of the new Governor, a new House of Burgesses was called for.

Young Jefferson had been a lawyer for two years now. He had probably found, as so many young men do, that the achieving of one ambition does not make you satisfied for life. The practice of the law was not big enough a task to use up all his energy or all his learning. His reading, especially of Greek and Latin writers, had given him ideals of patriotism and service that were too wide and varied to be fulfilled in the daily humdrum business of helping people who had become entangled in the law. Then there was the example of the many Randolphs, relatives of his, and of his friend Patrick Henry. There was his memory of Henry's speech on the Stamp Act. There was his position in the community as the son of his father. As a large landowner he was already a vestryman of the church in Charlottesville and a justice of the peace. In short, Thomas Jefferson was almost obliged to run for a seat in the new House of Burgesses.

Elections were leisurely affairs then, and there was a particular etiquette to be observed if one was a candidate. Jefferson had to make a personal visit to each of the voters in Albemarle County and courteously solicit his vote. No man would vote for a candidate who had been so rude as not to ask him to do so. And Jefferson was obliged to keep open house and detail a servant for the special task of keeping the punch bowl full throughout the three days of the election. Otherwise he would have been thought too stingy to make a good Burgess. During those three days of mild excitement he stood at the polls with the other candidates, and he bowed low when he heard a vote cast for himself. There were no secret ballots.

To be entitled to vote, a man had to possess a certain amount of property: fifty acres of land, or twenty-five acres with a house on it. Originally the size of the house had not been specified, with the result that the building business became very lively just before each election. One man claimed the right to vote after having put up a doll's house. But this had been too much for the Burgesses, and now a certain size of house was plainly stated in the voting law. On the other hand, all who could were compelled to cast their votes, unless they were willing to pay a fine of one hundred pounds of tobacco.

So after supplying the voters with lunch and punch for three days, Tom learned that he was duly elected to the position once held by Peter Jefferson. He was only twenty-six years old.

When the new House of Burgesses met, the first day was to be taken up, according to traditional usage, with an address from the Governor; the second by a reply from the House. In this reply it was customary to renew the expressions of loyalty to England and to outline the special needs of the colony. Because of his reputation for style and learning, and as a courtesy to his new membership, Jefferson was selected to draw up the reply to the Governor's address. Resolutions were adopted by the House instructing Jefferson in the points to be covered.

This job was very much to Jefferson's taste, and he worked at it that very first night with great zeal. The next morning he read his composition to the committee in charge, proudly pluming himself on the neatness of his phrasing and the general finish of his performance. But Jefferson's first experience in statesmanship was most ungratifying. The committee did not like what he had written.

What they had wanted was a flowing, flowery discourse, an address of welcome full of metaphors and Latin quotations. Instead, Jefferson had simply repeated the resolutions of the Burgesses in short, clear, forceful terms. The committee's frowns and head-shakings hurt the pride of the young man who was to become one of the greatest writers of the eighteenth century. Being the sensitive sort of person he was, he probably told himself that he did not belong in politics and would not last long at it.

So the task was given over into older hands. The head of the bar drew up a reply to the Governor's address in the approved style. But the excitement that soon followed made the young statesman forget his first disappointment. On the third day of assembly the Burgess passed a set of resolutions condemning taxation without representation and protesting against the practice of trying colonists accused of treason in London, away from their own homes. Furthermore, the House called upon all the thirteen colonies to work together as one in seeking redress for their grievances against England. This last was by far the most important and the boldest action the members had yet taken.

Two days later the Governor's secretary entered the assembly hall and announced: "The Royal Governor commands this house to attend His Excellency in the Council Chamber." The hundred members rose in a body, tramped after the secretary to the other end of the building, and ranged themselves round the Governor's throne-like seat. Jefferson, standing among them, observed with interest the Governor's solemn expression. He had some inkling of what was about to come.

"Mr. Speaker and Gentlemen of the House of Burgesses," the Governor began majestically, "I have heard of your resolves and augur ill of your effects. You have made it my duty to dissolve you and you are dissolved accordingly."

So it had come at last! The rebellious Virginians were to be shown their place. Their protests were to be met with oppression. Thus Thomas Jefferson, after having served only five days as a legislator, was again a private gentleman.

But the Governor had by this act made the resolutions known to the world. Williamsburg that day and evening was filled with little knots of men gesticulating violently and talking hotly. Former Burgess George Washington was there and had his say, and ex-Burgess Patrick Henry had his.

Some of the members decided that the time for talk was past and the time for action come. Jefferson joined a group that had hit upon a plan for a striking back at England. These former Burgesses drew up an agreement to boycott English goods until the home country should be forced, through the loss of its rich American trade, to see that she could not proceed against her colonies with such a high hand. The boycott is one of the very few weapons which a weak colony can use effectively against its powerful possessor. Even now India sometimes uses it against England.

Not as the House of Burgesses, but as private gentlemen, these same Virginians met the next day in the Apollo Room of the old Raleigh Tavern and signed their names to a set of agreements. This is what Jefferson ran his eye over as he signed. He promised:

To be a great deal more saving and industrious than ever before. Never again, as long as time should endure, to buy an article taxed by Parliament for the sake of raising revenue in America, except certain low-priced qualities of paper without which business simply could not go on. Never, in short, until the repeal of these irritating taxes and laws, to import any article from Britain, or in British ships, which it was at all possible to do without. Finally, to save all his lambs so that he could do without English imports of wool.

A list of the things that Jefferson thus particularly promised to refrain from buying from England is interesting because it shows how many things the colonies depended upon the mother country to get for them. He now refused to buy: brandy, wine, cider, perry (pear cider), beer, ale, malt, barley, pease, beef, pork, fish, butter, cheese, tallow, candles, oil, fruit, sugar, pickles, candy, pewter, hoes, axes, watches, clocks, tables, chairs, looking-glasses, carriages, cabinetwork, upholstery, trinkets and jewelry, plate and gold, silverware, ribbons, millinery, lace, India goods except spices, silks except in thread, cambric, lawn, muslin, gauze, calico, cotton or linen stuffs above fifty cents a yard, expensive woolens, broadcloths and narrow cloths, hats, stockings, shoes, boots, saddles and all leatherwork.

Of the 108 former members of the dissolved House, eighty-five signed the agreement. And in the elections for the new House, these eighty-five won back their seats; the others did not. For the Governor had been impressed by this dignified revolt and had written to the King's ministers counseling them to treat the Virginians with moderation. And it happened that just at this time the political party that came into power in England was opposed to the policy of annoying the colonists. So the Governor called for a new House, promising that there should be no more taxation without representation, and Jefferson found himself again among the Burgesses, where he stayed until that body came to the end of its existence.

V

THE MANOR AND THE LADY

WHEN Tom Jefferson had played with Dabney Carr on the crown of his *monticello* and had talked of building a house on it, he began something that was to occupy his free moments for the rest of his long life. At fifteen, of course, he was thinking merely of a regular planter's house, like Tuckahoe. But the older he grew the more ambitious became his plans.

To start with, the building of a mansion on top of a hill six hundred feet high was itself an original plan. Planters usually erected their houses low down to be near the river. While still in college, Jefferson used to steal time from his summer studies to superintend the leveling of his mountain top, and so the great work started.

Among the things most ardently discussed by Fauquier, Small, and Wythe at their weekly meetings was the beauty of buildings in Europe. Lacking the buildings themselves, these men would take out or refer to Palladio's very popular book on architecture. Palladio was an architect of the sixteenth century who had fallen in love with the classical Roman style of building. He had written a book containing illustrations of Roman temples and of Italian country villas built by himself on Roman models. The book was full of measurements, façades, ground plans, and ornamental details.

Tom listened breathlessly to these debates. The moment he saw Palladio's book he was captivated by it. There was something about the simple grandeur of the Greek and Roman style that appealed to his nature just as classical literature did. This was the kind of building that seemed to go naturally with democracy on the one hand and culture on the other.

Tom made Palladio his textbook. He studied the work, practiced drawing, and made hundreds of sketches. For he was one of those blessed people who are not only extremely clever with their brains but particularly adroit with their hands. He had watched his father make surveying charts. And was not mathematics the passion of his soul? So his mechanical drawing was already excellent during his student days, though he never became proficient at freehand drawing.

In all Virginia, when Jefferson was studying law, there were no architects. Houses were built without previous plans on paper. A planter who wanted a new mansion would call in his master carpenter, point out someone else's house, and tell him he wanted one like it.

But Jefferson worked out all his plans for Monticello on paper first, like an architect. His plan included the whole grounds. From Palladio he had learned that even the outbuildings should be so treated and ornamented that they seemed to belong to the main building, and not to be accidentally thrown together. Why should a Southern planter, who needed so many outbuildings, surround himself with a heap of ugly accidents that spoiled the appearance of the main house?

While working over his plans, Jefferson had put up a little house on Monticello, the cottage that he had dreamed would be big enough for Belinda and himself. That year he had also begun to lay out his new orchard, a typical Jefferson orchard, by the way, for it contained almost everything he could think of—pears, cherries, New York apples, peaches, nectarines, quinces, pomegranates, figs, and walnuts.

However, in 1770, when Jefferson was serving his first term as a Burgess, Monticello was still almost entirely on paper. He had changed his plans again and again, but he was too busy to make more than a start at the actual building.

One day Tom and his mother were visiting at a neighbor's when one of his servants came running with bad news. Shadwell had caught fire and everything was in ruins!

"Were none of my books saved?" was Jefferson's first question.

"No, master," answered the slave, and then added with a triumphant grin: "But we saved your fiddle."

When he wrote John Page about the fire, Jefferson estimated that he had lost a thousand dollars' worth of books. But it was the *books* and not the *cost* that he lamented. He immediately wrote to his agent in London for a book catalogue, ordered one book after another, and in ten years had gathered together a new library of 1250 volumes, not including music books or the law books he kept in Williamsburg.

Now the building of Monticello was not to be put off any longer. That summer Jefferson's mother, his sisters, and his brother went to live at the overseer's house, while he himself stayed in one of the building sheds on the mountain watching over the progress of the work.

It was a gigantic task. Not only were there trees to fell and underbrush to clear, but so many of the materials had to be manufactured right there. Every planter expected to make his own bricks, and nails were wrought on the spot. While he supervised the work and explained his plans to the builders, Jefferson busied himself making a few articles of furniture, for he was also handy with tools.

A year later, the work was still going on. Writing to a friend for the loan of a master builder, Jefferson described his life on Monticello. "I have lately removed to the mountain. I have here but one room, which like the cobbler's, serves me for parlor, for kitchen and hall. I may add, for bedchamber and study, too. My friends sometimes take a temperate dinner with me and then retire to look for beds elsewhere."

All of a sudden the work that had been going on steadily for years began to seem too slow to Jefferson. His brain began to boil with architectural ideas. The notebooks in which he jotted down his plans were bursting with the suggestions he stuffed into them. A strange change had come over the careful builder: he was in a hurry to finish his home.

These plans that he scribbled so furiously into his notebooks, as he sat lonely on his mountain top of an evening or in some dull tavern while traveling from one county courthouse to another, were curiously romantic. They certainly read more like the schoolboy who had written long-winded complaints about Rebecca Burwell to the long-suffering Page than like the work of a member of the House of Burgesses whose speeches were not flowery enough for his elders.

All this worry about springs and parks; whether he should have waterfalls or fountains, pebbles from Hanover or shells from Burwell's Ferry! Should he have a statue of a reclining figure near the spring? Should the springhouse be made in the form of a little Greek temple with a Latin inscription over the doorway, or a Chinese pagoda with an inscription in English? Perhaps a couch of moss near by, planted all around with jasmine, honeysuckle, and sweetbrier? What curious ideas for a springhouse where butter had to be kept fresh!

At times he let himself become faintly melancholic and thought of laying out a beautiful graveyard. In his notebook he wrote: "Choose out for a burying place some unfrequented vale in the park, where is 'no sound to break the stillness but a brook, that bubbling winds among the weeds; no mark of any human shape that had been there, unless the skeleton of some poor wretch, who sought that place out to despair and die in.' " He planned to put his cemetery among venerable oaks, and plant gloomy evergreens roundabout. In the center he would build a small Gothic temple. Half of the graveyard would be for the family, the other for strangers and servants. He even mused on the inscription for some favorite servant's grave. And in the middle of the temple he wished to have an altar.

This, for instance, is how he imagined he would want the grounds to look:

Keep it in deer, rabbits, peacocks, guinea poultry, pigeons, etc. Let it be an asylum for hares, squirrels, pheasants, partridges,

and every other wild animal (except those of prey). Court them
to it, by laying food for them in proper places. Procure a buck-
elk, to be, as it were, monarch of the wood; but keep him shy,
that his appearance may not lose its effect by too much familiarity.
A buffalo might be confined also.

What was it that had got into the young lawyer and politician, making him have such outlandish architectural visions;
making him forget the classic simplicity of Palladio and instead imagine the sort of home found only in romantic novels;
making him so kind to hares and buffaloes? Well . . .

There lived in Charles City County, on his estate called The
Forest, a prominent lawyer by the name of John Wayles. Jefferson had met him often in the courts of Williamsburg, and they
had learned to like and respect each other. Mr. Wayles invited
Mr. Jefferson to visit him at The Forest.

Living with Mr. Wayles was his daughter Mrs. Martha Skelton, a young widow of twenty-three, of exquisite charm and
beauty. She had a lovely figure, a graceful carriage, auburn
hair, warm hazel eyes, a lively intelligence, and the kindest of
hearts. She was an accomplished musician, taking lessons on
the harpsichord from Domenico Alberti, a famous Venetian
artist. And she was an excellent manager of her father's great
Virginian household.

No sooner did Jefferson make this lovely lady's acquaintance
than all his love for music suddenly blazed out into an un-
quenchable passion. Signor Alberti he engaged almost on the
spot to give him advanced lessons on the violin, and the fiddle
his servants had saved out of the Shadwell fire was all at once
not good enough.

Tom's cousin, John Randolph, owned a very fine violin.
And Cousin Randolph was quite mystified at the impetuous,

not to say impolite, way in which Cousin Jefferson insisted on his selling it. But for all his begging Randolph would not part with it. However, he said, if Tom would be patient, he would leave him the blasted thing in his will. Now Tom was to stop bothering him.

But Tom was not a lawyer for nothing. Yes, he would stop pestering John, but would John sign a contract about that will, and accept something in return? John Randolph had been a lawyer even longer than Tom, so, of course, he agreed. Between them they cooked up a very legal-looking document and got Patrick Henry and George Wythe and a glittering list of Virginian leaders to sign it as witnesses. If John died first, Tom was to have his fiddle. If Tom died first, John was to choose for himself eight hundred pounds' worth of Tom's books. Then they all adjourned to the Raleigh Tavern and drank a toast to each other's health and long life.

Jefferson was now rushing the completion of the small brick house that was to be the southeastern pavilion of Monticello. The big house itself was barely begun, and he dropped the work on it to interest himself in furniture.

First of all there would have to be a clavichord. Since his sister Jane's death, Tom's family had not seen him so serious about music. But suddenly he canceled his order for the instrument. He had seen a fortepiano, and would have one of those instead. For the fortepiano, or pianoforte (our modern piano), was something new in Virginia and was just beginning to replace the old clavichord. And if anything was new and better, Jefferson was sure to want it in preference to the old. Besides, as he wrote, he found "the workmanship of the whole very handsome and worthy the acceptance of a lady for whom I intend it."

So the secret was out.

Tom Jefferson had evidently learned his lesson once, and hence his hurry. For Martha Skelton, like Rebecca Burwell, was besieged by suitors, but this time Tom was no stammering boy. He had made his mark in the House of Burgesses. He could talk to her of music and of books. For the best part of a year this busy young man was a most frequent visitor at The Forest.

One night, the story goes, two of Tom's rivals happened to meet on the doorstep of Martha's house. They had each come to propose to her. As they looked each other up and down, their ears were assailed by strains of music coming from the drawing room. In it, happily intermingled, they heard Mrs. Skelton's harpsichord and Mr. Jefferson's violin and Mrs. Skelton's voice and that of Mr. Jefferson. For a few moments the two suitors listened to the harmony of these various sounds and then, without a word, they put on their hats and left The Forest.

On New Year's Day, 1772, Martha Wayles Skelton and Thomas Jefferson were united in marriage.

After the festivities at The Forest, the newlyweds set out in a coach for Monticello. There was a light snow, but it increased in depth as they advanced up the country. Finally they were obliged to quit the chaise and proceed on horseback. Having stopped for a short time at Blenheim, eight miles from Monticello, where only an overseer lived, they left at sunset to pursue their way along the only road, a mountain track, on which the snow lay in places two feet deep.

When they had battled their way to the small building which was all that had as yet been completed of Monticello, they found, instead of ruddy fires lighting up the windows, the house in total darkness. What a cheerless welcome for a young bride! Jefferson tenderly lifted Martha, numb with cold, from her saddle, stumbled with her into the house, and with tinder and flint lit a candle.

The servants, when it had grown so late, had not expected their master and his new wife to come that night, especially in such weather. So they had carefully extinguished all the fires and retired to their own cabins roundabout.

Poor Martha never forgot that dreadful moment when she saw the dreary house without light or warmth. But after Tom had put up the horses, he came back, built a small fire, and rummaged around until, with a cry of delight, he found a bottle of wine behind a shelf of books. Refreshed and warmed by the wine, Martha began to look on this strange homecoming as a jolly lark, and they were soon singing as merrily as they had ever done in The Forest.

The next morning Jefferson took Martha all over the place, showed her his plans on paper, and pointed out where the main house and the gardens were to go, where the park and the fountains, the orchards and the bridle paths were to be.

But they lived in their little pavilion, which is now known as the "Honeymoon Lodge," all that winter, for building work could be carried on only in the summertime.

VI

ARE AMERICANS
ENGLISHMEN?

AT about the time Tom Jefferson became a married man, his friend and brother-in-law, Dabney Carr, became a father again. Jefferson found Carr's enthusiasm slightly amusing. "Carr speaks, thinks, and dreams of nothing but his young son," Jefferson wrote Page. "This friend of ours, Page, in a very small house, with a table, half a dozen chairs, and one or two servants, is the happiest man in our universe. Every incident of life he so takes as to render it a source of pleasure."

Dabney Carr was indeed a happy mortal, happy in his wife

and family, happy in his practice of the law, and happy in the
promise all his friends held out for him. He was living and
practicing in Louisa County in 1773 when he was elected to
the House of Burgesses. Carr had always been interested in
public speaking, and Jefferson, who was himself a much better
writer than a speaker, was very proud of his friend's fine voice.
Although seven years younger, Carr was considered Patrick
Henry's most formidable rival in oratory as they argued
against each other in the Louisa County courthouse.

Like Patrick Henry eight years before, Carr came riding
into Williamsburg during a time of special excitement, when
the colonies were angry at still another inconsiderate act on the
part of the mother country. The cause of excitement this time
was the "*Gaspee* incident" of Rhode Island.

The year before a British man-of-war, the *Gaspee,* had for
some time been lying in ambush on the sea-road between
Newport and Providence. Like a pirate, the commander had
without warning descended upon and boarded every craft that
came out of these harbors: packets, market boats, ferryboats,
coasting schooners, everything that floated. He was searching
them for smuggled goods and contraband. Now the feelings of
the Americans against England's navigation laws had reached
such a pitch that smuggling had become a positively respectable profession. The sympathies of the colonists were not with
the British commander, and the Rhode Islanders felt very
warm about what they regarded as his high-handed procedure.

Rhode Island was the only one of the thirteen colonies that
elected its own Governor. This Governor protested to the commander of the *Gaspee,* stating that, unless the Governor was
shown a warrant, the commander's searches and seizures were
lawless, pure piracy.

One day the regular mail packet left Newport for Providence without informing the commander of the *Gaspee*. The *Gaspee* gave chase for twenty-three miles and then ignominiously ran aground. The captain of the packet gleefully told the adventure in Providence. Mr. Brown, the most influential merchant in the town, heard and chuckled. He knew that the tide would not let the *Gaspee* off the reef before three o'clock. He sought out eight boats, each commanded by a sea-captain, and with muffled oars they rowed out to the imprisoned *Gaspee*. They took off the sailors and men and set fire to the ship.

At such a shocking act of defiance the law-abiding Tories were indignant. But in a way they were as glad it had happened as were the smuggling rebels. For now, the Tories said, they will learn their lesson; punishment will be swift and sure, and we will have no more dangerous talk against the government.

A commission arrived from England with orders from the King that all those who had been responsible for the burning of the *Gaspee* and all the witnesses on both sides should be brought in a King's ship to London, where the trial would be held. But, although every boy in the streets of Providence knew just who had been in those eight boats, the commissioners could find no one in the whole city to tell them a thing.

Promptly the English Parliament passed a law, by the wording of which, if anyone so much as touched a button of a mariner's coat or the oar of a cutter's boat or the head of a cask belonging to the fleet, he was made guilty of a crime that could be punished by death and was to be transported to England for trial. Again Parliament had blundered, for now all the colonies were concerned, Virginia among them.

When Dabney Carr rode into Williamsburg and sought out Jefferson, they could scarcely speak of anything but the *Gaspee* affair and the new law. Nor could anyone else in the House of

Burgesses. But Carr had not listened to the debates for very long before he agreed with Jefferson that the endless discussions would come to nothing. They decided to call on Patrick Henry and the two brothers, Henry and Richard H. Lee, to meet them privately at the Raleigh Tavern to discuss plans of action.

"An attack on any one colony should be considered as an attack on the whole," said Jefferson when they had met. "But we must have some means of communication by which we will know what the other colonies are doing."

With the approval of the other three, he drew up resolutions for the forming of permanent Committees of Correspondence between the colonies. Samuel Adams was doing the same thing in Massachusetts. If England intended to treat them as one, they must learn to act toward England as one.

As the resolutions were Jefferson's, the others wished him to propose them to the House, but he was very anxious for Dabney to do it. Dabney as yet had had no occasion to speak, and Tom wished the members to hear and recognize his brother-in-law's fine talent.

At the next meeting of the House, Carr gave his speech proposing the Committees of Correspondence. It was beautifully delivered. Jefferson felt as pleased with his success as though Dabney were his son. The resolutions were carried; delegates, including Jefferson, Carr, and Patrick Henry, were appointed to meet other delegates from all the other colonies at some central point.

Carr went home to tell his wife about his maiden speech. She and the children were very proud of him. Martha was ill in bed at the time and she wished Dabney could stay with her a little while, but he had to be off again as he had some law business in Charlottesville. He bade her a tender good-by and remounted his horse. Martha raised herself on her elbow to catch sight of his face once more through the window and get him to smile to her, but all she could see was his moving hat as his horse trotted down the road.

Hardly had Dabney arrived in Charlottesville when he was taken violently ill with bilious fever. Before he could be taken home, he died, and, before Jefferson could be informed, they buried him at Shadwell.

At the terrible news Martha Carr had an attack of brain fever. For days, which lengthened into months, she suffered from a horrible nightmare. Whether awake in the day or asleep at night she saw a moving hat. It was feared that she would lose her mind, but after months of anxious care she recovered her reason.

Carr left three sons and three daughters. Jefferson took them and Martha Carr to live with him at Monticello. Thereafter he considered the children as his own. He had Dabney's grave moved to Monticello and buried under their oak, so fulfilling the promise he had made to Dabney fifteen years before. On his tombstone Jefferson planned to have carved, after the usual names and dates, this phrase: "To his Virtue, Good Sense, Learning, and Friendship, this stone is dedicated by Thomas Jefferson, who of all men loved him most."

Several months after the death of Dabney Carr, there arrived in Virginia a man who was to become a very dear friend of Jefferson's. His name was Philip Mazzei; he was an Italian; and he had come to America to see whether he could grow grapes for wine and olives for oil on the virgin continent.

Everyone knows the names of the Frenchman Lafayette, the German Von Steuben, the Pole Kosciusko, and of their services to the revolutionary colonies. And the memories of these men have been cherished by America. But because Mazzei was not a soldier, the unselfish aid he gave this country has been left out of the history books.

Mazzei really came to Virginia for the same reason as did the English planters—to set up a great estate like those back home. Only he thought of an estate in Tuscany, where they might think of one in Sussex. He had had an interesting and active life. Graduating from the medical school at Florence, he had practiced for several years in Turkey and Asia Minor. Then he had been the Grand Duke of Tuscany's special agent, or ambassador, to the Court of St. James's in London.

From there it had seemed to him that the English North American colonies were an ideal place to cultivate the products of his homeland, and that the Americans would probably be glad to learn the art of growing them. When Mazzei met Jefferson he was thirteen years older than that young man of thirty, but they became friends at once, on the basis of many common interests.

In the first place, this foreigner had traveled, and came from a land which Jefferson longed some day to see. Then, too, Jefferson had been studying Italian, and here was a chance to speak it. Mazzei, however, spoke English quite well, and the result was that Jefferson was a little bashful of bringing out his halting Italian before him. But Mazzei had imported a number of skilled Italian workmen and cultivators, who spoke not a word of English and on whom Jefferson was not afraid to practice his conversation. There are few things as delightful as finding your simple sentences in a foreign language understood perfectly by those to whom that language is native.

The meeting between Mazzei and Jefferson came about because the land the former chose for wine-growing bordered on Monticello. It seemed to him a paradise for grapes. Jefferson was so infected by his new friend's enthusiasm and was himself so anxious to see new benefits come to Virginia that he gave Mazzei two thousand acres of his own land.

Mazzei's experiments promised great things. His workmen found two hundred varieties of wild grapes. The shoots of some of them produced so many vines when transplanted and in a single year grew such great branches, that Mazzei's chief workman, Vicenzo Rossi, said to him once: "Master, don't write of this to our village, because they won't believe it, and you will pass for a liar." A hundred years later, when the famous vineyards of France were destroyed by a great plague, it was shoots such as these from America which were used to build those vineyards up again.

Mazzei had not been in Virginia long nor spent much time in Jefferson's company before he found himself growing more interested in politics than in wine. His duties as the Duke of Tuscany's agent in London had given him a better understanding of English government than most of the Americans had. He told Jefferson what he knew about the leading politicians in London, their views, and the true state of affairs there. Jefferson thought this information so important that he induced Mazzei to write it up. Jefferson translated his articles into English and had them published in the *Virginia Gazette*.

Later, when events grew more and more ominous, when the people who protested at England's treatment of the colonies began to call themselves "patriots," Mazzei threw in his lot with the Virginians. In nearly every county voluntary companies of militia were being formed, and Mazzei joined Jefferson in enlisting in the Albemarle regiment.

When British troops finally did land at Hampton Roads, Mazzei was among the volunteers hastily mobilized to defend the land. American methods of warfare were something new to Mazzei. There were few guns in Virginia except fowling pieces, and what ammunition there was each volunteer made at his own farm. Mazzei owned three hunting rifles. He armed one servant, but Vicenzo raised such a protest at not being taken along, that he gave him his other gun. And so they set out for Hampton Roads, Mazzei discovering on this march that what Jefferson had told him about night air was true— one did not necessarily take cold by sleeping out of doors.

At Orange County the company was joined by two young brothers named Madison, the older one, James, being then twenty-two. When they all reached Hampton, they found they had already gained a victory without firing a shot. Hearing that so many men were on their way to meet them, the English had hurriedly re-embarked.

Patrick Henry was in command of the Virginians. He called his militia together and made them an eloquent speech in praise of their immediate answer to their country's call. They were the minutemen of Virginia. And finally he added a few special words of praise for the three Tuscans who had thrown in their lot with them. When Mazzei translated this into Italian for the benefit of his assistants, Vicenzo became an American patriot on the spot.

In the meantime, though Dabney Carr was dead, his speech had done its work, and Jefferson's plan for Committees of Correspondence had been carried out. Among the first pieces of important news carried along this early grapevine system was the half-serious, half-comic story of the Boston Tea Party. How the young hotheads of Virginia roared when they heard that a whole cargo of English tea had been brewed in Boston harbor by a band of wild Indians! Older men shook their heads in distress, but Jefferson knew that events would move very quickly now, and he began to prepare for them.

Sure enough, word came from England that a law had been passed closing the busy port of Boston to all trade. The law was to go into effect June 1, 1774, and British troops were being sent to enforce it.

Hastily the same little group—without Dabney Carr—who had pushed through the Committees of Correspondence gathered together to devise a new measure of protest. They found what they wanted by searching through some old Puritan accounts. The next day the House of Burgesses passed a bill appointing June 1 as a day of fasting and prayer in Virginia. It was based on a model taken out of Puritan history.

The new Governor, Lord Dunmore, had by now formed one very irritating habit. Every time the House passed a bill which he considered the least bit objectionable to England, he dissolved the House and told the members to go to their homes. Nor was he behindhand this time. When the bill was brought to the royal Governor for his signature, he promptly dissolved the House of Burgesses. This was no more than Jefferson and the others expected. This time they were prepared.

The members, instead of going home, called for a Convention. Virginia's charter said nothing of any convention, and so, if one were called, the Governor could have nothing to do with it. It was illegal, outside the law, and so could say and do what it pleased. The purpose of this Convention was to elect delegates who would meet with delegates from the other colonies every year, thus forming a Continental Congress, a great advance on the Committees of Correspondence. Since the Congress was also illegal, the King could not even recognize it, let alone interfere in its decisions.

Naturally every county elected the same people to this Convention that it would have elected to the House of Burgesses. Duly elected from Albemarle County, Jefferson mounted his horse late in July and set out for Williamsburg.

On the road he was overcome by a serious attack of dysentery. Too ill to move, especially on a jolting horse over the rough roads, he was compelled to take lodgings on the way. He lay in bed frantic with disappointment.

He had prepared a rough draft of some resolutions which he felt he simply must deliver to the Convention. He had intended to finish them during the meeting. If only Dabney were alive! How often they had discussed together the principles in that rough draft. With his golden tongue Dabney would have made the others see how important these principles were, and would have wrung their assent from the delegates.

There was nothing to do now but send the drafts on by express. He was too weak to work on them. Fortunately there were two copies, one of which he sent to Patrick Henry, the other to his cousin Peyton Randolph, who was to be chairman of the Convention.

Patrick Henry either did not care for the resolutions or he was as usual too lazy to read them. At any rate he never mentioned them to anyone. But Peyton Randolph put them on the table, and most of the members read them.

These resolutions contained some views that Jefferson had been thinking out since his student days. For one thing, remember that he came from the Piedmont. He never thought of himself as an Englishman. He remembered his father as a Virginian, an American. All this talk of the colonists' rights as British subjects left him cold. His ancestors had not chosen

England as a birthplace. They just happened to be born there, and, when they grew old enough to know their own minds, they came away. In fact they had come to America because, for one reason or another, they did *not* like England.

So England and America, though they had the same King, were not the same country. Did the Saxons and the Danes who settled England owe absolute allegiance to Denmark and Saxony, whence they came? George III was also King of Hanover in Germany, but this did not mean that Hanover belonged to England or that England belonged to Hanover.

Moreover, neither England nor the King had bought the new territory on the western shores of the Atlantic. The colonists had taken land in a wild and sparsely populated country. They had not inherited it, but by their own hard work had carved out farms and cultivated them. These lands belonged to them and to no one else, least of all to anyone living in England.

Now this was really heresy. By English law, all this land belonged to the King. He was supposed merely to have made a gift of its use to certain individuals. Jefferson's opinion was exactly the opposite. He said that the King had merely been chosen by the colonists to help *them* run the country. He was the government they had decided to use rather than another. If he did not serve them well, they could just as easily choose another government.

Jefferson's resolutions showed how much he had been influenced by his readings in the old Anglo-Saxon law. He pointed out that it was only after the Norman Conquest that the King was considered to own all the land of his subjects and could give them out at his pleasure. Well, the colonists had done their own conquering; they alone owned their country.

These resolutions, for the instruction of delegates to the first Continental Congress, made a deep impression on many

ARE AMERICANS ENGLISHMEN?

members of the Convention. But for the time being Jefferson's views seemed too bold; in fact, treasonable. Later they would have to remember these resolutions, but now all they dared insist upon was that they were Englishmen, had the rights of Englishmen, and could not be taxed without representation. So the Convention voted for a different, tamer set of resolutions and sent them together with delegates to the Continental Congress in Philadelphia.

But this was not the end of Jefferson's resolutions. In England they were considered to be the best statement of the American position. The American agent who represented the House of Burgesses in London published the resolutions in a pamphlet under the title of *Summary View of the Rights of British America*. Edmund Burke, the great English statesman, who was a friend of the colonists, saw the pamphlet and, after making a few changes, used it in one of his famous speeches. The net result for Jefferson was that the English government put his name down on the roll of dangerous subjects to be made outlaw—along with the two Adamses, John Hancock, Patrick Henry, and other leading patriots.

VII

THE DECLARATION

IN Philadelphia the Continental Congress discussed ways and means of forcing the mother country to listen to her colonists' demands. It was decided to try commercial weapons. First, the boycott: after December 1774 the colonists would cease to import English goods. Then, if that should fail, the embargo: they would refuse to export their products to England.

The newspapers were filled with news of the boycott and its effects. Appeals were made to the patriotism of the ladies, and accounts were given of weddings in which not a single article of British manufacture was used: all the refreshments coming from the bride's gardens and fields, even the wedding gown woven as well as sewn at home, and so on.

Of course, with no goods allowed in from England, there would be a scarcity of many things, and so the Congress had urged patriotic merchants not to take advantage of this situation by charging too high prices. Here was work for the Martha Jeffersons as well as the Thomas Jeffersons. The ladies were not to permit profiteering, though that is not the word they used. And sometimes they did their work very well indeed. For instance, the newspapers told of one shopkeeper who had raised the prices of his tea outrageously, knowing that no more tea would be admitted. The women of the town came in a body and offered him a fair price. He refused it. Then the women took hold of him, trussed him up in his own shop, appointed one of themselves to do the weighing, and divided up the tea at the price they had offered.

Williamsburg had a little Boston Tea Party of its own when a group of people destroyed a cargo of tea and tried to burn the ship into the bargain, for it had been warned not to try to land. And some of the other newspaper accounts were full of fun, as when they told of a barber who, after shaving half of a customer's face, discovered him to be the captain of a British man-of-war, and refused to finish the job.

Jefferson, too, had a small problem of his own. Between one boycott and the next he had sent to England for fourteen pairs of sash windows and a parcel of extra glass to mend them with. As the English glaziers had kept them a month in order to harden the putty in the window frames, the second boycott went into effect while they were in a ship on their way over. Jefferson hastened to inform the committee of the case, and to tell them to do with the windows whatever they wished.

In each county of Virginia there was set up a Committee of Public Safety to see that the decrees of the Continental Congress were enforced, since the King's officials were to be expected to do nothing of the sort. Jefferson was now extremely busy, for he was the president of the Committee of Public Safety in Albemarle County as well as county lieutenant.

These committees kept in touch with each other through their own mail service, for the royal mail was not to be trusted. In the first place we have seen in Jefferson's own case how careful he had to be to disguise Belinda's name for fear of unscrupulous and inquisitive mailmen. But now these mail officials not only opened and read letters; if there was any suspicious patriotism in them the letters were turned over to the royal authorities, who would calmly destroy them and arrest the senders. William Goddard, who had had his Maryland newspaper barred from the mails because of its support of the colonists' cause, struck back by starting his own mail service. Soon his men were delivering all messages that it was dangerous to entrust to the King's men. These riders, when they met the royal mail riders on the road, would often have bloody fights.

The Continental Congress had also urged the colonists to discontinue all extravagance and dissipation during the boycott, especially gaming and horse-racing. Now the gay Virginia planters could not all at once become Massachusetts Puritans. But at their dances and card parties they made up for this disobedience by singing liberty songs, while round the well-filled punch bowl they drank only liberty toasts. A favorite toast was very arithmetical:

> Addition to the Whigs,
> Subtraction to the Tories.

> Multiplication to the friends of Liberty,
> Division to enemies of America.

On the 10th of May 1775 the second Continental Congress convened with Peyton Randolph again its president. But Randolph was also speaker of the House of Burgesses, and, when Governor Dunmore called a special session of the House, Randolph had to hasten back to Virginia.

A detachment of cavalry rode out to meet the President of the Continental Congress returning by coach to Williamsburg. Bells were rung, and that night there were "illuminations" or fireworks displays. The Raleigh Tavern was filled with gentlemen drinking liberty toasts.

The next day the House settled down to consider the special business, which concerned Lord North's conciliatory proposals. The English government offered to refrain from any further taxation of the colonies by Parliament if the colonies would in turn each agree to help England in case of war and make provision for the support of British soldiers. Now Lord North refused to consider the colonies as in any way united; he had addressed his propositions to each colony separately. Moreover, he insisted that each colony must pledge itself to help put down rebellions in any other colonies. And finally the colonies must agree to certain measures that would mean the destruction of New England's entire sea trade.

It was indeed fortunate that the Continental Congress was already in working order and had agreed upon the principle that a blow aimed at one of the colonies was an injury to all. Instead of sending its reply to Lord North, the Virginia House decided to frame an answer and submit it first to the Congress, so that all the Colonies could speak as one.

To Peyton Randolph and, indeed, to the House as a whole, there seemed to be one man best fitted for the task of framing

Virginia's reply—that man was Thomas Jefferson, the author of the famous *Summary View*. Not only was he now recognized as a legal artist, but his attitude toward England was absolutely clear and unwavering. Furthermore, Jefferson had already been chosen to take Randolph's place in Philadelphia while the latter conducted Virginia's affairs. So he would be taking his own ideas to the Congress.

From Williamsburg it now takes a few hours to go by train to Philadelphia. Jefferson's journey lasted ten days. He traveled in a very light gig with two spare horses. He had to stop at five ordinaries. Twice the road led through such wilderness that he had to hire guides to aid him. Since every colony had a different system of currency, he had to change all his money when he came into Maryland, as we now do when we go from one country to another. Nor did each colony have a fixed system of coinage; in Maryland he found in use the English shilling and guinea, the Spanish dollar, the pistareen, and the half jo. He had to go through a similar process on reaching Pennsylvania.

At length he arrived in Philadelphia, engaged lodgings at the home of a man named Ben Randall, and treated himself to dinner at the City Tavern. Ben Randall was a carpenter and cabinet-maker, and Jefferson had a job for him. For Jefferson had brought with him from Monticello the plans and drawings for a portable desk he had invented in his spare time. Randall made it while Jefferson stayed at his home. It could be folded up into the size of a large book, had a drawer for paper, ink, and quills, and could be opened out one way as a reading table and another as a writing desk.

The morning after his arrival Jefferson took his seat in the Congress. He felt far from important among the gentlemen there. After all he was only a substitute for his cousin, and the next to the youngest member present, being but thirty-two years old. But he was met with a warm welcome by some of the leaders, for his reputation for patriotism and scholarship had preceded him. John Adams noticed him and wrote in his diary: "Duane says that Jefferson is the greatest rubber-off of dust that he has met with."

The second Continental Congress, which had now been sitting for six weeks, was a feverish collection of men. In the first place they had no legal right meeting in this way. In the second place they would surely be held responsible and perhaps be hanged for the violent events that had taken place that year. Official or not, a war with the mother country was on. Just before the meeting of the Congress, a battle had been fought at Lexington, Massachusetts, between British regulars and farmers. And on the very day the second Congress opened Ethan Allen had led his Green Mountain Boys in an attack on Fort Ticonderoga and had captured it "in the name of the Great Jehovah and the Continental Congress!" That June there was fought a fierce battle at a place called Bunker Hill in Massachusetts between some British troops and twelve thousand Americans called out by the local Committee of Safety.

Sitting with Jefferson as another delegate from Virginia was Colonel George Washington, head of Virginia's militia. He attended the sessions in uniform. When the Congress found itself definitely committed to a course of treason against England, with battles like that of Bunker Hill already a fact, it chose this colonel as the commander-in-chief of the Continental armies.

Jefferson's *Summary View* had been handed around at the Congress. Though it had seemed too radical when he wrote it, the pamphlet now appeared to suit the situation very well indeed. So it is not surprising that in five days Jefferson found himself delegated to perform a very important and delicate task. He and John Dickinson were ordered to prepare an Address on the Causes of Taking Up Arms. The Congress was at last admitting that it would resist force by force, and Thomas Jefferson was given a hand in justifying this step to history.

John Dickinson, like Jefferson, was a literary artist in legal matters. He has been called "the penman of the Revolution"; he had written most of the petitions to the King. But otherwise the two committee members were nothing alike. Dickinson was cautious and conservative. He would have nothing to do with talk about independence from England, or the natural rights of Americans. When he saw Jefferson's first draft of the Address, it was as if a red flag had been waved in front of a bull. No, sir, he would not permit it! Why, this red-headed Virginian was egging the colonies on to Revolution!

So Dickinson rewrote the Address with milder, more conciliatory phrases. Only the last four paragraphs were left of Jefferson's fiery protests. The bomb of the Revolution was given a longer fuse; it would take a longer time spluttering before it exploded.

The more radical members of the Congress, the patriots, however, had found their man. They recognized in Jefferson "a happy talent for composition." Here was one upon whom they could call to present their case in the most elegant style and yet in its truest, most advanced light. As the Congress went beyond the cautious policies of Dickinson, it relied more and more upon Jefferson's pen.

The answer to Lord North's propositions of conciliation was considered to be the most important task of Congress. Vir-

ginia's reply, as drawn up by Jefferson, was acknowledged to
be the best model. So, when the committee for this particular
task was selected, we find, as we expected, Jefferson's name together with Benjamin Franklin's, John Adams's, and Richard
Henry Lee's. Franklin got the most votes, and Jefferson the
most after him. He had leapt immediately into popularity
with these Americans from all the thirteen colonies.

Lord North's proposals were rejected scornfully as insulting,
misleading, and not in fact conciliatory at all. England still re-
tained the *right* to tax whether she did so or not. She still im-
posed duties upon the colonies while she refused to allow them
to trade with other countries than herself. The attacks upon
Boston were inhumane. The answer was a more dignified expression of exactly what Virginia had wished to say.

On the first of August, the Congress being adjourned, Jefferson got into his carriage and made the ten-day journey home.
He was just in time to bid good-by to his friend and kinsman
John Randolph. John was going to England to live. He was a
Tory and disapproved of the threatening Revolution against
England. Jefferson bore him no ill-will. He had always believed that no man should be compelled to live in a country
with which he was not in sympathy, that it should be every
man's privilege to choose whatever citizenship he desired, no
matter where he chanced to be born. That was precisely how
he and his ancestors had become Americans.

Before he took ship John Randolph finally relinquished
the violin that Jefferson had so much wanted. John accepted
thirteen pounds and canceled the old arrangements of the
wills. But now Jefferson was too busy to do much practicing.
Nor was he in the mood, for the next month he lived through
still another family tragedy, this time the closest of them all.
His baby daughter, aged one and a half years, died.

Congress met again in September, but it had been sitting three weeks before Jefferson could come back to Philadelphia. His little daughter's illness and death had held him in Virginia. He was in Congress that December when the news came that the King had declared the American colonies in a state of rebellion and had accused them of seeking to establish an independent empire.

This was good news to the men who were of Jefferson's opinion. Now, if the King said so, perhaps the cautious conservatives would believe in the Revolution, too. Immediately after Christmas 1775 Jefferson left for home. There was work to be done in Virginia.

Jefferson was one of the greatest underground agitators of all time. Not being an orator, he could not sway the multitudes with fiery speeches, but he had a genius for organizing great bodies of opinion for action by quiet, simple means. He could talk to influential friends and acquaintances logically and persuasively. He could write letters. In the meantime he collected money for gunpowder and conducted the affairs of his Committee of Public Safety. He was now also head of the militia of Albemarle County. But his main business was to make Virginia prepared for the next decisive step of the united colonies.

In the midst of these labors, sorrow again visited the Jefferson home. His mother died that March.

There was a simple funeral. Congress had asked the colonists, for the sake of economy, to avoid the usual pomp of such ceremonies. In Virginia it was customary to present all friends and relatives with black gloves, and the ladies with black scarves. The funeral procession was the occasion of a grand display of gloomy trappings. Everyone had new suits made all of black. But Jefferson observed the requests made by Congress. He wore only a simple black band on his hat.

When in May 1776 a convention was called in Virginia to consider the question of independence, the success of Jefferson's labors, and the labors of the men like him, became apparent. The Convention voted unanimously to instruct its delegates in Congress to declare the united colonies free and independent States. In Williamsburg the church bells were rung, guns were fired, and the British flag over the State House was hauled down to make place for one with thirteen stripes.

As soon as he was sure of this vote, Jefferson hastened to Philadelphia to resume his seat. Virginia was safe; the next important work lay in Congress. Jefferson took rooms again with his old landlord, Ben Randall the carpenter. This time Jefferson found his fellow Congressmen in a daring, fighting mood. They had now all caught up with John Adams and Patrick Henry and Thomas Jefferson. They had all read, as had nearly every person in the colonies who could read at all, a pamphlet that for boldness and fire quite eclipsed Jefferson's scholarly *Summary View*.

While in London Benjamin Franklin had met a man named Thomas Paine, whom he persuaded to go to America, the land of opportunity. Paine had been in this country little more than a year when he wrote *Common Sense*, a pamphlet that put the arguments for independence so simply, so tellingly, that there seemed to be no answer to it. This was in January 1776. In a short time the clumsy presses of the day had labored to turn out a hundred thousand copies of the work.

Early in June, then, in obedience to the instructions they had received from home, the Virginia delegates proposed to the Continental Congress that a Declaration be drawn up stating that "these united colonies are and of right ought to be free and independent." The motion was seconded by John Adams of Massachusetts.

In the great debate that followed it became evident that no one denied America's right to independence or even the fact that America was already independent. Was not the Congress at that very moment directing a successful war against England? But was it good policy to put the fact into words? It was the same old situation that Jefferson had seen come up again and again when bodies of men gathered to deliberate upon the policies of nations. Statesmen simply hated to put facts into words, as if they were so many ostriches refusing to see what was under their noses.

Besides, not all the colonies were ripe for such a step. The middle colonies—New York, New Jersey, Pennsylvania, Delaware, and Maryland—as well as South Carolina were still in "the half-way house of Dickinson," as Jefferson called it. They had not yet instructed their delegates to go as far as those of Virginia and Massachusetts. But the public clamor for a statement of the colonies' rights to freedom had become so loud that Congress decided to draw up a Declaration at once, while it waited for the tardy colonies to catch up with the others. No time was lost in selecting a committee to write the Declaration. On it were John Adams, Benjamin Franklin, Roger Sherman, Robert Livingston, and Thomas Jefferson, who received the most votes. They set to work immediately and of course selected Jefferson, the legal artist, to do the actual writing.

Just at this time Jefferson was wishing he could be in two places at once. For, perfectly certain that independence would be declared, Virginia had decided to make itself a new constitution. Now Jefferson was a man born to write constitutions.

All his thinking and his studies had fitted him to set up rules for the conduct of just states, for the protection of men's rights.

But at a moment of such great historical significance Jefferson could not desert Philadelphia. Several of the Virginia delegates were hastening home, and to one of them, his old friend and teacher George Wythe, Jefferson entrusted a sketch of a constitution that he had dashed off.

When Wythe reached Williamsburg, he found the framers of the Virginia constitution quite fatigued with their labors. They had just accepted a document drawn up by James Madison and George Mason, and were simply too tired to go over the whole thing again. However, they took Jefferson's preamble and tacked it on to their own work. This preamble included a list of reasons for separation from England, and it was really a sort of first draft to what Jefferson intended to put into the general Declaration of Independence.

In his private life Jefferson was not a happy man just then. His daughter's death in September had been followed by his mother's end in March. And ever since last November, Lord Dunmore, royal Governor of Virginia, had been arming slaves and indentured servants and egging them on to attack the homes of rebel planters. They had burned Norfolk, and Jefferson never knew when they might be pillaging in Albemarle County. He had to rely for his family's protection on the Committee of Safety he had organized. To top everything, he received grave news of his wife's health. It took so many days for news to come from Monticello; his wife might be lying desperately ill while he knew nothing of it; she might be dying.

These thoughts lay heavily at the back of his mind when Jefferson began to write, to cut, to polish, to balance a composition that would become one of the most famous pieces of literature in the world. These thoughts may have given the work its passionate nobility, as great sorrow often does. When he wrote down the wrongs of England for all the world to see, he felt his accusations so strongly because his own happiness was now in danger through England's actions.

For eighteen days Jefferson tried to think of nothing but what he was then writing. And in that time he never turned to a book or pamphlet, though of course his mind was stuffed with books and pamphlets. But he had no ambition to be original; he was trying to put in neat, clear terms what America thought. And because he let America, this newborn nation, speak through him, he was a hundred times more original than he would have been by being simply clever.

Jefferson had moved to more commodious lodgings in the home of a Mr. Graaf. Here he sat for eighteen days over the portable writing desk Ben Randall had made for him, laboring over one of the great pages of history. Later he had to alter a phrase that did not suit Adams, or put in an idea suggested by Franklin. Finally the paper was ready to be put on the table before Congress.

Now, while Jefferson listened to the debate on his composition, he learned what embarrassment was. Some of the gentlemen in Congress were very frank in expressing their opinion of parts of Mr. Jefferson's writing. For instance, he had, among other charges, accused the King of refusing to let the colonists stop the cruel capture of slaves. But some of the Southern colonies and some of the Northern ones, too, which enjoyed a flourishing trade in the transportation of Africans, would not be pleased by such a statement, being in this respect quite of the King's opinion. So this particular censure was struck out. And so it went for a few days.

Dr. Franklin was sitting next to Jefferson during one of these episodes and noticed from the expression on his face how the young man was taking some of the comments on his work. To cheer him up Franklin told him a little story that, he said, explained why he, for one, would never accept a job like Jefferson's if it had to be passed on by a public body. It seems that when Franklin was a young journeyman printer a friend of his decided to open a hat shop. First he had himself made a handsome signboard which read: "John Thompson, Hatter, makes and sells hats for ready money," and had a picture of a hat on it. Then he asked his friends how they liked it. The first man he showed it to told him to take the word "Hatter" out, because the next words already said he made hats. Out came the word "Hatter." The next friend told him to strike out the word "makes," since his customers would not care who made them as long as he sold them and they were good. The word "makes" was struck out. A third friend thought the words "for ready money" quite useless as it was not the custom of the place to sell on credit, and every buyer expected to pay cash. The useless words were crossed out. Now the sign read: "John Thompson sells hats." "*Sells* hats!" exclaimed the next friend. "Nobody expects you to *give* them away!" So out came that word. And, of course, the word "hats" went with it, since there was already a picture of a hat.

Jefferson's Declaration did not suffer quite so annihilating a fate. Perhaps this was due in part to the accidental fact that Congress was meeting in Carpenter Hall. Near by stood a livery stable, from which a horde of horseflies ascended continuously to bite the gentlemen in their silk-stockinged legs. Discussions were punctuated with undignified slaps of hands and fans. The heat and the flies may have served to remind the members that, after all, they agreed with all that Jefferson

had written and that this was no time to be quibbling over unimportant details.

On July 4, 1776, the Continental Congress adopted the
Declaration of Independence as corrected. Many of the members were in a jovial mood, relieved to find themselves in agreement and to be over the petty annoyances of argument. John
Hancock scrawled his name so large that a signature has ever
since been humorously called a "John Hancock." The British
government had a price on his head, and this was an added
gesture of defiance. "There," he said, "John Bull may read my
signature without spectacles." And Franklin, when he stood up
to sign, is supposed to have said: "Gentlemen, now we must all
hang together, or we shall all hang separately."

Otherwise there was not much excitement that day, no fire-
crackers as there have been ever since. No one then thought
of that day as a great holiday. Three or four days later the
Declaration was read in a public square in Philadelphia, ever
since called Independence Square. Soon copies were being
printed in every town of the thirteen former colonies. Jefferson
had copies made especially for his friends George Wythe and
John Page.

The greater part of the Declaration consists of specific
wrongs committed against the colonies by the King and his
government. But the most important, the best remembered
and most quoted part consists of the short introduction to these
grievances. For in this first part is the doctrine that a nation
has at all times the right to change a government that does not
suit it and that no longer performs the duties which a government should.

This was not only treason; it was heresy. For despite the
numerous changes of kings in England's own history, some

of them accompanied by violence, it was still assumed that kings ruled by divine right, that they were given by God to the people to be obeyed. Even supposing that a king *might* commit wrongs; this was absolutely no excuse for refusing to obey him.

But the Declaration of Independence of the new United States held that the purpose of a king, or of any government, was not to be obeyed but to provide for the life, liberty, and pursuit of happiness of his subjects or its citizens. Any government that did not provide for these rights had no claim to be supported. Such a government was in itself criminal, and the crime that a government may commit upon its citizens is known as tyranny. Hence the long list of wrongs to prove to the rest of the world that King George's government had been tyrannous. The colonists withdrew their consent to be governed. It was a new doctrine of the *divine right of the governed*.

It is from this point of view that we must read the phrase, "all men are created equal." People may sometimes be heard to scoff at this phrase. Are all men of the same height or have they the same brain? Aren't some stronger, some wiser than others? But this cannot be what Jefferson, who was himself one of the wisest of his own day, meant. He meant that, in so far as all men are equally governed, so all governments receive their powers from the consent of all men equally. If you and I have the same duties, must obey the same laws, then we must have the same rights and privileges. And among those are the rights to life, to liberty, and to the pursuit of happiness. Some Congressmen may have thought that Jefferson should have included the right "to property" in that last phrase, but Jefferson knew that the owning of property was only one way of pursuing happiness. There might be others.

AIL MEN
are
created
free &
equal.

Æ 1776

VIII

THE INNER REVOLUTION

THE American colonies in signing Jefferson's document had declared themselves in revolt against Great Britain. The Revolution was now open and aboveboard. What does it mean to have a revolution?

For the colonies it meant two things, just as the Declaration had two parts. First, to King George III they said: For such and such crimes or acts of tyranny we renounce you. You are no longer our king. We intend to be free and, if you try to stop us, we will fight. And, since England most certainly did intend to put a stop to such rebellious nonsense, the Revolution meant War. This may be called the Outer Revolution, and the hero of this part of the Revolution is the soldier, George Washington.

But the Declaration also began with a different kind of "nonsense." It spoke of the rights of human beings that no government could take away. It defined governments differently from what they actually were anywhere in the civilized world. It was addressed to the whole world, and it contained statements that could have been used to justify revolutions in every nation of Europe. In short, it was trying to bring about a revolution in men's minds. This may be called the Inner Revolution, and its heroes are the thinkers, Benjamin Franklin, Thomas Paine, and Thomas Jefferson.

Both these revolutions were now started in America. They would have to be fought side by side. But the soldier's revolution would be more dramatic and it would be settled sooner. And without its success the other revolution could not take place. That is why we always think of soldiers when we mention the American Revolution. Thomas Jefferson was to have a taste of the warrior's revolution, too, but the thinker's revolution was to be his lifelong task.

So now, the Continental Congress having completed its most important task, Jefferson's eyes turned once more to Virginia. He refused to be re-elected to the Congress. George Wythe followed his example. The two of them hastened home as fast as they could drive their horses. For the laws of Virginia were about to be rewritten. Now she was a free State. She had elected Patrick Henry her first Governor. Under the King it had been impossible to pass reforms through the House of Burgesses, now the House of Delegates. But in a revolution the minds of men are fluid and willing to accept change.

How grateful Jefferson was for this rare opportunity! Now he knew that all his studies of the Greek, Roman, Saxon, and French laws had been in preparation for this moment. Now the many barbarous old laws of Virginia must fall. They must give way to others that would go with the new principles of freedom and happiness for all.

All the way home Jefferson's mind was grinding out one new law after another like a machine, turning over one old abuse after another like a new plow. How seldom does the reformer have a chance to begin from the beginning, to toss overboard all the old accumulated rubbish, to clean society's house! And now all the ideas that had been fermenting and growing in Jefferson ever since Dr. Small had taught him to think of such things had their chance against the stupid habits of thought, which people tolerated only because they were lazy. No one is lazy during a revolution. No wonder that Jefferson loved the American Revolution, looked upon its principles as something holy, and ever afterwards felt friendly to revolutions wherever they might occur.

Ambition drove him, too. Long afterwards, Jefferson wrote to a friend, in describing this period, that in his earlier years "the esteem of the world was perhaps of higher value in my eyes than everything in it." It was his particular form of "the pursuit of happiness."

Revolutions do this to people, too, for revolutions are like a fire under a pot or a ladle stirring in it. The pot is society, and the ladle and the fire bring things up from the bottom, where they have been dead, to violent activity at the top. People who never had a chance before discover new talents in themselves and new ways to exercise them. Napoleon once said of the French Revolution that it opened all careers to talent.

Jefferson was, of course, no Napoleon. He did not wish to make himself a dictator. He did not seek power for himself. He sought it for the people, so that their lives would be wider, freer, more self-reliant, and happier. The "esteem of the world" that he wanted so much—and the desire for which was to cause him so much heartache later—was the honest gratitude of a free people. He wanted to be like one of those Greek and Roman patriots whom his reading had made him venerate.

Also it may seem strange that Jefferson was more interested in the laws of Virginia than in those of the whole nation. But it must not be forgotten that the thirteen former colonies were not yet a nation by any means. Even after the Declaration of Independence, the Continental Congress was not making laws for all. A traveler abroad would describe himself as a Rhode Islander or a Virginian rather than as an American. In fact, he might be annoyed if you forgot what State he came from, just as a man from Argentina will be annoyed if you call him simply a South American, or as an American is now annoyed if someone in Italy calls him an Englishman. Very few Americans could see, as Benjamin Franklin did, a truly united nation in these thirteen independent States.

Jefferson had been back in Virginia a month when he received a very tempting message from Congress by express. He was informed that Congress had elected him, along with Silas Deane and Benjamin Franklin, to go to the French court to negotiate treaties of alliance and commerce with France.

Now Jefferson was torn with desire. At the back of his mind there had always persisted the hope that some day he would go abroad. For three days he kept the express waiting while he tried to make up his mind. Finally he decided against it. His wife's health was too poor to allow her to cross the ocean, and, if Philadelphia was too far away from her, Paris certainly was. Then, too, the battle over Virginia's legal reforms had just begun.

The legal revolution that Jefferson had in mind was not a task for any one man. He had to have friends, supporters, teachers, and disciples. Dabney Carr would have made an ideal collaborator, but he was gone. There was, however, a stanch little group around Jefferson of old friends and new ones, who were leaders in Virginia and had some of the qualities that Jefferson lacked.

There was nothing finer in Thomas Jefferson's life than his friendship with George Wythe, or "the learned Mr. Wythe," as he was called by all those who knew him. In 1776, Wythe was about fifty-two years old, Jefferson's senior by eighteen years. From the day that Dr. Small had introduced these two, they had been great admirers of each other. It was while reading law under Wythe that Jefferson acquired his ideals of the legal profession.

For Wythe was a lawyer who actually took delight in small fees, sometimes returning part of the money he had received if, after the case was over, he thought the sum excessive. If he thought his client was in the wrong, he would simply drop the case. He was by nature a man without personal ambition and without desire for wealth. His passion was for study, for deep research in the ancient languages, exact sciences, and the law. He was an astronomer, a mathematician, and one of the ablest Greek scholars in America. His favorite amusement was to compose Greek poetry on the fly leaf of his notebooks. It can be seen that Wythe and Jefferson never wanted for a common subject of conversation.

Jefferson considered Wythe the best and most moral man he knew, and Wythe in turn idolized his former pupil. For public business, however, Wythe lacked two of Jefferson's most useful qualities: tact and patience. He could never conceal his annoyance at the opposition in a committee meeting. We have already seen how he acted at Patrick Henry's impudent request to be made a lawyer without knowing the law.

George Mason, another of Jefferson's elderly friends, and author of Virginia's constitution, resembled George Wythe in personal nobility, but his talents were more social. Like Washington he was extremely fond of fox-hunting. He was very handsome and cut a fine figure in a ballroom.

Mason had also been elected to the Continental Congress, but just then his wife had died and he was so grief-stricken that he could not leave his family. But he had carried on the good work at home. His Bill of Rights in Virginia's new constitution had served as one of Jefferson's models when he drew up the Declaration. Mason supplied the little group of stanch revolutionists with the fiery oratory it needed. He ended one of his letters to his son, at that time in Paris for his health, with the sentence: "God bless you, my dear child, and grant that we meet again in your native country as free men; otherwise that we may never see each other more is the prayer of your affectionate father."

Revolutions also need young men, who will carry on the work of mature men, just as mature men must base their work on the study and experience of older men. Jefferson's circle soon attracted the ideal young man for its purposes. This was James Madison, then twenty-five years old. Jefferson could always rely on this lieutenant to see any plans or measures carried through when he himself was obliged to be absent. Madison was always seeing things through. Though not as brilliant in speech or in writing as some of the others, he was untiring and persistent, and his ideal of the patriot was Jefferson.

These men, then—Jefferson, Wythe, Mason, and Madison —were the center of the movement to revolutionize Virginia's laws. Patrick Henry, and others as well, would sometimes join them to put through special measures, but these four men were constant in their aim to build up a democratic state. For, they felt, freeing the colonies from the English King was not the heart of the Revolution. States may be free and yet the people living in them be slaves. The real Revolution consisted in freeing these people from English ideas of government, from aristocracy, and in giving them a democratic form of government such as Europe did not have. The people themselves must be allowed to decide in each case what best served their rights to life, liberty, and the pursuit of happiness.

England was ruled by an aristocracy, and the aristocracy had its power, its wealth, and its social position in the ownership of large tracts of land. To keep the aristocracy limited to a small number of powerful people, these tracts of land were not allowed to be divided up. The whole of each nobleman's estate, together with his title, passed down intact to his eldest son. The other sons could shift for themselves, usually by becoming officers in the army or clergymen in the Church of England.

When the early settlers came to Virginia, it was natural that they should think of living under this same system. Those who had had no chance in England of being among the favored few land-owners—many of them younger sons and many merely of the middle or lower classes—now had their first opportunity to become powerful. Land could be had almost for the asking, and they carved out vast plantations for themselves in the Tidewater region. The huge grants of land passed from eldest son to eldest son.

These great landlords considered themselves the aristocrats, the untitled nobility, of the New World. They lived in splendid mansions and were magnificent in dress. They could be recognized by their periwigs and knee breeches, while the mean or lowly born wore the bobwig and plain baggy trousers. They insisted upon certain expressions of respect when they were addressed, and, even though they had no titles, they had worked out complicated systems of rank. Even at Harvard College the students were seated according to rank, John Adams being fourteenth in his class of twenty-four. To the Southern aristocrats their estates were as much a part of themselves as their noses, as closely connected with their names as their own fathers. There is a story of John Randolph of Roanoke setting his dogs on a man who dared to ask him the price at which he would sell his estate.

The Tories who opposed the Revolution came largely from this class of land-owners. Not having a king at hand, they created their own little court by flocking around the royal Governor. The latter usually chose councilors of state from among them. True, there were not enough positions to go around for so many of them, but the possibility of being chosen some day made each of them most devoted to the King's government, more loyal to England than to Virginia.

Now Jefferson saw at once that the power of this class lay in the laws that protected their system of inheritance. He would much rather have seen America populated and governed by sturdy independent farmers, with farms not so vast that they had to be cultivated by slaves. Besides, he considered the inheritance laws themselves very unjust.

If a man died without a will, everything went to his eldest son. This was called the law of primogeniture (*primo*—first; *genitura*—birth). It all depended on this eldest son's good heart whether he would take care not only of his younger brothers and all his sisters, but also of his mother. Moreover, he could not always give his brothers any of his land even if wanted to. For the land might be "entailed." This meant that by some provision of his great-grandfather's will, the land must always stay intact and could never be broken up. The great-grandfather's dead hand forbade any heir from getting rid of any part of the estate he had inherited. Hence, this law of entailment was also called "the law of the dead hand." The heir could not sell his estate or give it away; he must pass it on to *his* eldest son, at least as large as he had received it. Generation after generation the estates might grow larger but they could never grow smaller.

These devices had been invented in feudal times, and Jefferson felt that they did not suit the modern world, especially not the American part of the world. They had undoubtedly been useful, he said, for providing armies under the conditions of the Middle Ages, but in the eighteenth century they only created hardships, and helped keep up a hereditary aristocratic class that was repugnant to the best principles of the Revolution.

Even in England, he pointed out, the dead hand had become such a burden on the country that as early as 1473 a law was passed making it possible to break the entail in some instances by going to court. But the Virginians were trying to be even more feudal than the English; they had passed their own law rejecting this type of relief and had gone the English one better by permitting Negro slaves to be entailed along with the land and houses. And, of course, the larger the estates grew under this system, the more did slaves become necessary.

So Jefferson and his friends set out to abolish this law of primogeniture, this "law of the first-born." It is an unfair law, they said. Why should accident of birth give the one son, who might after all be the stupidest and meanest of the lot, such an advantage over his brothers and sisters and mother that they were forced to live on his bounty? It must be remembered that families in those days were very large, it being no uncommon thing for a household to have ten children.

Curiously enough, the two great champions of the abolition of this law of inheritance had both benefited by it. Jefferson was an eldest son. George Mason's father had died without leaving a will, so that George had to accept the whole of the property, leaving his younger brother and sister penniless. Fortunately, Mason's mother, by dint of much saving, had got enough money together to buy the younger children ten thousand acres of wild land at a few shillings an acre, so that they might feel themselves equal with their older brother.

Jefferson's two measures, repealing the law of primogeniture and the law of entail met with the most bitter opposition. Even Patrick Henry joined in the protest. But Jefferson's most serious opponent was Mr. Pendleton, who, though he had finally joined the Revolution against England, was otherwise firmly attached to the ancient order of things.

Pendleton was a skilled politician with the patience of Job. He attacked Jefferson's radical proposals with oratory and with stratagems. In the debate he reduced the impatient George Wythe to a positive fury. Whenever the bills seemed finally about to pass, Pendleton would tack on an amendment which would turn their meaning upside down. He became such a nuisance to the radicals that they always referred to him as "Moderation" Pendleton. "Old Moderation" could always be depended upon to show them that, no matter how well considered their ideas, they were going too far.

But Jefferson's patience was equal to Pendleton's, and at last his measures were about to become a law. Hereafter, when a man died without leaving a will, his children would share the inheritance equally, and his dead hand would not prevent them from doing with it as they pleased. When "Moderation" saw that nothing could stop this from happening, he grasped at a last straw of compromise.

"At least," he said, "let us keep by the old biblical law and let the oldest son have twice as much as the rest."

"No," Jefferson replied, "not unless he can eat twice as much or work twice as hard."

And so Jefferson won his first big battle against the enemies of change. He had started the heavy omnibus of Virginia's laws rolling toward democracy. But from this time on he had sworn enemies who never forgave him, who never lost an opportunity to wreak their hatred on him. It was the beginning of a class hatred against him that never died as long as he lived. Fifty-five years later John Randolph of Roanoke could still attribute all the evils he saw or imagined in Virginia to the triumph of Jefferson and his "leveling system," as he called it.

Jefferson's next concern was the naturalization of foreigners. In proposing his bill, Jefferson repeated some of the statements he had made in his *Summary View:* that every person had the right to reside in whatever country he chose as long as he obeyed its laws, and that all that should be necessary for a man to give up his old citizenship was to declare his intentions and move. We have all become Americans, Jefferson argued, by moving from Europe or by having our parents move, and we should not suddenly close this privilege just because we ourselves are safely intrenched here.

His bill provided that any foreigner who desired to become a citizen of Virginia could do so after two years' residence by declaring in court his intention of living in the State thereafter. The wife of a naturalized citizen became a citizen with him, and so did his children who were under age. All minors who migrated to Virginia without father or mother became citizens without any legal steps when they came of age.

America had always been an asylum for Europeans dissatisfied with their home countries or persecuted in them, and Jefferson meant to see that Virginia at least would keep this noble purpose forever. The bill was easily passed.

The next great battle was not won with such ease. For Jefferson and his friends now set about establishing religious freedom, an idea so new and advanced that to many people it seemed shocking, if not blasphemous.

Most American colonies had become more or less accustomed to religious *tolerance,* that is, people were allowed to profess whatever religion they chose without being considered criminals. They could worship in their own churches in their own way. But they did not always have religious *freedom.* In every European country there was one religion that was held to be the State religion. Even if you were not persecuted for practicing some other religion, you were not a good citizen if you did so. You could not hold office; you were deprived of many rights and privileges; and, although you supported your own church, you paid taxes also for the maintenance of the State church to which you did not belong. In every European country, too, including England, the established State church was closely bound up with the ruling aristocracy.

Now, as a matter of fact, Virginia did not even have religious tolerance. Of course, she had an established church supported by the State, and of course that church was Episcopalian or "Church of England." And of course the landed aristocracy would permit no tampering with it.

The Southerners were not Puritans. Sunday in Virginia was not the solemn dreary day it was in New England. There were pretty strict laws about attending church on Sunday, but once the service—not too long—was over, your duty was done and you could do what you pleased with the rest of the day. The Episcopal Church did not forbid cards or dancing or any of the gentlemanly forms of entertainment. Your neighbor would not feel it his duty to report you to the elders for extravagance and luxury—as he might have in Massachusetts —if you had been so worldly as to buy a handsome carpet for your living room. And the clergy were gentlemen, too. They drank wine and even danced. In fact, once you belonged to the established church and attended services, no one could interfere with your private life.

But not belonging to the established religion was quite a different matter. While the Puritans had been hanging witches in the North, Episcopalians in Virginia were persecuting Quakers. The Quakers did not believe in baptism; they kept their hats on in church; they held other dangerous and suspicious notions. The Episcopalians felt they must put a stop to a religion that followed such vile and heathenish customs. Laws were promptly enacted fining anyone who did not baptize his children, punishing those who kept their hats on in church. Finally Quakers were forbidden to come to the colony at all. Any Quaker who showed up in Virginia was put in jail,

2

2 when he had served his sentence he was banished. If he
came a second time, he was to be put to death. As for the
Quakers already in Virginia when the bill was passed, no more
than five of them over the age of sixteen were allowed to meet
together at any time. That would break up their vicious
churches!

Now that the New Englanders were becoming more tol-
erant, a sudden wave of religious intolerance seemed to be
sweeping over Virginia. This time the persecution was being
directed against the Baptists. Madison, who was a graduate of
Princeton, wrote to a Northern friend:

"I want to breathe again your free air. . . . That diabolical,
hell-conceived principle of persecution rages among some;
and to their eternal infamy, the clergy can furnish their quota
of imps for such purposes. There are at this time, in the
adjacent county, not less than five or six well-meaning men in
close jail for publishing their religious sentiments."

Truth to tell, the magistrates did not know what laws to
invoke against the pestiferous Baptists, for they did baptize and
they did remove their hats in church. But since the Baptists
annoyed most by their fervent, open-air preaching, the magistrates usually convicted them of "disturbing the peace." This
accusation seemed to cover as many sins as it does now under
the new name of "disorderly conduct." Said the prosecutor in
one case: "May it please your honor, these men are great dis-
turbers of the peace. They cannot meet a man upon the road
but they must ram a text of Scripture down his throat."

Once Patrick Henry heard about some Baptists who were
being held in prison awaiting trial. He rode fifty miles to
defend them. Coming into the courtroom during the trial he
picked up the indictment as if by chance, seemed to look
astounded, shook his head incredulously, and launched forth

in one of his most famous speeches that began: "May it please your worships, what did I read? Did I hear an expression that these men whom your worships are about to try for misdemeanor are charged with *preaching the Gospel of the Son of God?*" Needless to say, when Henry was through getting over his amazement, the Baptists were freed.

Only half of those residing in Virginia really belonged to the established church, yet all paid it taxes equally. Furthermore, to be legally wed one had to be married by an Episcopalian minister.

"It does me no injury," Jefferson said, "for my neighbor to say there are twenty Gods or no God. It neither picks my pocket nor breaks my leg. . . . Is uniformity of opinion desirable? No more than face or stature. . . . Millions of innocent men, women, and children since the introduction of Christianity have been burnt, tortured, fined, and imprisoned, yet we have not advanced one inch toward uniformity. The effect of this coercion has been to make one half of the world fools and the other half hypocrites."

Practically all the Burgesses were Episcopalians, and, as one of them snobbishly said: "I trust no Virginia gentleman would care to go to heaven except by the established faith." However, the moderates were willing to go half way with Jefferson in his desire to remove all religious restrictions and disabilities. They admitted, for instance, that it was unfair to tax people for a church they did not belong to. Why not, they said, let people specify which churches they wished their taxes to go to? Would that not be religious freedom? For, if churches, any churches, were not supported by the State, religion would vanish from the face of the earth, and mankind would grow wicked and dissolute.

Even Washington wrote to Mason: "Although no man's

sentiments are more opposed to any kind of restraint upon religious principles than mine are, yet I confess that I am not among the number of those who are so much alarmed at the thought of making people pay toward the support of which they profess."

But Jefferson said No. This was not a matter for compromise. You had freedom or you did not. There was no third way about it. Any bargaining might some day be used as a basis for religious persecution. There must be no loopholes. Religion and religious support must be made purely voluntary. If religion was important, there need be no doubt that the people could be trusted to take care of it themselves without compulsion.

For eight years this struggle continued. At last, when Jefferson was in France, Mason and Madison got his bill for the establishment of religious freedom passed. It was the hardest battle that Jefferson and his lieutenants had ever fought. And Jefferson was always particularly proud of this victory. Later this principle of absolute religious freedom was inserted into the Constitution of the United States as the first amendment of the Bill of Rights, chiefly through the efforts of James Madison.

Once while writing about slavery in Virginia, Jefferson said he trembled when he remembered that God was just. There were during the Revolution about 250,000 slaves in Virginia. Jefferson himself owned more than a hundred and fifty. He had never bought any; they came to him with his father's and his wife's estates.

The slaves in America were nearly all African Negroes. The stronger tribes in Africa had always enslaved the weaker ones, but on a small scale. Then came the white men, who offered these stronger tribes such valuables as firearms, rum, calico, and various gewgaws in return for their slaves. In a short while the capturing of men, women, and children became a great trade. The strong tribes no longer sought slaves to do their own work; they captured them only to sell to the white traders, and in ever-increasing numbers. Finally not a single tribe on the African coast could live happy, decent lives, for they all went about with the terrible fear of capture.

Before the coming of the white trader, the slaves' lives were wretched enough, but at least they knew they would live among people like themselves, in a country like their own, and would do work such as they were accustomed to. But now their destination was a horrible mystery; they knew only that they would be put aboard the great white-winged boats and taken away from Africa, which was after all the whole world to them. So there were many tribes who never allowed themselves to be enslaved. They killed themselves first; or they killed their captors and masters.

The white men could soothe their own consciences by claiming that they themselves never engaged in the brutal business of *capturing* slaves, that the Negroes themselves *enslaved* each other, that they, the white men, only bought with good money, fairly and squarely, what was other men's property. But they could not so easily dismiss the charge of brutality, for the slave ships were built and manned and owned by white men, and the transportation of slaves from Africa to such markets as Virginia was one of the most brutal aspects of the whole business.

The ships were unspeakable. The Negroes were chained together, the sick with the healthy, and crammed between decks like sardines in a can. Here they could not even stand up, the ceilings were so low, or move about freely, so tightly were they packed together. For the shipmaster expected a certain large percentage of them to die during the long passage, and he took no chances of arriving with a small unprofitable cargo. He therefore often filled his ship with twice as many slaves as it was originally made to hold. Any infectious disease would spread like wildfire under such conditions.

The miserable savages could only wonder: "Did the white men, a strange race without women, live always on the water? Were they being taken somewhere to be eaten?"

The Negroes came from different parts of Africa's vast continent. They spoke hundreds of different languages and included dozens of different races. They could not always understand each other. They varied widely in color, size, and features. Some were giants in height, others pygmies. Some were the most abject savages, others rather nighly civilized. Their skins ranged from yellow to deepest black. Some of the slaves were so frail of build that they could not stand the heavy labor of the fields, but they often made good carpenters and coopers. The American Negro today is the result of the mixture of these many races. It is therefore a truly American race, to be found nowhere else, not even in Africa.

By 1776, however, nearly all the slaves in Virginia spoke English, and most of them had been born in America.

Many Southern patriots looked with distaste upon the institution of slavery. Owning slaves troubled Wythe's conscience so much that once, practically on the spur of the moment, he freed all of his own. George Mason said that his own Virginia should not be permitted to join the United States of America unless it abolished slavery. But this was very far from being the opinion of the majority of planters. The latter even passed laws to prevent idealistic hotheads like Mason from doing anything rash. Thus it was a law in Virginia that

no slave could be set free on any pretense whatsoever unless
the Governor and his council gave his owner a special permit
to do so.

When Jefferson first became a Burgess under a royal Governor, he had begun to work against the slave system. His
first cautious proposal was a measure permitting freed slaves
to live in Virginia. The measure was defeated and Jefferson's
supporters were only heaped with abuse and called traitors
for their pains. Jefferson had then decided that nothing pro-
gressive could be done about slavery as long as a king still
ruled the country. He decided to bide his time.

So, when Jefferson was writing the Declaration of Independence, he included among the crimes of the King the
charge that he had obstructed the colonists' attempts to limit
the system of slavery. But he discovered that many colonists
thought exactly as did the King's governors on this matter.
He was, much to his annoyance, forced to cross out this charge.

But the Declaration still stated that all men were created
free and equal, and this in one of the few countries in the
world where slavery was permitted! As soon as Jefferson got
back to Virginia, he set about the task of removing this in-
consistency. At first he wanted to attack the problem directly
at its heart by simply having slavery abolished. He told his
friends Mazzei and Mason that this was demanded by humanity, by justice, and by the principles of the Revolution.

He said that "to keep in slavery beings born with equal
rights to us and who do not differ from us in anything but
color is an injustice both barbarous and cruel, and even shame-
ful," especially when these very Negroes were helping the
former colonists to gain their own freedom.

But Jefferson's friends pointed out many circumstances
that made such a forthright step as abolition seem impossible.

First there was the opposition of the Virginia planters. Then Mazzei thought that, at a time when in some regions the slaves outnumbered the whites two to one, it was a dangerous proceeding suddenly to free them. The process should be more gradual. Mason wanted the Negroes to be educated before they were freed, and thought that their masters should be obliged to prepare them for liberty. Finally, Jefferson's own former experiences with the slavery question convinced him that the only sure way of abolishing slavery was to get the slaves actually out of the country. For he thought that the people who had once been slaves would never be allowed to live in peace side by side with people who had once been their masters.

In the end Jefferson worked out an elaborate plan for ultimately turning America into a free country that would answer all these objections:

All Negro children who were born from now on were to be free and to belong to no one but their parents. Thus the planters could not claim that they were being robbed of anything they had paid for. These children were to stay with their parents until they were old enough to be trained in a trade. Then at public expense they would be taught farming, handicrafts, or science according to their ability. When the boys were twenty-one and the girls eighteen, they were to be supplied with tools, seed, cows, horses, and firearms and be sent to some suitable colony, preferably in Africa. Considering what America had got out of these people, this was only a fair return. This colony was then to be declared a free nation by the American government. Finally, at the same time, America would be sending out ships to Europe to bring free white colonists to take the place of the slaves.

Jefferson took several years to work out the details of his

plan. In the meantime, he fought for small advantages. But his every attack on the slave problem came up against the stone wall of the planters' opposition. It was not until 1782 that Jefferson's original measure, permitting freed slaves to live in Virginia, was pushed through by Madison, after a compromise. The act now read that an owner might free a slave if he guaranteed that the freedman would not become a public charge. In eight years this act resulted in the freeing of ten thousand slaves.

As for the larger plan, which if enacted might have saved this country from the Civil War, it did not even start to take place until 1822, when James Monroe, a friend and pupil of Jefferson's, was President of the United States. In that year Jehudi Ashmun brought some freed slaves to the West Coast of Africa, where they started the nation of Liberia. But by now it was too late, for the cotton gin had been invented and slaves had become much too valuable to be allowed to go free.

If Jefferson felt that the difference between a slave and a free man should show in his education, it may be imagined what his feelings were about education for his fellow-countrymen. In the ideal state which Jefferson was now trying to help build in Virginia, everyone capable of learning at all must be educated, be he rich or poor. How else could the citizens understand their rights, be able to maintain them, and exercise with intelligence their parts in self-government?

Tom Jefferson had himself attended every type of school that existed in Virginia. At Tuckahoe he had been a pupil at a "field school," so called because it was held in an abandoned tobacco field. Then he went to two Latin schools, whence he had gone on at last to William and Mary College.

From first to last Tom's education had been paid for. For,

if there were no truant officers in Virginia, neither were there free public schools, except for three or four little religious ones founded by some charitable people.

Children of poor parents were usually apprenticed to farmers, tradesmen, or merchants. Since there were no orphan asylums, children left by their parents' death without money were apprenticed away by the courts. The law required that masters teach their apprentices to read and write. Boys had also to be taught some arithmetic, but this was considered unnecessary for girls. Of course, some masters were kind while others were cruel. One could not pick up a newspaper without seeing advertisements offering rewards for runaway apprentices:

Run away from the subscriber in Staunton, Augusta County, the 4th Instant (March) an indented boy, named

MOSES BARTHOLOMEW

aged 15 years, about 5 feet 4 inches high, of dark complexion, pitted with small-pox, very slim made, with dark short curled hair; had on when he went away, a brown double breasted jacket with sleeves, and a coat, red plush breeches, yarn stockings and plated buckles. He had a down look and is small of his age. He rode a small sorrel horse with one eye and a large blaze in his face.

Whoever fetches the servant and horse will receive three pounds paid by me.

Jefferson laid out a plan for public schooling that covered the whole system of education. Though the plan seemed too radical to be acceptable to the Virginian legislators, it is in many respects the system we have today. In other respects we have not yet caught up with it.

Each county was to be divided up into wards five or six miles square. Each ward was to support a school and a teacher with taxes collected from people who owned property, whether they had children or not. This is exactly how our modern schools are supported. Each child, rich or poor, was entitled to attend this school to learn reading, writing, and arithmetic. But most surprising of all, these public schools were to admit girls! This radical idea had not yet penetrated even into Boston, which was then the most advanced city in regard to public education.

Then in different parts of the State there were to be established twenty "grammar schools," which would teach Greek, Latin, geography, and advanced arithmetic, very much like our high schools. The brightest student from each ward school was to be sent to a grammar school on a scholarship. After a two years' trial, the brightest of these students were to be continued at advanced courses in the grammar school.

At the end of six years, half of the students were to be dismissed, some of them to become grammar and ward school teachers. The other half would be sent to William and Mary for a three-year course in whatever sciences they chose. Thus the brightest boys would be educated entirely by the State.

Of course, William and Mary would have to be reformed to allow for this new system. Jefferson had never considered it a satisfactory college. And after Dr. Small's departure it had seemed to go from bad to worse. The professors played cards all night long at the ordinaries and were often seen drunk on the streets.

Jefferson wanted to make a pure college of it, abolishing the Latin school, whose work would now be done by the grammar schools. The old Indian school, which never had done any good, would also have to go. A better use for the money would be to send teachers out to the different tribes. They would not only instruct the Indians in the principles of Christianity—as the fund required—but would also collect the Indians' laws, customs, and languages (Jefferson's never-resting curiosity about the first Americans again cropping up). When the missionaries had done their work in one tribe they could be sent on to another, and so on.

Finally, Jefferson sought to have the State lay aside a certain amount of money every year for books, paintings, and statues. For he proposed the revolutionary idea of a public library and a public art gallery!

As in the case of slavery, Jefferson's educational proposals did not have much luck. They were adopted only after many years, and then only piecemeal, and never in their entirety. In 1796 Jefferson's friends finally managed to get passed that part of his education bill dealing with the lowest grade schools, but only with an amendment that made it quite worthless. The amendment left it to the magistrates of each county to decide whether they should have ward schools or not. As the magistrates were the big land-owners of the counties and as the cost of education was to be borne by the wealthy classes (who had private tutors for their own children), very few ward schools were established.

And so Jefferson had to be satisfied again with merely planting the seed which would bear fruit much later. Eventually, he knew, his ideas must conquer. In the meantime he threw at the heads of the aristocrats one proposal after another which, like the one about public education, had for their purpose the destruction of every ancient aristocratic privilege and the blocking of every future one, so that a foundation might be laid for a government truly republican and democratic.

Now that there was no king, no court, no English Parliament to look after Virginia's laws, everyone realized that some revisions would have to be made in the present statutes. For this task of adapting the old code of laws to a republican form of government, the Virginia legislature selected their three best writers of laws: Thomas Jefferson, George Wythe, and Edmund Pendleton.

Jefferson was given the most ancient British laws to re-model, those that were older than the founding of the colony of Virginia. Wythe took the British laws up to the Declaration of Independence. And Pendleton was put in charge of the laws passed by Virginia herself.

Jefferson saw that the first big sweeping reform would have to do with the death penalty. For life was cheap in the English law of those days, much cheaper than a little property. Here are a few of the crimes that the British laws punished with hanging: high treason, also petty treason, murder, beating, wounding and preventing shipwrecked persons from saving their lives, night robbing with cruelty, robbing in general, forging, cattle stealing, malicious maiming of cattle, plundering a wreck, stealing in home or shop, mail theft, destroying wool or silk in a loom, sending threatening and anonymous letters, entering marriage falsely in a parish register, forging a marriage license and publishing same to be true, breaking down the head of a fish pond, destroying trees in plantation, sacrilege, deer and rabbit stealing, impersonating seamen to obtain their wages or prize-money, setting fire to ships or dockyards or mines or delphs of coal, destroying instruments used in manufacturing of cottons, silks, etc., breaking prison, petty theft (this might mean of a loaf of bread), together with a variety of minor offenses.

As a matter of fact, most of these laws were not very well enforced in England, for juries would often acquit a man for stealing a sheep rather than see him hanged for it. But the laws were there, and sometimes they were enforced for all their brutal, medieval character. Jefferson, Wythe, and Pendleton, for once unanimous, recommended the abolition of the death penalty for all crimes except murder and high treason. But it took the legislature eleven years to make this recommendation law.

In going over the ancient laws Jefferson was forcibly reminded of the difficult time he and Dabney Carr had had as students in following the involved language of "old Coke." He saw again how the complicated wording of the laws, with their parentheses within parentheses and their *saids* and *aforesaids,* their *bys, ors,* and *ands,* made them hard even for lawyers to understand and absolutely incomprehensible to the ordinary man.

Jefferson therefore determined that, while he was rewriting these laws, he might as well cast them into as simple and clear a style as he was capable of. Wythe joined him in this. Students of the law in Virginia today have Jefferson to thank if their studies are somewhat easier than elsewhere.

For three years these three men cut and pruned and rewrote. When the legislature was not in session Jefferson took his work home with him to Monticello, much to the happiness of his children and his wife, who was now never entirely well. In the intervals of rewriting the law he would teach the children. Besides his own two daughters, Martha, almost seven, and Mary, aged one year, there were their Carr cousins, whom Jefferson had adopted.

Finally, in February 1779, each of the three men completed his task. They met together and went over Jefferson's and Wythe's parts word by word, weighing every phrase and correcting every expression until all three were satisfied. When they came to the third part, it was discovered that Pendleton had not seized Jefferson's and Wythe's idea of simplifying the wording of the laws. Pendleton had copied the laws as he found them, merely dropping out the parts of which he disapproved.

Urgent family business called Pendleton away from the midst of these conferences, and he asked the other two to rewrite what he had done. Time was short, but they hastened to do so, with the result that the whole code of Virginia was practically written by the old teacher and his pupil.

The "Revised Laws" were put before the Assembly in the form of 126 separate bills. As usual the faithful Madison took up the colossal task of getting them passed: By plugging and hammering away he managed in six years to get 56 of them adopted.

IX

WAR-TIME GOVERNOR

WHILE Jefferson and his friends were fighting to make their country a better place to live in for future citizens, the war was going on which would decide whether America was to be a country at all. The news that poured in from the various fronts was disheartening enough. But late in 1777 there came the joyous surprise of Burgoyne's surrender at Saratoga. This great news had among other things two important results for our story. First, it brought France in as an ally of the young republic. Secondly, four thousand prisoners of war were sent to be quartered in Virginia.

The troops with their officers who were encamped in Albemarle County, within sight of Monticello, included many Hessians. Jefferson saw them arrive after seven hundred miles of dreary march, and he was struck with pity for the dismal condition and prospects of these men, mostly impressed soldiers whose hearts were not in their task. "The spell of weather," he said, describing the gloomy picture of their arrival, "was the worst ever known within the memory of man."

But soon there appeared a bright side to the situation. Among the German officers, who had no cause to bear the revolutionary colonies ill-will, were men of true European culture, and soon the Jeffersons had formed many delightful new acquaintances in the neighborhood.

The Germans have always been a musical people, and this alone endeared them as persons to Thomas Jefferson, the violinist. He threw open to the officers his gardens, his house, his library. It may well be imagined that he also did not lose this golden opportunity to practice the German language.

Some evenings Mrs. Jefferson played her new harpsichord while several officers grouped around her and sang. A certain Captain Bibby enjoyed his duets with Jefferson so much that, after the war, when he settled down in New York as an American citizen, he always proclaimed Mr. Jefferson as one of the best amateur violinists he had ever known.

Martha Jefferson was very helpful to Baroness Riedesel, the wife of the Hessian general, in getting her started at housekeeping during her internment in Virginia. The Baroness was an immense woman who startled the Virginia ladies by riding her horse astride like a man. Her misuse of the English language kept Madison in funny anecdotes for a long time. But her acquaintanceship with the managing of an aristocratic European household must have been a source of much interest to the colonial dames.

Baron Riedesel determined that his troops should make the best of this sad turn in the fortunes of war. He distributed among them a thousand dollars' worth of seed, with the result that the whole barracks was abloom with gardens. This in turn resulted in the Hessians' considering their imprisonment as the happiest part of their entire military career.

Some of the officers went to great expense in making over the houses allotted to them as quarters, deciding to wait out the duration of the war in comfort. Even General Phillips, commander of the English prisoners, whom Jefferson described as the proudest man of the proudest nation, entered into the spirit of neighborliness. Acknowledging Jefferson's politeness he sent him the following invitation: "The British officers intend to perform a play next Saturday at the Barracks. I shall be extremely happy to have the honor to attend you and Mrs. Jefferson in my box at the theater should you or that lady be inclined to go." He was careful to end his letter with great *personal* respect; he was Mr. Jefferson's humble servant.

Jefferson wrote a friend: "It is for the benefit of mankind to mitigate the horrors of war as much as possible. The practice, therefore, of modern nations, of treating captive enemies with politeness and generosity, is not only delightful in contemplation, but really interesting to all the world—friends, foes, and neutral."

At one time when this generous relationship between the vanquished and their victors was in danger of being destroyed, Jefferson came to the aid of the prisoners, thus rewarding their very decent conduct. Some Virginians had raised the cry that the four thousand war prisoners were eating up too great a share of the short food supplies of the State, and that they should be sent somewhere else. Jefferson at once wrote in protest to Governor Patrick Henry, saying that it would be a breach of faith to send these soldiers away, just when they had got fairly settled, had planted vegetable gardens, and had made investments in improving the land. Moreover, he pointed out, if these men used up some of Virginia's rations, on the other hand they distributed a great deal of gold and silver which were then very much needed by the State.

Virginia was indeed hard up for money. Whenever Jefferson entered into a discussion of events with Mazzei, it always wound up with the consideration of plans for raising money. Mazzei had much faith in a scheme of his own. His former patron, the Duke of Tuscany, was a very thrifty person, and Mazzei knew that three years before the Duke had ten million crowns in gold lying idle in his treasury. The Duke of Tuscany was the brother of Queen Marie Antoinette of France, and the Queen was said to be enthusiastic over the American Revolution. Therefore, Mazzei reasoned, Duke Leopold, who was besides a very liberal ruler, might also be sympathetic. Mazzei had already sent the Duke his own translation of the Declaration of Independence.

Now Mazzei offered to return to his native land, at his own expense, and get Duke Leopold to lend his idle gold to the Americans. Jefferson wrote to Adams at the Continental Congress about the plan. He received no reply. Evidently Adams was not interested in borrowing these ten million crowns. But why not borrow them for Virginia, which had such terrible need of them? There was nothing to lose in trying.

So Mazzei was sent by Virginia. He was authorized by Governor Henry not only to get the money but also to buy supplies with it for the Virginian troops. He bore letters from Virginians to friends in Europe, including the one from George Mason to his son in Paris.

Mazzei sold all his household goods at public auction and his house to Baron Riedesel. Luckily, the Italian was on board ship before the Hessians' horses trampled down all his precious vineyards. Had he known of this piece of criminal carelessness, he would have lost some of the fine ardor with which he set out on his mission to aid the colonists.

Mazzei's vessel had not got very far when it was captured by a privateer. Mazzei was taken as a prisoner to New York. It was some time before he could set out for Europe again, and when he finally got there his mission was unsuccessful.

John Page and Thomas Jefferson had kept their friendship unbroken since the time they were boys at college together, when Tom had made John the confidant of his laments over Belinda. Page lived on a magnificent estate in the largest mansion that had ever been built in Virginia. He had had great political successes; at one time he was appointed to the royal Governor's council, the honor so much coveted by his class. But from the beginning of the struggle between Virginia and its King, Page had sided with the colony.

Now that they were each thirty-six years old, the two friends suddenly discovered that they were rivals. Both were candidates for the governorship of Virginia. The Governor at this time was elected by the legislature, not the people. Neither Page nor Jefferson had much to do with their own candidacies. Each was nominated by his own friends, and the rivalry was really between these two sets of friends, for neither of the two old schoolmates lifted a finger in his own behalf. For the custom then was for candidates to high executive posts not to do any canvassing of votes on their own account. Beating your own drum was considered vulgar and inconsistent with the exalted dignity to which you aspired.

So Jefferson and Page simply waited for news of the outcome at their respective homes while their respective friends had it out on the floor of the Assembly. Jefferson won the election by just a few votes.

Page at once wrote him a letter of congratulation, to which Jefferson replied: "It has given me much pain that the zeal of our respective friends should ever have placed us in the situation of competitors. I was comforted, however, with the reflection that it was their competition, not ours, and the difference of the numbers which have decided between us was too insignificant to give you a pain or me a pleasure, had our dispositions toward each other been such as to admit those sensations."

In 1779, when Thomas Jefferson became Governor of Virginia that State embraced much more territory than it does now. It extended as far west as the Mississippi and included all the land that we now call Virginia, West Virginia, Kentucky, and a great part, besides, of what is now Ohio, Indiana, and Illinois. In other ways, too, Virginia was practically a nation in its own right. It could borrow money on its own account, and, two days after Jefferson's inauguration, Virginia ratified a treaty with France, quite as though it were an independent power.

Jefferson's first year of office—the Governor's term was for only one year—was spent in Williamsburg. Here he had his old college of William and Mary under his eyes. He had not forgotten the educational reforms he advocated, and, when he was made a "visitor" or director of the college, he immediately began to put them into effect.

He abolished the grammar school and the two divinity schools. He made George Wythe the first professor of Law in America. Among Wythe's most famous pupils were John Marshall, father of the Supreme Court, James Monroe, and Henry Clay. A cousin of James Madison, also named James Madison, was made professor of Mathematics and Science, and Mazzei's friend Charles Bellini, who knew French and Italian perfectly and German and Spanish passably, was given the chair of Modern Languages. An old college-mate of Jefferson and Page named Charles McClurg, who had returned from Edinburgh with a doctor's degree, was made professor of Medicine. Making a good university out of a poor one was an agreeable task. Jefferson's other duties were not so pleasant.

The alliance with France had a few undesirable consequences as well as many good ones. For one thing there was a change of spirit on both sides. Now that France was to send over troops, volunteering on this side dropped off. There was not now such a feeling of desperate need as there had been.

On the other hand this alliance made the English more ruthless. Now they feared that the colonies would become French possessions, they fought harder and also went more systematically about the business of laying waste the land. They hoped perhaps that, even if they lost, the country would be valueless to the French. Also Burgoyne's surrender had to be made up for, and the South, since it was less populated, seemed more easy to conquer.

Before this, during Patrick Henry's term as Governor, there had been no serious fighting in Virginia. Now the British were coming up from the south through North Carolina. Jefferson determined to keep them out of Virginia at all costs. To do this he had to put all his hopes in General Gates, who was opposing the English army in North Carolina. He sent Gates all the resources in men and ammunition he could spare. He was encouraged in this course by General Washington.

But many Virginians looked on with anxiety as Virginia's means of defense poured into the Carolinas. It still was hard for some people to think of the American army as a whole, or the whole war as a single campaign. Virginian soldiers should be fighting Virginia's battles, that is, in Virginia, they thought.

Jefferson, however, felt that above all the British general, Cornwallis, must be kept out of Virginia if she was to be spared from devastation. When firearms gave out, smiths were kept busy making axes and tomahawks for General Gates. They tried to supply his requests for belts, but leather had become so scarce that people were stealing the tops of cartridge boxes to sole their shoes with. To transport these supplies Jefferson called upon all the planters to donate any wagons they could possibly spare from absolutely necessary farm work. He first of all contributed his own wagons at Monticello. Mrs. Jefferson sent out an appeal to the women of Virginia to sacrifice their jewels and money to the cause, as she did herself. In the midst of his frenzied duties Governor Jefferson remembered the map of Virginia that had been made long ago by his father and Professor Fry. He began a search for it.

While still straining every resource to send Gates supplies, Jefferson received the dreadful news that the Americans had been disastrously defeated at Camden, South Carolina. In one battle all the materials that Virginia had spent two months in collecting were lost to the enemy. All their sacrifices had been in vain. The British would now invade Virginia. Jefferson's critics raised a louder murmur.

Fortunately for Jefferson's peace of mind, the Virginian forces had carried out at least one successful campaign. In accordance with the new British plan of wasting the South, a British general named Hamilton had spent the winter of 1779 persuading the chiefs of some Indian tribes to attack the

Americans. The Virginians were especially incensed against Hamilton because of the way in which he encouraged the tribes to fight. They took no prisoners, preferring scalps, and, of course, drew no sharp lines between soldiers and civilians, men and women. It was reported that white soldiers had led the Indians in some of these brutal massacres. Colonel George Rogers Clark, a former neighbor of Jefferson's, had been sent into the western forests with a tiny army of 130 frontiersmen to take Hamilton. Though the feat seemed incredible Clark actually did surprise and capture Hamilton with all his white forces early in the spring. Hamilton and two other officers were brought to Williamsburg, the others released on parole.

The feeling against Hamilton was very bitter, and Jefferson shared it to such an extent that he now did something that seems quite foreign to his nature. He had the three prisoners loaded with chains and put in a cell. This was because Hamilton's cruelties had gone beyond the necessities of war. As a matter of fact this treatment of Hamilton had a rather good effect, for it led to a better treatment of American prisoners by their British captors.

Hamilton was finally exchanged, but his defeat had done its work. From now on Virginia did not have to guard its western frontier against invasion. It could turn its whole energies to stopping the British army advancing in the south.

Meanwhile, the victorious British in the Carolinas were taking several months to reach the Virginia border. Again and again they were checked by guerrilla troops. At the same time Virginia was being threatened on a new front, and Jefferson's critics were now loudly saying that they had warned him what would happen if he sent Gates all Virginia's means of defense.

A dozen armed vessels had anchored in Chesapeake Bay.

They landed troops. Virginia held its breath, but nothing happened. These ships had been ordered to wait for Cornwallis, and the Carolina guerrillas were keeping Cornwallis away. The ships set sail again after waiting more than a month. They had done very little damage, but, while they were anchored near by, hundreds of British prisoners had escaped to them. Jefferson decided to send those that remained to Maryland. His personal relations with them continued to be most pleasant, and with one German officer he later maintained a correspondence for ten years.

No sooner did Virginia seem safe again than a messenger galloped into the capital to say that twenty-seven warships had been sighted entering Chesapeake Bay. The messenger had not waited to make out what flags the ships flew. This was Sunday, December 21, 1780. It was not until Tuesday that the Governor learned that the ships were *not* French, as everyone had fondly hoped, but British, and that they were making their way up the James. Instantly Jefferson called out the militia and gave orders to remove all war supplies to a point above Richmond, where the James was not navigable because of rapids.

Thursday evening the Governor received news that the British troops under the renegade Benedict Arnold had landed. Jefferson found himself alone, all the members of the government being away on duty or engaged in removing their families from danger. There was not in Virginia a military force large enough to stop Arnold's troops. And Jefferson himself was no soldier.

Sending his own family, the youngest child of which was then two months old, to a relative in Tuckahoe, he mounted a horse and raced to the war supplies. The great thing, he knew, was to keep these from Arnold. He superintended the transportation of the supplies across the river for some hours;

then at midnight he galloped off to Tuckahoe to see that his family was safely put across the river.

By that time it was daylight. Man and horse, both tired and unfed, galloped back to supervise the transport of the last stores from Richmond across the James. Before they could reach their destination, the overstrained horse sank dying at the roadside, where Jefferson was compelled to abandon it. With the saddle and bridle across his shoulder, he walked quickly to the nearest farmhouse and asked for a horse. The only animal left was a yet unbroken colt. But Tom Jefferson had not spent so much of his lifetime on horseback for nothing. The colt was caught, saddled, and was galloping for Richmond before it had time to be properly frightened.

Just before reaching Richmond Jefferson discovered that it was already in the hands of the enemy, and turned off just in time to follow the stores. Then he hunted up Baron von Steuben's camp to get the advice of the only trained commander within reach.

Arnold was in Richmond trying to cripple the town in the shortest possible time. He burned a cannon foundry, quantities of tobacco, some public warehouses, and a few private buildings; threw five tons of powder into the canal, and ruined as much of the military equipment as he could find.

Meanwhile, the Virginia militia was massing around him. Luckily for Arnold, the wind shifted, so that he could board his ships, sail down the river and away. The raid was over.

Jefferson had been in the saddle for three and a half days when he rode into Richmond on the heels of Benedict Arnold. He must now take up a job that was as little to his liking as a task could well be. For from this time on Jefferson was virtually a military dictator. All civil government had practically ceased to exist.

Virginia was now being harried on all sides. To the east
Benedict Arnold was pillaging the State in spite of Steuben's
and Lafayette's attempts to check him. To the south Cornwallis and Tarleton had at last burst across the border and
were sweeping northward. In the western counties the Indians
were again on the warpath, it was said. Finally the British
fleet swooped down unexpectedly here and there on the coast.

In response to repeated calls for help Washington had at
last sent "the boy Lafayette" to Virginia. This youthful major-
general had already been in America four years before he
entered Richmond in March 1781. He had always wanted
to meet the author of the Declaration of Independence, and
now he had a chance to come to his aid! From their first meeting Jefferson and Lafayette became dear and lifelong friends.

Hurriedly the legislature met and empowered the Governor
to call out the militia, to confiscate wagons, horses, food, equipment, clothing, and Negroes. He was also to arrest disloyal
Tories. He was to issue money. In short, the man who had
fought with every weapon to make men free was given such
tyrannical powers as no royal Governor had ever enjoyed.

The capture of Virginia's legislature and her Governor
would have been a feather in any British general's hat. Four
times in Jefferson's second term of office the legislature had to
flee before the enemy. First in January 1781 when Arnold
sacked Richmond; then in March; and then again in May,
when the enemy armies were so close that the few members
who were left decided after that to meet in Charlottesville
near Monticello.

The fourth time was the closest call of all. The legislature
had agreed to convene in Charlottesville on May 24th. Jefferson's term was up on June 1st, and elections had to be held

at once. But because of the constant danger, there were never enough legislators gathered together at any one time to permit of a legal vote. Elections were postponed and postponed; the month of May passed; Virginia was without a governor.

Because Monticello was so near to Charlottesville, Jefferson had staying at his home several of the members of the legislature. One early morning during the first week in June, Jefferson's guests were awakened by galloping hoofs. It was Captain Jack Jouett. He had been at the Cuckoo Tavern in Louisa County when he saw through the window General Tarleton's White Dragoons pass down the main street. He had recognized them by their white uniforms. Jumping into the saddle of a swift horse, Jouett had taken a short cut to warn them, thus becoming the Paul Revere of Virginia.

The Jefferson household and its guests sat down to an unhurried breakfast. The legislators then left for Charlottesville, called a meeting, adjourned it, and the members set out for their homes. On the way seven of them were captured.

Jefferson told his family to prepare for a journey. He closeted himself in his study to sort out his papers, some for burning and some to take with him. He was immersed in this work for two hours when a neighbor rode up to tell him that the enemy troops were just beginning to climb the mountain. Jefferson then sent off his family, in the care of a young man who was studying law with him at the time and accompanied by some servants. They were to go to the plantation of Colonel Coles, some fifteen miles away.

At the first warning earlier he had sent his favorite horse to be shod at the smithy in Shadwell. He now ordered it to be brought to a certain place between Carter's Mountain and Monticello. After lingering a bit more among his papers, he took up his telescope and went by a short cut to get his horse.

Hearing no sound of an approaching regiment, he walked a little way up Carter's Mountain to a rock where he could get a better view of Charlottesville. Kneeling down and aiming his telescope, he could see nothing suspicious. There was no need for such hurry, he thought, and was already on his way back for some more of those papers, when he noticed that his sword was missing from its sheath. First he would return to the lookout rock to see whether he had dropped it there. There, sure enough, he found it. But when he took one last look through his telescope he also found the streets of Charlottesville swarming with dragoons.

Coolly he mounted his horse and followed his family.

Actually his escape was much narrower than it seemed. For he had barely been out of the house five minutes when it was entered by White Dragoons under the command of Captain McLeod. Martin and Cæsar, two slaves, were busily engaged in hiding the plate and silver under a loose plank in the floor. Cæsar was standing under the floor while Martin handed the things down to him. When Martin saw the white coats coming through the orchard, he whispered something to Cæsar, dumped in all the remaining valuables, and then closed down the plank.

Cæsar had been raised with Tom Jefferson and could be depended on. Martin, who was only twenty-six, had appointed himself his master's body servant, though Jefferson always refused to use a valet. However, when Martin was around he would let no other servant perform any personal service for Jefferson. And if anyone other than Jefferson gave him orders, he would receive the commands with a sullen expression and rarely carry them out.

Martin received Captain McLeod and showed him through the house. When they came to the study, where Jefferson kept all his papers, McLeod gave it a hasty glance, locked the door, and gave the key to Martin. "If anyone asks you for the key," he said to the servant, "tell him I have it."

Except for some wine which a few soldiers took out of the cellar to drink, nothing in the house was touched during the eighteen hours the soldiers stayed there. When one of the drinking soldiers cocked a pistol at Martin's head and said: "Tell me which way your master is gone or I fire," the slave replied: "Fire away, then," and nothing happened.

When McLeod finally left, Martin let Cæsar out of his voluntary prison. For eighteen hours Cæsar had sat without light, little air, and no food, and had made not a sound.

The events at Monticello were quite unusual, and were probably owing to McLeod's character, for Tarleton himself had a very bad reputation. At Elkhill on the James River, another plantation of Jefferson's, the British acted in an entirely different manner. Jefferson himself described the havoc that Cornwallis wrought at this place:

He remained in this position ten days, his own headquarter being in my house, at that place. I had time to remove most of the effects out of the house. He destroyed all my growing crops of corn and tobacco; he burned all my barns, containing the same articles of the last year, having first taken what corn he wanted; he used, as was to be expected, all my stock of cattle, sheep, and hogs, for the sustenance of his army, and carried off all the horses capable of service; of those too young for service he cut the throats; and he burned all the fences on the plantation so as to leave an absolute waste. He carried off also about thirty slaves. Had this been to give them freedom, he would have done right; but it was to consign them to inevitable death from the smallpox and putrid fever, then raging in his camp. This I knew afterwards to be the fate of twenty-seven of them. When I say that Lord Cornwallis did all this, I do not mean that he carried about the torch in his own hands, but that it was all done under his eyes; the situation of the house in which he was, commanding a view of every part of the plantation, so that he must have seen every fire. I relate these things on my own knowledge, in a great degree, as I was on the ground soon after he left it.

When the dispersed legislature finally met together again on June 7, the State of Virginia had been without a Governor for a week. The members were irritable and nervous. They had been made to flee before advancing British troops four times. They had to have someone to blame, and it was only natural that Jefferson should come in for a good share of spite.

Hadn't they told him not to send all their supplies and men to General Gates in the Carolinas? Now, see where they were, harried on four sides by the foe. The legislators who were busily crying, "I told you so," were now joined by the older enemies of Jefferson, the conservatives, the men who had fought against the abolition of the entail, who hated him for winning religious liberty for Virginia.

Finally these rumblings and mutterings came to a head. George Nicholas, a young representative from Jefferson's own county of Albemarle, rose up and accused the former Governor of failing in his duty by allowing Benedict Arnold to terrorize the State.

Immediately there was uproar. Jefferson's friends jumped to his defense. But Jefferson himself was profoundly shocked. It seemed so obvious to him that he had always worked for the State's best interests both in the present and the future. He had not realized that in doing so he was making personal enemies of his political opponents.

Amazed and hurt, he got a friend to secure from Nicholas a list of the formal charges the latter intended to bring against him. Through the same friend he sent Nicholas the answers he intended to make. Then he retired to the country to brood over the ingratitude of his State.

For thirteen years he had been in public service. Generals Washington, Gates, Green, Lafayette, and Steuben had applauded his wisdom and promptitude in these last harrowing years. These were the men who really knew the conditions, for they had all co-operated with him in the defense of the State. Jefferson could not shake off his sense of injured amazement.

Before he retired for good, as he thought, he answered one more challenge to his principles and did his State one more service. At this last meeting of the legislature one party began to agitate for a dictator. "The very thought," said Jefferson, "was treason against the people, was treason against mankind in general." He united his friends, who were still in the majority, to defeat the project.

He knew, however, that what the country needed at its head in these warlike times was, if not a dictator, at least a soldier, but one legally elected. So he turned his last political efforts to the election of General Nelson as his own successor.

General Nelson had been one of the mainstays of Jefferson's administration. He supported it with his name, his military talents, and money from his vast estates. When he was elected, he went very conscientiously about his task of being a military emergency Governor. Virginia had a taste of the dictatorship it seemed to want.

Nelson forced men into the army, impressed wagons, horses, slaves, and supplies. When at Yorktown his own mansion was captured by the British, he had the mixed pleasure of ordering cannon balls shot through the windows of his own dining room where English officers sat at his table drinking his wine and eating his food.

General Nelson succeeded in pleasing his countrymen no

better than the previous Governor, although he had sacrificed health and fortune for them. After holding his office six months, he threw it up and he, too, went before the Assembly to answer charges made against him.

In the meantime Jefferson was still on his wife's estate Poplar Forest, in Bedford County, waiting for the Assembly to convene again. Then he would go to face his accusers, answer them, and retire to private life permanently, never to accept public office again.

Near the end of June, while still waiting at Poplar Forest, Jefferson was thrown from his horse and was so seriously hurt that he was unable to sit a horse or journey by carriage for a month after. His mind was bathed in gloom. Everything seemed to conspire against him.

In August, Lafayette brought Jefferson a letter from the President of the Continental Congress. It contained exciting news: Jefferson had been appointed to represent the young United States abroad.

For once Martha Jefferson's health was good enough for her husband to take her to Europe. Then, too, this meant getting away from Virginia, where he had been so deeply offended, and going to a land he had longed to visit ever since he had been a boy listening to Governor Fauquier's tales. But he could not go until he had personally answered those accusations. He declined the offer, and wrote Lafayette about it.

I lost an opportunity, the only one I ever had, and perhaps ever shall have, of combining public service with private gratification; of seeing countries whose improvements in science, in arts, in civilization it has been my fortune to admire at a distance, but never to see, and at the same time of lending some aid to a cause which has been handed on from its first origination to its present stage by every effort of which my poor faculties were capable. These, however, have not been such as to give satisfaction to some of my countrymen; and it has been necessary for me to remain in the State till a later period in the present year than is consistent with an acceptance of what has been offered me.

Before the legislature met again, the war was over. Cornwallis had surrendered at Yorktown. Virginia was free of its invaders; it was deliriously happy; it did not remember its petty grudges. When, a month later, in November, Jefferson ran for the Assembly in Albemarle County, he was elected without a dissenting vote.

Grimly Jefferson rose up in his place. The House would be pleased to remember that accusations against him had been hinted at the last session. Would the members in question please repeat the accusations? He was prepared to meet and answer them.

There was no reply. George Nicholas had purposely stayed away. After a silence, Jefferson calmly read off the points as he had received them through his friend. Then he answered them point by point. He sat down.

Immediately another member stood up and offered a resolution thanking Jefferson for his "impartial, upright, and attentive administration." It was passed unanimously by both Council and Assembly.

But at the next meeting of the House, Jefferson did not appear. True to his vow, he had returned to Monticello, determined to spend the rest of his life as a private citizen. There were some things, of course, which Jefferson could not know. He could not know, for instance, that at thirty-eight he had not yet completed even half of his life; and he could not know that he had just barely begun to fulfill his early desire to be a citizen of the world.

The friends who had been indignant at the treatment Jef-

ferson had received at the hands of political adversaries, were
now becoming indignant at Jefferson's own pride and exaggerated sensitivity. They knew how important he was to them
and to their plans for a democratic republic. They did not
hesitate to chide him to his face. James Madison, who loved
his teacher so deeply, could still write to a friend:

Great as my partiality is to Mr. Jefferson, the mode in which
he seems determined to revenge the wrong received from his
country does not appear to me to be dictated either by philosophy
or patriotism. It argues indeed a keen sensibility and a strong
consciousness of rectitude. But his sensibility ought to be as great
towards the relenting as the misdoing of the legislature, not to
mention the injustice of visiting the faults of this body on their
innocent constituents.

James Monroe, too, wrote directly to Jefferson and told
him what the people were saying. Jefferson answered him that
he had examined his heart and was convinced that every fiber
of political ambition had been torn out, that he thought he
had a right to withdraw after thirteen years of public service,
and that his family now needed him. If the disapproval had
been of well-meaning but uninformed people, he said, he
might have comforted himself. But that it should come from
men who had worked with him and had known his aims was
a shock for which he had not been prepared. "I felt," he ends
the letter, "that these injuries had inflicted a wound on my
spirit which only will be cured by the all-healing grave."

George Nicholas, some time later, published a letter containing a handsome apology. He accused himself of having
been hasty, hot-headed, and unjustified in the statements he
had made on the floor of the house during those panicky days
of the war. Now Jefferson was left with almost no excuse for
sulking in his retirement.

Ceiling Decoration Monticello

X

RETURN TO BATTLE

WHAT fortified Thomas Jefferson in his resolve to stay out of politics was the fun he got out of being home. There were so many interests he had had no time for while at Philadelphia and Williamsburg and during the feverish two years of his governorship.

First and foremost among these hobbies was the completion of Monticello and its grounds. Jefferson had never given up tinkering with his home even when to most eyes it looked quite finished. He was forever having inspirations that required adding something here, altering a detail there. The latest addition was the building of a walk round about the mountain.

147

In the spring of 1782 Jefferson entertained a distinguished and appreciative visitor. The Marquis de Chastellux was a major-general in command of one of the French armies in America. What impressed Jefferson even more was that he was one of the Forty Immortals—as the members of the French Academy, the chief learned body on the continent of Europe, were called. The Marquis later wrote a book about his American experiences and he had this to say of Monticello:

The house, of which Mr. Jefferson was the architect, is rather elegant, and in the Italian taste, though not without fault; it consists of one large square pavilion, the entrance of which is by two porticoes ornamented with pillars. The ground floor consists chiefly of a very large, lofty saloon, which is to be decorated entirely in the antique style; above it is a library of the same form. Two small wings with only a ground floor and attic story are joined to this pavilion and communicate with the kitchen, offices, etc., which will form a kind of basement story, over which runs a terrace. My object in this short description is only to show the difference between this and the other houses of the country; for we may safely aver that Mr. Jefferson is the first American who has consulted the fine arts to know how he should shelter himself from the weather. Let me describe to you a man, not yet forty, tall, and with a mild and pleasing countenance, but whose mind and understanding are ample substitutes for every exterior grace. An American, who, without ever having quitted his own country, is at once a musician, skilled in drawing, a geometrician, an astronomer, a natural philosopher, legislator, and statesman.

The Marquis spent some time at Monticello. He tells of going with Jefferson to dinner at the house of a friend who had a tame wolf, ten months old, as playful as a young dog. He also talks about going to the park to observe the deer which Jefferson had raised (instead of buffaloes as he had romantically planned), which were so tame that they ate corn out of their master's hand.

One evening after Mrs. Jefferson had retired, Chastellux and his host, in the company of some other French gentlemen, were conversing over a bowl of punch when the subject of Ossian came up. A Scotchman named Macpherson had published some very beautiful epic poetry which he claimed to have translated from the original Gaelic manuscripts written by the poet Ossian fifteen hundred years before. Macpherson's poems had been translated into all the modern European languages. Even many years later they were the favorite reading of such great men as Goethe and Napoleon.

Jefferson had loved Ossian's poetry ever since his discovery of them in his student days. So much so, that he actually wrote to a relative of Macpherson's, who had once lived in Virginia, asking him to procure if possible a Gaelic grammar and dictionary and to request the "translator" for a manuscript copy of the original poems in Gaelic. It is to be feared that Macpherson would have been quite embarrassed if the request ever reached his ears, but the whole incident is typical of Thomas Jefferson. If he loved something, he must delve back to its original source; if he was tremendously interested in a book, he could not be satisfied by a translation.

Well, here was Jefferson almost forty, still adoring Ossian's poems, and what was his great pleasure to find that Chastellux was also a passionate admirer. Some of the Frenchmen present were not acquainted with Ossian, but fortunately they knew English very well, and so first Jefferson would recite a stunning passage from memory and then the Marquis would recall another. Finally they got down the book, and late into that night they took turns in reading it aloud over the punch bowl.

This was one of the Marquis's happiest evenings in America, but it was a fair sample of how they spent that visit. "Sometimes," the Marquis wrote in his account of it, "natural phi-

losophy, at other times politics or the arts were the topics of
our conversation, for no object had escaped Mr. Jefferson; and
it seemed as if from his youth he had placed his mind, as he
had done his house, on an elevated situation, from which he
might contemplate the universe."

In becoming a gentleman farmer, Jefferson was fulfilling
one of his two ideals of the completely satisfactory life. His
second ideal was the life of the scientist. Already in his college
days Jefferson had learned from Professor Small to prefer exact
information to hazy general statements. So for five years he had
kept a very close account of the amount of rain that fell in the
neighborhood, the coldest temperature and the hottest as revealed by the thermometer, and the direction the winds blew.

Such facts make up the science of meteorology, the science
of climate and weather. Jefferson's early tables were not the
crude efforts of a careless boy; they would be just as under-
standable today as any recent bulletins of the United States
Weather Bureau, and just as useful. For it is from such information that reliable almanacs may be made up.

Even now at Monticello Jefferson recorded the appearance
and disappearance of snow and ice, of the leaves of the different trees, of the buds and fruits of the orchards, of the
ticks and fireflies, and of many birds. He observed the day of
the year that each of the vegetables and fruits and berries
reached his table.

All this information went into notebooks. Every conceivable
fact of interest about Virginia that Jefferson ever heard had
gone into those notebooks. Every observation that might be
useful to himself or his neighbors he jotted down. If he learned
of something strange from the Indians, he noted it down, for
queer and out-of-the-way information was his special passion.

The result was that he became something of a walking encyclopedia, as the Marquis de Chastellux had been fascinated
to find.

Now it happened that Monsieur Barbé-Marbois, the secretary of the French legation in Philadelphia, had been instructed by his government to collect all the important facts
and statistics about the American States. The logical person
to go to for such information about Virginia was, of course,
Jefferson, and to him the secretary went.

Jefferson sat down happily to the task of composing a report on the State of Virginia for the French government—and
in the end he wrote an important little book. He called it
Notes on the State of Virginia and every page shows the passions of a naturalist. Even now it makes interesting reading.
There are accounts of all the birds and beasts of Virginia, all
the Indian tribes; and there is a chapter on plants that lists
all those used for medicinal, eating, or ornamental purposes.
This book is the forerunner of those great libraries of scientific
reports which are nowadays issued by every State government
as well as the Federal government of America.

So thorough was Jefferson's description of the natural resources, the products, the inhabitants, the boundaries, and the
laws and customs of his State that, without intending it, he became America's first real geographer. For the sake of complete-
ness he added to his work a copy of his father's map of Virginia.

But he was not satisfied with a mere dusty report of things
as they were. He added a picture of Virginia as he hoped she
would some day be. The future was more important to Virginia than her past or present. So we also find in this work
Jefferson's pet theories on slavery, education, and religion. He
included all the measures he could not get passed while a lawmaker, especially those on the gradual abolition of slavery.

For Mrs. Jefferson the two years of her husband's retirement were filled with both pain and happiness. Since the birth of her second child she had never quite regained her strength, growing weaker and weaker with time. On the other hand, Jefferson was now always with her to take care of her. That second year he spent most of his time nursing his beloved wife, taking turns with her sister, Elizabeth Wayles Eppes, and with Martha Carr, his own sister.

Suddenly Martha Jefferson's condition became alarming. For four months her husband was never out of call. When he was not at her bedside, he was working in a little room which opened directly beside the head of her bed.

On September 6, 1782, Martha Jefferson lost her long dreary fight for life. As his wife died, Jefferson had to be led fainting into the library. There he remained unconscious for so long that his sister feared he would never revive. But he recovered, closed the doors, and began to walk about the room. All night he walked and walked, up and down, trying to numb his mind to what he knew was the greatest loss he had ever suffered. His daughter Martha, a little girl of ten, stole into the library. Her presence seemed to bring him some comfort. At last he sank down exhausted on a straw pallet that had been brought in for him during his fainting fit.

For three weeks Jefferson kept to his room. Little Martha tried never to leave him alone. When at last he left his room and mounted a horse, she accompanied him on her own pony. From that time on he was incessantly on horseback, rambling about the mountain, following the least frequented roads, forging through the woods. It was during these lonely rides, as she silently witnessed her father's bitter grief, that Martha came to have her great lifelong love and respect for her father.

Mrs. Jefferson left, besides her namesake Martha, two other

little daughters—Mary, who was four, and Lucy Elizabeth, an infant. Thomas Jefferson promised himself to be both father and mother to them. He hoped to heal his grief for Martha by caring for her children.

One day Jefferson herded together his family of nine children—daughters, nephews, and nieces—and took them to an out-of-the-way plantation called Amphill, lent to him by its owner. They were all to be inoculated against smallpox.

Smallpox, the most contagious of diseases, was a terrible scourge in the eighteenth century. Not only were the deaths from it tremendous in number, but five persons could not casually come together without at least one of them showing the ravages and disfigurements of this disease on his face. This was before the discovery of vaccination, but it had already been noticed that those who once had the malady did not very easily catch it again. From the Orient had come the idea of giving people a mild case of smallpox to prevent their having severe or fatal ones. This was called inoculation.

Many people bitterly opposed inoculation because mild cases sometimes became severe ones, and thus helped spread the disease to others. That was why Jefferson sought out a secluded plantation. He was a firm believer in the value of smallpox inoculation. At the age of twenty-three he had himself made a journey to Philadelphia in a one-horse chaise to be inoculated by the famous Dr. Shippen.

Now at Amphill Jefferson became both scientist and nurse. He had always been a good first-aid surgeon, being able in an emergency to sew up an ugly wound or set a slave's broken leg. He nursed the children through their illness, and as a scientist had the satisfaction of carrying through a successful experiment.

The country's affairs were now being run by the Congress established by the Articles of Confederation, which had finally been ratified in 1781. While still at Amphill, Jefferson received word from this Congress that he had been appointed a minister and was to go to Paris to help Benjamin Franklin and John Jay conclude the final treaty of peace with England. Jefferson's friends, knowing of his wife's death, now hoped that he would be willing to return to public life.

As a matter of fact, Jefferson was more than willing. He was eager. Without his beloved companion he no longer wished to spend his life at Monticello in country pursuits that would always remind him of his great loss. Here was an opportunity to lose himself in hard work and important services. He decided at once to take Martha with him, and to leave the other children with relatives. His oldest girl had become quite inseparable from him.

It was midwinter when Jefferson hurried to Baltimore to embark on the French frigate that was to take him abroad. He looked forward to the trip with intense pleasure, for one of his fellow-passengers was to be the Marquis de Chastellux. But he found the frigate frozen in the ice, and the English fleet still blockading the harbor. Before these difficulties were overcome, the belated mails arrived with the news that the first draft of the peace treaty had already been signed. Jefferson wasn't needed. Was he destined never to see France?

Jefferson returned to Monticello. There he spent a dismal summer. He had lost interest in improving his estate. The notebooks that had hitherto been so full of observations contained only one brief entry: "September 2nd and 3rd. White frosts which killed vines in the neighborhood—hills of tobacco in the north garden—fodder and corn." He worked hard as usual but he no longer took any joy in his work.

In the meantime, Jefferson's friends were still busy at getting him back into the thick of politics. That summer he was chosen to represent Virginia at the Congress of the Confederation. His duties began in November.

One of the Congress's pressing tasks was to establish a money system for the new nation. During his first trip to the Continental Congress Jefferson had noted the number of different kinds of coin that were used and how difficult it was to remember how much a Maryland coin was worth in Pennsylvania. Besides the coins of various States there were also used English, Dutch, and Spanish moneys, to say nothing of the use of tobacco for currency in the South.

It was natural at first to think of adopting the British system of coinage. Four farthings make one penny, twelve pennies make one shilling, twenty shillings make a sovereign or one pound; besides which, twenty-one shillings make a guinea, two shillings make a florin, and two and a half shillings make a half crown. At the thought of this jumble, Jefferson and several others threw up their hands in dismay. Here was a brand-new republic starting from scratch—why not create a sensible system while they had the chance?

When Gouverneur Morris proposed the decimal system we now have, Jefferson immediately agreed with him. This meant that each coin could be reckoned in terms of the other coins by tens. Ten mills make one cent; ten cents make one dime; ten dimes make one dollar; ten dollars make one eagle; and so on. But Robert Morris, the financier of the Revolution, had figured on making the cent so small a coin that it should be worth about $\frac{1}{1440}$ of a Spanish dollar. This small unit would allow all the other coins, English, Dutch, and what not, to be divided by it without leaving fractions.

Here Jefferson disagreed. It would be difficult to reckon prices with such a small unit. A loaf of bread, for instance, would be worth 72 units and a bullock 115,200 units. Besides there was no need to bother about other coinage systems, since they would all eventually disappear when our own money was established. Let us take the most common coin in use, he said, one with which everyone is familiar, and make it our unit. This is the Spanish dollar.

And so the dollar became the basis of our currency. The word *mill* comes from the Latin and means a thousandth; the word *cent* means a hundredth; and *dime* means a tenth.

The most important work done by Jefferson at this Congress was the plan he drew up for the government of the Northwest Territory, which had been surrendered by Virginia to the Confederacy. First of all his plan proposed that all territory now owned or later to be acquired by the United States should be divided up into States. This provided a framework for the growth of the country. It made expansion a national instead of a State question. It prevented the creation of two different kinds of citizens, some belonging to States and some to the United States only. Jefferson obviously had at the back of his mind a dream of a vast empire, composed of many great States, closely bound up together.

Furthermore, Jefferson's plan provided for the government of these territories before they became States. The inhabitants might create their own temporary governments as long as they fulfilled two conditions. First, these governments must be republican in form and must admit no person to citizenship who held a hereditary title. Secondly, after the year 1800 there should be no slavery in any of this territory.

Finally, any part of this territory could be admitted into

the union as a State "on an equal footing" with the original thirteen, as soon as it had as many free inhabitants as the least populous of those original thirteen States.

When Jefferson presented this plan to Congress, it was adopted and ratified—but only after a little amendment had been inserted which spoiled the whole idea for its author. This amendment removed the conditions about hereditary titles and slavery. To his chagrin Jefferson saw even his own two fellow members from Virginia vote against the slavery clause.

In spite of these changes, the adoption of Jefferson's plan for the treatment of United States territories makes him the father of the American system of State-making. It is thanks to him that a citizen of California is precisely the same kind of American citizen as the citizen of Massachusetts.

The last great task Jefferson engaged in while at the Congress was also intended to unite and strengthen the new republic. He proposed that ministers be sent to all the European nations to negotiate commercial treaties. Europe should learn to look upon the United States as a single nation.

It may be difficult to realize just how insignificant America was at this time, and how unimportant she was considered in world affairs for a hundred years to come. Since English merchants had always carried on America's trade, few people knew even the products of the young country.

Jefferson drew up a list of "Instructions" for American ambassadors at all foreign capitals. The remarkable thing about these instructions is that they contained not only rules for making commercial treaties but also a set of regulations for the more humane conduct of wars. American ministers were to try to get all the European governments to pledge themselves to follow these regulations.

These instructions show that the Americans had not lost their idealism the moment they gained the ends for which they had revolted against England. There was a sincere desire to prove that they deserved their own freedom by the new note of liberalism and reason that they could thus bring into the crooked world of international diplomacy. The Inner Revolution was still going on.

Jefferson's regulations forbade privateering, the molesting of neutrals, and the injuring of farmers, fishermen, or other civilians. There was to be no confiscation of property, no crowding of prisoners into unhealthy places, no ravaging of seacoasts. War, in short, was to be kept purely a matter of armies, of soldiers and sailors.

These "Instructions" were very highly thought of by soldiers like Washington as well as by the civilian patriots in Congress. They were adopted whole-heartedly, much to Jefferson's relief, for he was beginning to be irritated by the shortsightedness and quibbling over details in the nation's legislature.

Congress was now meeting in Annapolis, Maryland. Martha had been left by her father in Philadelphia, where she could attend school. Jefferson wrote regularly to his Patsy, as he called her, and his letters were as full of counsel as they were of affection. They also give us some idea of what Jefferson considered the proper education of an eleven-year-old lady.

Annapolis, Nov. 28th, 1783

My dear Patsy—

After four days' journey, I arrived here without any accident, and in as good health as when I left Philadelphia. The conviction that you would be more improved in the situation I have placed you than if still with me, has solaced me on my parting with you, which my love for you has rendered a difficult thing. The acquirements which I hope you will make under the tutors I have provided for you will render you more worthy of my love.

With respect to the distribution of your time, the following is what I should approve:

from 8 to 10, practice music

from 10 to 1, dance one day and draw another

from 1 to 2, draw on the day you dance, and write a letter next day

from 3 to 4, read French

from 4 to 5, exercise yourself in music

from 5 till bedtime read English, write, etc.

Communicate this plan to Mrs. Hopkinson, and if she approves of it, pursue it. I expect you will write me by every post. Inform me what books you read, what tunes you learn, and inclose me your best copy of every lesson in drawing.

A friend of whom Jefferson had asked news of his daughter wrote him that she was doing well in body and mind but that her only fault seemed a little carelessness in dress. At once Jefferson sat down to write a note to Patsy:

Annapolis, Dec. 22nd, 1783.

I omitted in that letter to advise you on the subject of dress, which I know you are a little apt to neglect. I do not wish you to be gayly clothed at this time of life, but that what you wear should be fine of its kind. But above all things, and at all times, let your clothes be neat, whole, and properly put on. Do not fancy you must wear them till the dirt is visible to the eye. You will be the last one who is sensible of this. Some ladies think they may, under the privileges of the dishabille, be loose and negligent of their dress in the morning. But be you, from the moment you rise till you go to bed, as cleanly and properly dressed as at the hours of dinner or tea. A lady who has been seen as a sloven or a slut in the morning, will never efface the impression she has made, with all the dress and pageantry she can afterwards involve herself in. I hope, therefore, the moment you rise from bed, your first work will be to dress yourself in such style, as that you may be seen by any gentleman without his being able to discover a pin amiss, or any other circumstance of neatness wanting.

XI

FRANCE

ON the day that Congress adopted Jefferson's "Instructions" for ministers abroad it also appointed him a sort of roving minister to Europe. His duties would be to explain his document to Benjamin Franklin and John Adams, who were already in Paris, and to aid them in drawing up new treaties. After so many false starts he was to go abroad at last!

Hastily Jefferson made his preparations. Martha he would take with him and place in a French school. His two younger children he left with Mrs. Eppes, his wife's sister. (Little Lucy Elizabeth died of whooping cough within the year.) To James

Madison he entrusted the care of Dabney Carr's oldest boy, Peter.

"I have a tender legacy to leave you," Jefferson wrote him. "It is the son of my friend, the dearest friend I knew. He is a boy of fine disposition, and of sound talent. I was his preceptor myself as long as I stayed at home, and when I came away, I placed him with Mr. Maury. There is a younger one. If I did not fear to overcharge you, I would request you to recommend a school for him."

Madison fulfilled this trust as he had so many others of his friend's. As long as Jefferson stayed in France, Madison wrote him long letters about the progress of the boys.

Just as Jefferson was about to sail, he received a letter from Lafayette. The young Marquis was leaving France at this time for a visit to America. Their ships would pass each other at sea. Lafayette's letter told how much he regretted losing this opportunity to introduce his old friend to the things he ought to see in France. Also Lafayette had been looking forward to a visit to Monticello, but that too was out of the question now. He ended his missive cordially and generously:

My house, dear sir, my family, and anything that is mine are entirely at your disposal, and I beg you will come and see Madame de Lafayette as you would act by your brother's wife. Her knowledge of the country may be of some use to Miss Jefferson, whom she will be happy to attend in everything that may be agreeable to her. Indeed, my dear sir, I would be very angry with you if either you or she did not consider my house as a second home, and Madame de Lafayette is very happy in every opportunity to wait on Mistress Jefferson.

On July 5, 1784, the day after the eighth anniversary of the signing of the Declaration of Independence, the vessel *Ceres* set out from Boston. On board were Mr. Thomas Jefferson and his daughter Mistress Martha, on a mission to the court of France. Another passenger was Mr. Nathaniel Tracy, owner of the *Ceres* and one of New England's merchant princes. From him the new minister could pick up a great many pointers on commercial treaties. There were only three other passengers.

They made a remarkably swift passage—only nineteen days to cross the Atlantic Ocean! And this in spite of the fact that they were becalmed for three days off the Banks of Newfoundland. The crew spent the three days while they waited for a wind in fishing for cod. The Banks are to this day the greatest cod fisheries in the world, and the catch was so plentiful that the cabin passengers were soon eating only the delicate portions of the cod's head and throwing the rest of the fish overboard. The ship had no salt to spare for preserving food.

As they approached England, Martha became violently seasick. At Portsmouth Jefferson had to take her ashore for some days until she had recovered. Then they boarded ship again, crossed the English Channel, and finally landed in Le Havre. France at last, after all these years! Jefferson took his time in going from Le Havre to Paris, soaking up impressions of the country, getting used to the idea that a boyhood dream had come true.

The Jeffersons first took lodgings in Paris so that they might get acquainted with the city before they settled down for good. Martha was shown all the sights of the exciting foreign town, until she became used to hearing nothing but French spoken around her. Then her father put her in one of the famous convent schools to finish her education as a lady. She was now twelve years old, and it was high time she learned how to conduct herself in a drawing room.

Panthémont, the convent school chosen by Jefferson, was

one where princesses and the daughters of the highest nobility received their education. This education was chiefly in music, dancing, etiquette, and languages. It was a charming place, where a girl could be quite happy. Busy as he was, Jefferson found time to visit Martha daily for two months until he was quite sure she had lost her homesickness.

For Jefferson was very busy indeed. First he had to explain to Franklin and Adams the new instructions for making treaties, including the new rules of warfare. Then the three ministers had to draw up special treaties to send to the many different courts of Europe. Most of this work was carried on in Franklin's home at Passy, a suburb of Paris.

Jefferson was delighted with Passy. He looked upon Franklin as America's greatest man, and Franklin had made himself so popular with the French court that the society that came to visit him was always brilliant and interesting. The old American philosopher was getting tired, however. He had asked for permission to return home, and instead Jefferson brought him more and bigger duties than ever.

Soon the three American diplomats had worked out a model treaty based upon Jefferson's "Instructions." Franklin struck off some copies on his own little printing press and sent them around to the French statesmen. When the Count de Vergennes, His Royal Majesty's Minister of Foreign Affairs, was shown the new treaty, with its humane provisions for the conduct of war, he must have smiled. These philosophers, these American idealists! They warmed one's cynical old heart, but did they really think this treaty of theirs would make any difference?

Unfortunately, the Count was right in his disbelief. France and the whole of Europe were just then on the brink of a twenty-year war, in which every ideal of humanity would be forgotten.

The first to sign the treaty with America was Frederick the Great of Prussia, who was something of a philosopher himself, though he was an old war-horse. Negotiations were started with Denmark and with Tuscany, Mazzei's native country.

Then Franklin finally received his permission to go home, and Jefferson was made ambassador in his place. The whole of Passy and a great part of Paris turned out to bid Franklin farewell. Because of his age, the Queen sent him her own traveling litter, a sort of sedan chair carried between two mules.

"You replace Dr. Franklin," said the Count de Vergennes, come to congratulate Jefferson.

"I succeed; no one can replace him," Jefferson answered.

The five years that Jefferson was to spend in France were as busy as any in his busy life. With Franklin gone home and Adams sent to England as American minister to that country, Jefferson became both ambassador and consul at Paris. That is, he took care not only of all diplomatic matters but also commercial ones.

Franklin had scarcely departed when the rumor began to spread that he had been captured by the Barbary pirates. This was, fortunately for the old philosopher, not true, but it might very well have been. The Mohammedan countries along the northern shore of Africa were inhabited by a race of people known as Berbers, whence came the name Barbary Coast for that whole region. The Algerian and other Barbary governments were supported by piracy. They terrorized the whole Mediterranean Sea. Unlike the private Christian pirates they were not satisfied with capturing all the booty and making their prisoners walk the plank. They were much more interested in the prisoners, for these made possible a vast slave trade.

To save their Mediterranean and African trade from complete destruction, the powerful nations of Europe had been compelled to pay tribute to these piratical governments. England had bought them off with lavish presents to the Dey of Algiers, to the Regency of Tunis, and to the Sultan of Morocco. The Dutch government humbly presented to "the glorious, mighty, and most noble King of Morocco" a little gift of "30 cables, 70 cannons, 21 anchors, 12 compasses, 285 pieces of sail cloth, 50 dozen sail needles, 24 tons of pitch, etc., etc." In other words the Dutch were expected to supply, and they did supply free of charge, the very means by which the pirates plundered the shipping of the world.

As long as the ships of the colonists had flown the British flag, they had been protected by the bribes and tribute paid by the British government. But now Jefferson began to receive alarming and heartbreaking news. In the spring of 1785 the crew of the American ship *Betsy* was captured, taken to Morocco, and held for ransom. Luckily for these men, their government was then on the very friendliest terms with that of Spain. And Spain had just made a handsome present to the Sultan of Morocco. So two little courtesies were exchanged. The Sultan made a return gift of his new American slaves to the King of Spain, and the Spanish government turned the freed sailors over to the American consul.

But a month later Jefferson received a letter from three American sea captains who had been captured with their crews by Algerian pirates. For seven years Jefferson struggled to get these men out of slavery.

There has come down to us a letter written by an American sailor who was captured by these Algerians, and it reads like the wildest fiction of adventure. This man had observed the approach of a ship that flew the Spanish flag. The few men on its decks were dressed like ordinary Spanish seamen. But suddenly, when this vessel had come very close, the Spanish colors were dropped, the Algerine flag was hoisted, and its hold began to belch forth swarms of dark, bearded men, with daggers in their teeth and two pistols in each belt. They boarded the American ship, overpowered the crew, whom they stripped to their underwear, and set about looting the vessel. The captive crew was then transferred aboard the corsair and was flung a few filthy rags to wear.

On reaching shore, these men became government slaves. As long as foreign ships in port offered a slight chance of escape, the slaves were loaded down with heavy chains. Ordinarily they wore only an iron ring around the ankle. Their daily ration was three tiny loaves of black bread and some vinegar, and on this diet they were whipped to backbreaking tasks. They were the longshoremen of Algeria, unloading the captured cargoes. They were the quarrymen, blasting rocks in the mountains. Fragments of these rocks, weighing from twenty to forty tons, were rolled down on huge sleds, which teams of two hundred or more slaves dragged for two miles to the city. At night the captives were crammed into the cells of the *bagnio* or prison.

When Jefferson received demands of ransom for these American sailors, his blood boiled. He thought it a disgrace for a civilized country to pay tribute to these pirates. He was all for making war on them. Why could not all the nations band together and conquer them? It should not be difficult. Why should a strong naval nation like England stoop to make presents to these brigands?

The reason was not far to seek, and it was not a pretty one. For Jefferson suspected that the British government was rather pleased to see the trade of small, weak nations eliminated by the pirates. But why could not these smaller nations league together and support a fleet of police boats of their own to blockade the Barbary ports? Jefferson's plan for a League of Nations seemed a good one to Portugal, Naples, Sicily, Venice, Malta, Denmark, and Sweden. With his own country Jefferson encountered more difficulty. Congress did not have the money to pay for a frigate, which would be its share of the police fleet. And Adams in England advised against making war.

Sick at heart, Jefferson had finally to agree to paying the ransom. But the moment the pirates got wind of the fact that the Americans were ready to pay, the price went up sky high. For freeing the twenty American sailors it had enslaved and for the promise not to molest American shipping, Algeria demanded $660,000.

To give the Algerians such a sum would only mean to encourage them to prey on American vessels. Congress agreed to spend $40,000. This affair had by now been dragging on for years. Unaware that Jefferson had been constantly and secretly negotiating for their release, the captured sailors sent him cruel letters in which they accused him of heartlessly prolonging their misery. At one time Jefferson had turned to the Mathurins, an order of monks who devoted themselves to the special task of redeeming Christian slaves. Nothing came of it. Indeed, it was not until long after Jefferson had returned to America, that the sailors gained their freedom. But Jefferson did not forget the indignities his country had suffered from the pirates, and when his chance came he revenged them.

Early in 1786 Jefferson received an encouraging message from London. England, wrote John Adams, seems at last ready to enter into a friendly treaty with her former colonies. Would Jefferson join Adams in London and help carry it through?

Jefferson was delighted at the prospect of winning back the friendship of the mother country. He hastened to London, where the two American ambassadors quickly drew up a brief treaty.

Coming from his kindly, warm-hearted Paris, Jefferson was shocked at the treatment he found Adams subjected to. "On my presentation, as usual, to the King and Queen at their levees," he wrote later, "it was impossible for anything to be more ungracious than their notice of Mr. Adams and myself." The British ministers, too, took their cue from their sovereigns. To the Americans' proposals the Minister of Foreign Affairs was cold, condescending, and evasive. He never seemed to be able to grant them their requests for an interview, always having pressing engagements at the time.

After seven weeks of this cool contempt, Jefferson gave up and returned to his French home. The only admirable things he had noticed in England were the gardens and the mechanical inventions, certainly not the manners. It is not surprising that Jefferson could never entirely forget this treatment of himself and his country. His stay had only increased his dislike and distrust of everything British and aristocratic. It only made stronger his friendship for the French.

Jefferson therefore sympathized with the French ministers when they complained that American trade went mostly to England, despite the fact that France was a better friend to the United States than was Great Britain. But France, Jefferson had to reply, had a very high tariff against imported goods. Americans could not sell their goods in France, and hence they could not afford to buy there. He urged the French to try out lower tariffs and even free trade. He himself became quite convinced of the superiority of free trade over tariffs, and was soon talking in favor of it everywhere, in the drawing rooms of society as well as in the audience chamber of the Count de Vergennes.

For, of course, Jefferson was not a diplomat twenty-four hours of each day. After a while he found more and more time to be the private gentleman, to meet people socially, to pursue some of his many personal interests. Lafayette, who after his return from America was always aiding Jefferson in his official work, was also his chief second in society, introducing him to the most fashionable drawing rooms, getting him acquainted with scientists and philosophers.

Being Thomas Jefferson, the more leisure he had from official duties the busier he became. He was over forty now, in the prime of life, and his mind was seething as never before with new ideas, problems, plans, questions, and answers. Whichever way he turned he always seemed to be doing something for the good of his country.

In the first place, like many an American visiting Europe since his day, Jefferson found the most appalling ignorance about his country even among the best-educated classes. Even as late as 1900 the uneducated Londoner had a mental picture of New York, in which Indians and cowboys made up a large percentage of the population. But the ideas about America that Jefferson discovered in the Parisian salons were much wilder.

There were scientists, for instance, who pointed out that, since America was a New World, it could not be quite dry yet. One popular writer on America, an abbé, who had of course never been there, described the prairies as vast tracts of slime and ooze over which rested a perpetual atmosphere of mist and steam. The men and animals who lived in this moist climate were therefore weak, stupid, and hairless.

Another and more popular class of writers on America took their ideas from the Swiss philosopher Rousseau. Rousseau had taught that civilization was the root of all evil, that man was everywhere born naturally good but was corrupted by society. If you want to find a truly noble man, he said, with a sly dig at the artificial aristocrats of Europe, go to the savage.

Though the writers who followed Rousseau did not actually go to the savage in the sense of paying him a visit, they did believe in his natural nobility. These writers thought of the New World as a continent that was young, fresh, and unspoiled. Not only were the redskins a brave and honest race, but even the white men who breathed the pure air of this country became good and virtuous. Look at the Quakers! they were never tired of repeating.

For the old feudal society of France was old and tired and about to collapse, though no one may have known it. It was natural for French thinkers to yearn for a young and vigorous society such as they imagined to exist in America. The American Revolution, too, seemed to prove that they had been right in all their romantic notions of a sturdy, simple, virtuous folk, incapable of any of the crimes of civilization.

All these writers, whether they praised or despised America, copied from each other until every trace of first-hand knowledge had all but vanished from their books. Occasionally there might be an account by an actual traveler, but unless it was filled with romantic nonsense it was not likely to be very widely read. Jefferson's old friend Mazzei, for instance, who had finally found his way back to Europe, did publish a sober book on America, but this honest description by a man who had really lived in the New World for years never became popular.

At any rate, when the Marquis de Lafayette led his friend into the Parisian salons, Jefferson found himself the center of a most tremendous interest. A real American, did you say? the ladies whispered behind their fans. A compatriot of that charming Dr. Franklin? And the author of the Declaration of Independence? Do please introduce us to him, the writers would beg, we have some very serious questions to ask him.

Jefferson was willing, indeed anxious to oblige. He considered it very important that these kind French friends should have a true picture of his country, not the impossible ones they seemed to like so much. He even agreed to edit and correct the articles on America they were putting into their Encyclopedia. But after he had corrected them, he saw these articles printed with the editors' corrections of *his* corrections. People simply would not believe anything as unexciting as the truth.

Then one day Jefferson heard that a certain printer was publishing a French translation of his *Notes on Virginia,* which he had written for the French legation in America some years before. Guessing in advance what wild statements the French translator would be putting into his mouth, Jefferson hastened to secure a copy. Sure enough, his worst fears were justified. There was only one thing to do. Jefferson put out his own edition, in English. That is how this book written in Virginia came to be published first in France.

Hand in hand with the French enthusiasm for everything American there went a vogue for what was called "republican simplicity." When Jefferson arrived in France in 1784, this cult of simplicity, this "back to nature" movement, was already well advanced.

Only a few years before women had been wearing the most elaborate headdresses in the most fantastic shapes. On one poor woman's head there might float a great frigate with every sail unfurled. Another lady's hair might depict the whole globe, with all the continents clearly marked. These coiffures were often so tall that the hairdresser had to mount a ladder to put on the finishing touches, and the wearer had often to bend double or kneel down on the floor when riding in a low coach. A famous hairdresser had therefore invented the "grandmother spring," with which, simply by pressing a button, one could raise one's coiffure by a foot. It got its name from the fact that it could save the young flapper of the day a scolding. On the way to the ball, she could visit her grandmother with a modest-looking headdress; but once she was out of the way of the old lady she pressed the spring, and presto! her headdress rose one or even two feet in the air, with all the battlements and turrets of a medieval fortress.

But now the ladies who read or heard about Rousseau no longer dumped a pound of white powder into their hair of an evening. The simple hairdress of curls was covered by a bonnet or by a wreath of roses. The gowns, too, were less voluminous and embroidered, and it even became the fashion to wear low-heeled shoes. Fortunate little Martha Jefferson, not to have to dress like a miniature lady! Her mother as a young girl had been kept from running and jumping by tight corsets, but Martha's simple taffeta dress allowed her some natural freedom of movement. Of course, a great many grownups thought this new freedom scandalous.

When Jefferson's friend Monsieur de Moustier was sent as ambassador to the United States, he took with him his sister-in-law Madame de Brehan. She was also a friend of Jefferson's, and a great admirer of everything American. She told Jefferson how delighted she was to leave the artificial atmosphere of the French court and to go to his simple and hospitable people. In vain did Jefferson try to warn her against her own ideas of what American democracy was like. He succeeded no better

than he did with the writers of the Encyclopedia. Her mind
had been made up by what she had read about America.

Hastily Jefferson wrote to his friends in America and
pleaded with them to be extremely natural with Madame de
Brehan, not to stand on etiquette with her but to treat her
cordially and simply. Again in vain. American society was not
going to lose this chance of showing off its best manners before a lady of the brilliant French court. In fact, this is a
habit that American society seems never to have lost since
the day that the United States rid itself of kings and courts
of its own.

The result was that Madame de Brehan, who came from a
city where republican simplicity was all the fashion, was quite
unhappy. She wrote Jefferson that society was much more
formal in Philadelphia and New York than it was in Paris.
No one called unless she called first, everyone dressed to kill,
and so on. She was quite hurt and disillusioned.

In spite of being so much lionized by French society Jefferson was often quite homesick during his first year in Paris,
once writing to a friend at home: "I am savage enough to prefer the woods, the wilds, and independence of Monticello to
all the brilliant pleasures of this gay capital." But eventually
Jefferson came to feel quite at home in the Paris that was the
world's capital of wit and ideas as well as of pleasures, especially after he had found some really intimate friends among
all these idolizers of everything American.

Franklin, before leaving, had introduced Jefferson to his
dear friend, Madame d'Houdetot. This lady came to admire
Jefferson at least as much as she had Franklin. For Jefferson
was not only an American and a philosopher; he also could
tell her about American plants and trees, in which she was

interested and of which the city-bred Franklin knew very little. Long after Jefferson had returned home, he continued to send Madame d'Houdetot bulbs, seeds, and plants.

Then there was the circle of Lafayette's wife, in which Jefferson met many interesting and learned men. Among them was Monsieur de la Tude, who had spent thirty-five years in the gloomy Bastille for writing in his youth four little lines of verse making fun of Madame Pompadour. Finally, the French officers who had served in the American Revolution were frequent visitors at the Embassy.

To all this hospitality Jefferson had to make proper and generous return. For a Virginian this was a pleasure as well as a duty. But he was sometimes hard put to it to provide such lavish entertainment as he himself received, especially on the salary of nine thousand dollars a year that Congress sent him, a salary which, incidentally, he himself had helped to fix.

For, as part of the "simplicity" rage of Paris, invitations to supper had almost gone out of fashion. Instead, at about nine-thirty or ten o'clock in the evening, the steward would come into the drawing room, inquire how many people had happened to drop in, and lay as many covers as there were people present—invited or not. It was no unusual thing for a great lady to serve eighty persons with supper at almost a moment's notice, and in certain popular homes there would never be less than thirty plates laid. So, though this might mean that a poet need never starve once he had been introduced to some lord, it also meant that entertainment was a tremendously expensive business, which is certainly a queer result of "simplicity," especially since the poor peasants on the estates had to pay for it all.

As cook and steward Jefferson hired a Frenchman named Petit, who became quite attached to him and wrote him out recipes for French dishes to send to friends in America.

Though himself a light eater, Jefferson had always taken an interest in the art of cookery. In Virginia, whenever he had tasted a delicious dish, he had always asked the hostess how it was made. So, too, while in France, he became interested in wine-growing and wine-making. After making a thorough study of the various vintages, he sent his findings to Adams and Washington.

Jefferson kept a constant stream of information flowing from France to America. Four colleges—Yale, Harvard, William and Mary, and the College of Philadelphia—received letters from him regularly on any new inventions and discoveries that he might have come across or heard of. He even suggested lists of books that he thought should be included in their libraries. Out of gratitude for these services Yale sent him an honorary degree in 1786 and a year later Harvard did the same. He was the first to send to America news of the success of Watt's steam engine "by which a peck and a half of coal performs as much work as horse in a day." He became excited, along with the rest of France, over the new experiments with balloons, and studied the new science of aeronautics.

Once a French mechanic came to Jefferson with the clever idea of standardizing the various parts of watches. To us it may seem natural that a broken part of a watch can be taken out and another ready-made part, exactly like it, put in its place. But in the eighteenth century each watch was so individual that, if it broke down, the watchmaker had to cut out a brand-new piece to replace the broken part. This man's idea Jefferson sent to Congress.

It was while in Paris that Jefferson met John Ledyard of Connecticut, who had accompanied Captain Cook on his famous voyage in the South Seas. He proposed to Ledyard that he explore the western part of North America, in which Jefferson was always keenly interested, by following a novel route. Ledyard was to pass through St. Petersburg in Russia, cross Siberia to Kamchatka, thence go by boat to Nootka Sound in Canada, and from there explore what we now call Oregon. Jefferson would get him the permission of Catherine the Great of Russia to cross her domains. The plan unfortunately fell through because the Empress refused to allow a foreigner to make so hazardous a journey. Ledyard went instead to explore the sources of the Nile, and died there, but Jefferson continued to wonder about the mystery of the western half of his continent.

Jefferson never tired of helping his friends and countrymen, especially if the cause of science and learning was thereby advanced. He kept in his inexhaustible notebooks a list of persons to whom he must send books on certain subjects. As each new volume of the famous French Encyclopedia came out, he subscribed to it for several friends. In the afternoons nothing gave him greater pleasure than haunting the bookstalls of Paris (which are as picturesque today as they were then) and finding rare books for himself or for his friends —books of law for his old teacher, George Wythe, for instance. He also liked to pick up engravings, plaster casts, and medals.

Sending gifts across the Atlantic was an anxious business. Would Madison receive "the most perfect watch" that Jefferson could find, which he had picked up for six hundred francs? And did the pocket telescope, the walking stick, and the chemical box arrive in good condition? When Mrs. Adams's daughter asked him to buy her two pairs of corsets, the errand embarrassed him only because she had forgotten to send him the size she wanted. For he was used to buying all his daughters' clothes, and was always sending Polly, his youngest, sashes and dolls from Paris.

Whenever he heard of a ship sailing to America, he would collect all the articles he had bought for friends or for furnishing Monticello, box them, and send them to the seaport. Then sometimes weeks later he would hear that the ship had sailed without his boxes. Professor Bellini once wrote asking Jefferson to get him a pair of spectacles, for they were not to be procured in America. The poor professor had to wait a year for his glasses. "A box of books lay forgotten at Havre the whole of last winter," Jefferson wrote him, "and your spectacles were with them. I packed the spectacles, three or four pairs of glasses adapted to the different periods of life, distinguished from each other by number and easily changed. You see I am looking forward in hope of a long life for you, and that it may be long enough to carry you through the whole succession of glasses is my sincere prayer."

Though all the farming Jefferson could now do was in the form of letters to his overseer, he never ceased to look upon himself as a planter. So it is natural that the superiorities of Europe over America that he observed most closely, and wrote most fully about in his notebooks, were agricultural superiorities. Whenever he saw a new variety of plant, he asked himself why America could not grow it. In Charleston and in Philadelphia there were already the beginnings of agricultural societies, and Jefferson encouraged these as much as he could by sending them from Europe nuts, roots, seeds, plants, and information. He sent them seed from the only kind of grass that is cultivated in Malta. He sent them acorns of the oak tree from the bark of which comes our cork. He sent them instructions on the planting of capers, whose buds are used in making sauces.

His fondest hope was to see the olive tree extensively culti-

vated in the Southern States. He wrote letter after letter on
this subject. The olive was easy to grow, it bore fruitfully, and
flourished in the poorest soil. It had a great variety of uses
as food. It took much less labor than any grain, and would
lessen the necessity for slaves. He sent bountiful supplies of
every variety of the plant and offered to contribute money
every year for experimenting with it. But like the caper and
the cork oak, the olive did not thrive in the South.

It was with rice that Jefferson was finally able to do something important for the agriculture of America. His own part
in this patriotic contribution was something of an adventure.

Not having lived in a Catholic country before, he had been
surprised at the amount of rice he found eaten in France. On
Fridays and in Lent, when Catholics would not eat meat, rice
was the staple food. This was especially the case in inland
countries where fresh fish was rare and costly, for transportation was slow and, as for refrigeration, it practically did not
exist. Most of this rice came from Italy. Jefferson was told that
it was of much better quality than the American rice.

So, when Jefferson once took a vacation trip to Italy, he
decided to keep his eyes open for rice fields. What was his indignation to discover that the Italians had a law forbidding
anyone to take out of the country any rice seed that had not
first been cleaned and polished so that it could not be planted
and grow! Jefferson thought such a law barbarous. For plants
are no one man's invention; they come freely from the bounty
of the earth and they belong to all mankind.

Jefferson decided to evade the law. Perhaps such an illegal
attitude came naturally to a former American colonist. His
Britannic Majesty's American subjects could never be got
to look upon smuggling as a very serious offense, in fact as any-

thing but a highly respectable business. Patriotism, a scientific interest in agriculture, and his detestation of anything that would deprive mankind of nature's benefits, all seemed to urge Jefferson to adopt a certain course. He hired an Italian muleteer to slip over the border with a couple of sackfuls of the seed.

The muleteer never succeeded in running the rice across the border. But Jefferson was not caught unprepared. Just for luck he had filled the pockets of his greatcoat with the best rice seed of the best rice-growing district in Italy, and the pockets of those days were the size of small knapsacks. When Jefferson got back to France, he divided the seed from his pockets into two parcels, and sent each of them by a different boat to Charleston, South Carolina.

Both parcels arrived safely. The seed was distributed among fifty planters or so, perhaps a dozen grains to each. The planters watched over their seed with the greatest care. When the precious rice plants came up, they were not entrusted even to the overseers but were tended by the planters themselves. That is how South Carolina came to grow rice that was as good as any in the world.

Jefferson followed the success of his Italian rice with pleasure and pride. Later he sent the planters in South Carolina rough seed-rice from the Levant, from Egypt, and even from Cochin China in the Far East. How did he come by unhulled rice from Cochin China? In Paris, Jefferson had befriended the young prince of that country and had made him promise to send some seed back when he returned to his oriental home.

Not all of Jefferson's scientific interests took such a practical or useful turn. The following story told by Daniel Webster may not be true, but it describes exactly the sort of thing Jefferson was *likely* to do if he took a notion to hunt down a scientific fact.

Among Jefferson's acquaintances in Paris was the great French naturalist Buffon, who was then about eighty years old, but who was still collecting materials for his famous book, *Natural History,* which was to appear in more than forty volumes. Jefferson is said to have given him much information about nature in America, and at one time to have procured for him the skin of an American panther, an animal Buffon had never heard of.

The story goes that Buffon, probably influenced by the theories of the abbé mentioned before, expressed the opinion that American animals were all weaker and smaller than those in Europe. On fire to disprove such an insult to his native continent, Jefferson wrote to General Sullivan in New Hampshire to send him the skin and skeleton of a moose, mightiest of the deer. Sullivan, also anxious to uphold the honor of his country, organized a hunting party. The expedition set out in the deep snows of New Hampshire, found a herd of moose, killed the biggest of the lot, and cleared a road twenty-four miles long to get it home. Then they cleaned the hide and skeleton, added the horns of five other deer—the biggest they could find—and shipped them off to France in a huge box, along with General Sullivan's glowing letter of the hardships endured.

In due time Jefferson received the box and the bill, more than a hundred and fifty dollars, for transportation. He made a wry face over the sum, but he had his satisfaction when Buffon, upon being presented with the massive bones of the moose, said: "I should have consulted you, Mr. Jefferson, before I wrote my *Natural History.*"

While in Paris Jefferson had formed the habit of stopping whatever he was doing at the stroke of one, and taking his daily exercise. This usually consisted of a long walk into the country, sometimes for seven miles. Returning one day from one of these rambles, he was joined by a friend, and so earnest was their conversation that he did not look where he was going. Suddenly he stumbled and fell on his right hand. A violent pain shot through his wrist, but he said nothing of it to his friend when he picked himself up. Holding to his wrist with the other hand he continued the conversation until they reached his door. Then he told his companion that he was afraid he had broken his wrist and must leave at once for the surgeon's.

It turned out to be a compound fracture, that is, the broken bone had been driven into the flesh, and it was never properly set by the surgeon. Jefferson's right wrist was ever after stiff and weak. For a man whose two chief pastimes were writing and playing the violin, this was a heavy blow. It remained to the end of his life a handicap that he never quite overcame. It stopped the violin playing for good, but he learned in time to write with his left hand almost as well as with his right. On the very day of the accident, we still find Jefferson faithful to his notebooks. With his left hand he entered among his items of the day's expenses the wages he paid his steward Petit, and the money he spent on buttons (24 francs) and gloves (4 francs).

After the surgeons had bungled the setting of Jefferson's wrist, they could think of no better remedy than that he should take the mineral waters of Aix in Provence, southern France. Jefferson did go to Aix, but needless to say the waters he drank did not cure his trouble. While in the south of France he decided to make an extended tour of the country round about as well as the nearby Italian States. It was on this trip that he smuggled out the rice for South Carolina.

Farther south in France is the city of Nîmes, a place that Jefferson had no intention of missing while he was in this region. Its attraction for Jefferson was the fact that it contained several famous Roman monuments. Chief among them was a temple which the French called "La Maison Carrée" (The Square House). When Jefferson had first seen this temple, he literally fell in love with its beauty. He returned time after time to spend whole hours gazing at it "like a lover at his mistress," as he wrote to Madame Lafayette's aunt. He wanted to see it from all angles and under all conditions, in sunshine, in mist, morning, noon, and twilight. The stocking weavers whose shops were in the neighborhood began to think he was an eccentric Englishman who intended to commit suicide on this romantic spot.

When Jefferson received word that Virginia was about to build a new Capitol in Richmond, he wrote at once begging that the building should not be commenced until he had submitted some plans for it. The commissioners in charge of the work wrote back that the building was already started. Jefferson was in despair. He sent letters to Madison pleading with him to stop the commissioners before it was too late. He had hired the best draftsmen and architects in Paris. They were working as fast as they could. They were working on a plan for a perfect State house. It was to be Jefferson's adaptation of the Maison Carrée at Nîmes.

Jefferson won his point. The building was delayed until he could send over a plaster model. Unfortunately the Virginia architects had ideas of their own which they incorporated in Jefferson's classic plan, with the result that many architects look upon the plaster model as more beautiful than the finished building.

1789 1776

XII

THE FAMILY ABROAD

WHILE on his four months' vacation from Paris, Jefferson wrote his Patsy long letters to keep her from growing too lonely in her convent. They were preachy letters, full
of sage advice, but Patsy loved them and was always complain-
ing to her father that he did not write often enough and that
he left wide margins which he might have filled up. She told
him how she spent her time and what were the most important
events going on in Paris.

Being disappointed in my expectation of receiving a letter from you, my dear papa, I have resolved to break so painful a silence by giving you an example that I hope you will follow, particularly as you know how much pleasure your letters give me. I hope your wrist is better, and I am inclined to think that your voyage is rather for your pleasure than your health; however, I hope it will answer both purposes. I will now tell you how I go on with my masters. I have begun a beautiful tune, done a very pretty landscape, and begun another. I go on slowly with *Tite Livy* [the Roman historian], it being in such ancient Italian [Latin] that I cannot read without my master, and very little with him even. As for the dancing-master, I intend to leave him off as soon as my month is finished. I am afraid you will not be able to read my scrawl, but I have not the time of copying it over again, and therefore I beg your indulgence, and assure you of the tender affection of yours,

M. JEFFERSON.

Please write often and long letters.

Patsy had been in Paris about two and a half years by then, and she was beginning to write English like a Frenchwoman.

My dear Papa—
Though the knowledge of your health gave me the greatest pleasure, yet I own I was not a little disappointed in not hearing from you. Titus Livius puts me out of my wits. I cannot read a word by myself, and I read of it very seldom with my master; however, I hope I shall soon be able to take it up again. I have not heard any thing of my harpsichord, and I am afraid it will not come before your arrival. They make every day some new history on the Assemblée des Notables. I will not tell you any, for fear of taking a trip to the Bastille for my pains, which I am by no means disposed to do at this moment. I go on pretty well with my Thucydides [the Greek historian], and I hope I shall very soon finish it. Adieu, my dear papa; be assured you are never a moment absent from my thoughts and believe me to be, your most affectionate child,

M. JEFFERSON.

To which "dear Papa" replied with longer sermons on the value of the habit of industry. "If at any moment, my dear," he wrote her, "you catch yourself in idleness, start from it as you would from the precipice of a gulf." He did not like to hear that she could not read Livy unaided. She must learn to be self-reliant.

It is part of the American character to surmount every difficulty by resolution and contrivance. In Europe there are shops for every want; its inhabitants therefore have no idea that their wants can be supplied otherwise. Remote from all other aid, we are obliged to invent and to execute; to find means within ourselves, and not to lean on others. Consider, therefore, the conquering your Livy as an exercise in the habit of surmounting difficulties; a habit which will be necessary to you in the country where you are to live, and without which you will be thought a very helpless animal, and less esteemed. Music, drawing, books, invention, and exercise will be so many resources to you against ennui. But there are others. These are the needle and domestic economy. The latter you cannot learn here, but the former you may. In the country life of America there are many moments when a woman can have recourse to nothing but her needle for employment. In a dull company and in dull weather, for instance, it is ill manners to read, it is ill manners to leave them. The needle is then a valuable resource. Besides, without knowing how to use it herself, how can the mistress of a family direct the work of her servants?

You ask me to write you long letters. I will do it, my dear, on condition you will read them from time to time and practice what they will inculcate. My expectations from you are high, yet not higher than you may attain. Nobody in this world can make me so happy, or so miserable, as you. Retirement from public life will ere long be necessary for me. To your sister and yourself I look to render the evening of my life serene and contented. Its morning has been clouded by loss after loss, till I have nothing left but you.

Martha could think of no higher happiness than to become what her father wanted her to be. But now she had the added duty of making someone else into that same sort of person. For her little sister Mary, now eight years old, was coming to join them in Paris, and Jefferson was going to put her entirely into Martha's care.

My dear Papa—

I was very sorry to see that your return would be put off. However, I hope not much, as you must be here for the arrival of my sister. I wish I was myself all that you tell me to make her; however, I will try to be as near like it as I can. I have another landscape since I wrote to you last, and have begun another piece of music. I have not been able to do more, having been confined some time to my bed with a violent headache and a pain in my side. The plague is in Spain. A Virginia ship coming to Spain met with a corsair of the same strength. They fought, and the battle lasted for an hour and a quarter. The Americans gained and boarded the corsair, where they found chains that had been prepared for them. They took them and made use of them for the Algerians themselves. They returned to Virginia, from whence they are to go back to Algiers to change the prisoners, to which, if the Algerians will not consent, the poor creatures will be sold as slaves. Good God! have we not enough? I wish with all my soul that the poor Negroes were all free.

Adieu, my dear papa, and believe me to be for life your most tender and affectionate child.

For more than two years the Jeffersons had not seen their little Polly. She had been left with her aunt, Mrs. Eppes. Mary Jefferson had become so fond of her aunt and of her two little cousins, especially of Jack Eppes, that she absolutely refused to leave Virginia, even to join her father. She was of such an extremely affectionate nature that Mrs. Eppes was afraid the parting would be too cruel for the child.

But Jefferson did not want his little girl to grow up forgetting her father and her sister. He knew that, once she was in Paris, she would like it as much as she did Virginia. So he always, in his letters to her, tried to keep before her mind the idea that she would soon be coming to see him in France. This is one of the earlier letters, and it is typical of all of them, even to the moral instructions and the advice on being ladylike addressed to a little seven-year-old girl:

Paris, Sept. 20th, 1785

My dear Polly—

I have not received a letter from you since I came to France. If you knew how much I love you and what pleasure the receipt of your letters gave me at Philadelphia, you would have written to me, or at least have told your aunt what to write, and her goodness would have induced her to take the trouble of writing it. I wish so much to see you, that I have desired your uncle and aunt to send you to me. I know, my dear Polly, how sorry you will be, and ought to be, to leave them and your cousins; but your sister and myself cannot live without you, and after a while we will carry you back again to see your friends in Virginia. In the meantime you shall be taught here to play on the harpsichord, to draw, to dance, to read and talk French, and such other things as will make you more worthy of the love of your friends; but above all things, by our care and love of you, we will teach you to love us more than you will do if you stay so far from us. I have had no opportunity since Colonel Le Maire went, to send you anything; but when you come here you shall have as many dolls and playthings as you want for yourself or to send to your cousins whenever you shall have opportunities. I hope you are a very good girl, that you love your uncle and aunt very much, and are very thankful to them for all their goodness to you; that you never suffer yourself to be angry with anybody, that you give your playthings to those who want them, that you do whatever anybody desires of you that is right, that you never tell stories, never beg for anything, mind your books and your work when your aunt tells you, never play but when she permits you, nor go where she forbids you; remember, too, as a constant charge, not to go out without your bonnet [because she would become tanned, a disgraceful condition for a lady's skin in the eighteenth century], because it will make you very ugly, and then we shall not love you so much. If you always practice these lessons, we shall continue to love you as we do now, and it is impossible to love you any more. We shall hope to have you with us next summer, to find you a very good girl, and to assure you of the truth of our affection for you. Adieu, my dear child.

To all such letters, with their suggestion of leaving her aunt, Mary's replies were the same, all written in a large childish scrawl:

Dear Papa—

I long to see you, and hope that you and sister Patsy are well; give my love to her and tell her that I long to see her, and hope that you and she will come very soon to see us. I hope that you will send me a doll. I am very sorry that you have sent for me. I don't want to go to France, I had rather stay with Aunt Eppes. Your most happy and dutiful daughter,

POLLY JEFFERSON.

Dear Papa—

I should be very happy to see you, but I cannot go to France, and hope that you and sister Patsy are well. Your affectionate daughter. Adieu.

MARY JEFFERSON.

Dear Papa—

I want to see you and sister Patsy, but you must come to Uncle Eppes.

POLLY.

In the meantime Jefferson was making the most careful preparations for his daughter's unwilling trip. When he thought of all the dangers that a ship ran—sinking, shipwreck, pirates—he almost decided to let the little girl have her way. By very diligent inquiry he found that most vessels lost at sea were either making their first voyage or had been sailing for longer than five years. He knew, too, that the Atlantic was least stormy between April and July. So he bided his time until he could make sure of just the right combination of things for Polly's trip, writing to Mrs. Eppes that he would rather live a year longer without his daughter than trust her to any but a good ship and a summer passage.

While her father was making all these careful preparations, Polly kept hoping and praying that he would change his mind. Mrs. Eppes wrote Jefferson that she had used every argument she could think of without moving the girl's stubbornness in the slightest. "Either of my own children," she wrote, "would with pleasure take her place for the number of good things she is promised."

Finally they had to resort to trickery. Just the right sort of ship being then in the harbor, Polly's trunks and bags were smuggled on board. She and her cousins were taken to the boat every day to play on its deck, until she had become quite familiar with it and its crew. Then one day all the children were sent to one of the cabins to take a nap. As soon as Polly was sound asleep, her cousins were quickly and quietly taken off the ship. When Polly woke up, she found herself far out at sea. She had been "shanghaied"! This was exactly the same trick that had been played on the Indian princess Pocahontas to get her to England.

With Polly was Isabell, a Negro servant girl, whom Jefferson had chosen as his daughter's companion because she had already had the smallpox. Though Polly had once been inoculated against smallpox, her father did not wish to leave anything to chance on this voyage.

But there was one hazard that Jefferson had forgotten. The master of the ship, in whose charge Polly was sent, was a Captain Ramsay. It was not long before the child's loving disposition had so attached her to this good captain that she decided to stay on the ship with him forever. The ship was only going as far as England, but Captain Ramsay, for his part, had grown so fond of the girl that he offered to leave his vessel and escort her himself to Paris. Jefferson would not have him put himself to so much trouble. Mrs. Abigail Adams would take Polly off the boat and forward her to her father. Amid tears of parting, Polly left her Captain Ramsay.

Then, of course, the thing happened all over again in London. This is what Mrs. Adams wrote to her sister:

I have had with me for a fortnight a little daughter of Mr. Jefferson's who arrived here, with a young Negro girl, her servant from Virginia. Mr. Jefferson wrote me some months ago that he expected them, and desired me to receive them. A finer girl for her age I never saw. I grew so fond of her, and she was so much attached to me, that, when Mr. Jefferson sent for her, they were obliged to force the little creature away. She is but eight years old. She would sit sometimes, and describe to me the parting with her aunt who brought her up, the obligations she was under to her, and the love she had for her little cousins, until the tears would stream down her cheeks; and how I had been her friend, and she loved me. Her papa would break her heart by making her go again. She clung round me so that I could not help shedding a tear at parting with her. She was the favorite of everyone in the house. She is a beautiful girl, too.

Jefferson had now returned from his travels in Italy with his wrist bothering him somewhat less. He had friends staying in England who were to bring Polly with them when they came to Paris, but he could not wait. So he sent his steward Petit after her. How glad Patsy and Jefferson were to see Polly again! She had grown a great deal in two years so that they could scarcely recognize her. Now the whole family was united again.

Martha left her convent school for a while to stay with her little sister until Polly should become used to her Paris home. Martha took Polly visiting to the convent several times, and, when the little girl seemed to have grown familiar with the place, both of them returned for good to study there. It was not long before the little American with the affectionate character had become a favorite at the school. First they called her Mademoiselle Polie, but, when they learnt that Polly was only a nickname for Mary, she became Marie. From then on even her American friends always called her Maria.

It was years before Maria was to see her Aunt Eppes and her cousins again, but her face would always kindle with love when they were mentioned. When she was told that Aunt Eppes had had another baby, who was to be called Mary, after her, Polly was overjoyed. She told her father she would teach the baby French when she returned home. She must write this to her aunt, too. But Maria did not take after her father in the matter of letter-writing. Dozens of times she would sharpen her quills, prepare her inkpot and sandbox, and sit down at her desk, pen in hand. Then, after racking her brains, she would call out: "Indeed, Papa, I do not know what to say, you must help me." But he never would, and so the letters were never written.

With Polly safely settled in school, Jefferson thought he could make another trip, this time to a country he had not yet visited. He went to Germany, noting down as usual on his travels anything that might possibly be useful for Americans to know, and studying the language.

One day he happened to pass through a town in which a Hessian garrison was quartered. Jefferson was recognized with an outburst of joy by one of the Hessian officers, Baron de Geismer. The Baron had been one of the prisoners who had been treated so kindly in Virginia. He at once called together his brother-officers, whom he had told of his adventures in America. Now Jefferson was overwhelmed with invitations and kindly attentions of every sort.

Shortly after Jefferson first came to Paris three young Virginians sailed for Scotland to attend the University of Edinburgh. They were Thomas Mann Randolph, his brother, and his cousin. Thomas was a grandson of Peter Jefferson's best friend William Randolph. His father was the Thomas Mann Randolph with whom Tom Jefferson had gone to school in Tuckahoe while his father was guardian of the young Randolphs there.

Three years later the boys were returning home in the spring, when Thomas Mann Randolph decided to stop at Paris and visit the Jeffersons. Martha and young Tom had known each other since they were little children. But, when he dropped in on them now, Martha was confused to see a grown-up young man, tall and lean, with brown skin and dark eyes. He looked strong and supple as steel, and at the same time showed a manner that was as polished, and a mind that was as cultured as that of any young gallant she had met in Paris. Tom, on his side, saw a girl cousin that had suddenly grown from a child to a tall and elegant young lady of sixteen. The two youngsters made an enjoyable summer of it, exchanging ideas, going out on excursions together. When the time came for Tom to leave, he did so with regret.

During the next year, the last the Jeffersons were to spend in France, Martha came to a very serious decision. She had begun to think about the world around her, and from thinking she had gone on to brooding.

It did not seem to Martha that the world was a happy place. All about her was suffering, and the rising complaints of the people against their king and their government. In the streets people were starving and blood was being shed. She was no longer homesick for Virginia, and indeed she might have reflected that with its slavery her home had no less wickedness and misery than France. There a shivering coachman slave might be bound by chains to his box on a winter night while his mistress made merry indoors at some party. From the sea there seemed only to come news of piracy and disaster, no better than on the land.

In the convent all was peace and quiet, gentleness and calm thought. She was at an age when many people turn most strongly to religion, and in Panthémont all problems seemed solved. Martha finally wrote her father asking his permission to stay in the convent the rest of her life.

A day passed. On the second Jefferson drove up in his carriage. He greeted his daughters with affectionate smiles. "Come," he said to them, "I am lonely. I have come to take you to live with me." Martha's school days were over. She was to take over the duties of her father's household, and Maria was to have private tutors at home. Jefferson never mentioned the incident again to Martha, nor she to him.

Some months before this, Jefferson had written home asking for a six months' leave of absence. But in America the whole government was then being revised. A new Constitution had been written and was being ratified. Jefferson was asked to stay on in France a little longer. Actually he had to wait almost a year, his permission to leave not coming until August 1789.

In the meantime events of tremendous importance were taking place in France. The Revolution had really started.

The winter of 1788–89 had been a frightful one in Paris, and the news from the rest of France was no better. The country was in the grip of a depression. In weather that was twenty degrees below zero, the government had to burn bonfires in the streets to keep the poor from freezing to death. Every day long lines of women and children stood before the bake-shops begging for bread. There was such a shortage of bread that among the aristocracy it became the smart thing for invited dinner guests to bring their own along with them.

Jefferson wrote a letter to America, which was published in the papers, asking for flour. America sent France 35,000 barrels of flour as a result of this appeal.

Many people think that Jefferson and the other American revolutionists took their ideas from the French philosophers, who started their country thinking about revolution. This was not so. Both Jefferson and Rousseau, for instance, were affected by their reading of the older English thinkers and of the writers of antiquity. Both took out of the air, as it were, their feeling that the old societies were rotten and doomed, that mankind needed a new start with new ideas of justice.

On the other hand, not enough is said of the influence of America upon France. Everything American was greeted with enthusiasm by the French. Paris doted upon those of her sons who had fought in the American War of Independence. Every reformer pointed to the United States as a model of reason and justice. When the French Revolution started, everyone's eyes were on America.

Not only was Jefferson America's official representative in Paris, he was himself a famous revolutionary. In French eyes, the writer of the Declaration of Independence was the great apostle of the religion of liberty. He was not simply a theorist, a man who talked large ideas; he was a practical statesman, a man who had drafted Virginia's Bill of Religious Freedom and had drawn up a complete plan for public education.

Liberals and reformers like Lafayette therefore thought it a great piece of good luck that Jefferson should be present at what promised to be the dawn of a new era in the history of France. This put Jefferson in a very difficult position. Sympathetic though he might be with Lafayette's political friends, and willing to give them the help they expected, he had after all been sent by his own government to the King of France. He was thus the King's guest, and it would be poor return for the hospitality he had received to aid in plots against the King's government.

On the other hand, Jefferson was very much indebted to Lafayette. After his visit to the United States in 1784, Lafayette had returned to become the protector of American interests in France. His tour of the States had been a great success. Everywhere he had been met with love and honor. When an American said "the Marquis," he always meant Lafayette. Ever since, Lafayette had worked for American interests with redoubled energy. He was the untiring friend of the whole American colony in Paris. He introduced Americans to the Court; every Monday he had their principal men to dinner; and in a thousand little ways he had made Jefferson's tasks easier.

Now he was turning to Jefferson for encouragement and advice. How could Jefferson refuse him? Once, for instance, the Marquis asked if he could bring a little party of eight men to Jefferson's house for dinner. When these nine Frenchmen sat down at Jefferson's table, they turned out to be members of the new Patriot Party who had come together to decide whether representatives to the new assembly ought to be elected or hereditary, and whether the King should be allowed to veto the laws they passed. After eating Jefferson's food and drinking his wine, they discussed these questions calmly for six hours. Jefferson held his tongue throughout. Afterwards he was afraid that in taking part, even silently, in such a seditious gathering he had not observed the proper etiquette for a Minister of the United States. So he went to the French Minister of Foreign Affairs and referred very delicately to what he had done. But it seemed that the Foreign Minister knew all about it and quite approved.

Again, in July 1789, at the supreme moment of the Revolution, when the Estates General had met to decide the future of the nation, this body paid homage to Jefferson. For the committee it had appointed to draft a constitution called on this foreigner to sit in at its sessions and favor it with his advice. This honor, too, Jefferson had to decline for diplomatic reasons.

Just about this time President Washington finally sent Jefferson permission to come home for a six months' vacation. By the time the news of this had reached Jefferson and he could get ready and find a ship for America, the months of July, August, and September slipped by. In these months the most exciting place in the world to be in was Paris. The Revolution was in full swing, and rumors were even thicker than events. Jefferson and his secretary were forever running down reports that thousands of people had been killed in street fighting, only to find that a couple of heads had been broken.

On July 17, he went out and inspected the ruins of the King's great grim prison, the Bastille. The populace of

Paris had attacked it and freed all the prisoners. Aristocrats were beginning to flee the country, and in the streets Jefferson could see excited throngs being harangued by fiery orators.

But go he must. His plans were all made, and in any case he intended to be back soon. So Jefferson paid parting calls on his many friends, and he and his two girls left for Le Havre, whence his boat sailed at the beginning of October. The trip home, which was not without its excitement, was later described by Martha:

In returning we were detained ten days at Havre, and, after crossing the Channel, ten more at Cowes, in the Isle of Wight, which were spent in visiting different parts of the island, when the weather permitted. We sailed on the 23rd of October 1789, in company with upwards of thirty vessels who had collected there and been detained as we were by contrary winds. The voyage was quick and not unpleasant.

They arrived at the coast of Virginia in a thick fog, almost ran aground, were nearly rammed by another ship, but made port safely.

We arrived at Norfolk in the forenoon, and in two hours after landing, before an article of our baggage was brought ashore, the vessel took fire, and seemed on the point of being reduced to a mere hull. They were in the act of scuttling her, when some abatement in the flames was discovered, and she was finally saved. Our trunks, and perhaps also the papers, had been put in our staterooms, and the doors incidentally closed by the captain. They were so close that the flames did not penetrate; but the powder in a musket in one of them was silently consumed, and the thickness of the traveling-trunks alone saved their contents from the excessive heat.

There were no stages in those days. We were indebted to the kindness of our friends for horses; and visiting all on the way homeward, and spending more or less time with them all in turn,

we reached Monticello on the 23rd of December. The Negroes
discovered the approach of the carriage as soon as it reached
Shadwell, and such a scene I never witnessed in my life. They
collected in crowds around it and almost drew it up the mountain by hand. The shouting, etc., had been sufficiently obstreper-
ous before, but the moment it arrived at the top, it reached the
climax. Then the door of the carriage was opened, they received him in their arms and bore him to the house, crowding
around and kissing his hands and feet—some blubbering and
crying—others laughing. It seemed impossible to satisfy their
anxiety to touch and kiss the very earth which bore him. These
were the first ebullitions of joy for his return after a long absence, which they would, of course, feel; but perhaps it is not
out of place here to add that they were at all times very devoted
in their attachment to him.

XIII

"A REPUBLICAN COURT"

A FEW days before Jefferson's ship left Le Havre, while he was busily packing up his possessions and bidding his friends *au revoir*, the first President of the United States named him the first Secretary of State.

Jefferson did not receive the official appointment until he landed in Norfolk. His first impulse was simply to refuse the honor. He was coming home for a short visit only. France was on the edge of great events, and it would be a pity not to be there when they happened.

But on the heels of President Washington's messenger, Jefferson received a visitor who had already once before made him change his mind just as he was about to retire from politics. This was, of course, James Madison, with the same old story. Jefferson's country needed him more in New York than it did in Paris. Great events were about to happen here, too, for Madison was sure that this time they had made a government that would last. As Secretary of State, Jefferson would be at Washington's right hand: as such he could help save the Revolution, make sure that the things they had fought for would be kept and the things they had fought against be thrown out.

Jefferson finally let himself be convinced. In the middle of February 1790 he formally accepted the post, and sat down to write his French friends that at their last meeting it should have been *adieu* and not *au revoir*. He was not coming back to France. By the way, his daughter, Mademoiselle Martha, was to be married next week to her cousin, Thomas Mann Randolph. They would undoubtedly remember the young man—he had visited the Jeffersons two summers ago. Yes, Jefferson approved of the match, though of course he had not arranged it as French parents would have. "Though his talents, disposition, connections, fortune were such as would have made him my first choice," wrote Jefferson, "yet according to the usage of my country, I scrupulously suppressed my wishes, that my daughter might indulge in her own sentiments freely." The ceremony would be performed by the Reverend Mr. Maury, the son of Thomas Jefferson's old schoolmaster.

Shortly after the wedding Jefferson left Monticello to take up his duties in New York, then the capital of the Federal government. It took him three weeks to get there, arriving March 22. He stopped at several towns on the way to talk with friends and to be honored by mayors. At Philadelphia he visited Franklin. The old man, shockingly thin but cheerful as ever, was confined to his bed. Jefferson had to tell him all about France and his darling Paris and the Revolution that was going on.

A month later Jefferson was very glad he had had this talk with his old friend. America's wisest citizen was dead. Congress put on mourning. In France the National Assembly proclaimed three months of mourning throughout the country, and memorial services were held by the leading patriotic clubs, by the various scientific societies, by the National Guard, the Masonic lodges, and the guild of printers. Statuettes of Franklin, carved from stones of the Bastille wall, were sold in Paris. It was one of Jefferson's duties as Secretary of State to write and thank the French National Assembly for "setting the first example of the representatives of one nation doing homage, by a public act, to the private citizen of another."

Coming to New York was like attending a reunion. One of the first social affairs Jefferson attended was the second wedding of his schoolboy chum and confidant, John Page; Fanny Burwell having died five years before. Madison was there, and John Adams, and so many of the men of the old Continental Congress. Only old Ben Franklin was missing.

During Jefferson's absence in France, his disciple Madison had become a famous person. The acknowledged "Father of the Constitution" was now the foremost man in the House of Representatives. There was therefore no better man to tell Jefferson what had happened at the Constitutional Convention, what problems had been solved, and which still awaited solution.

When Jefferson, in Paris, had first heard of the proceedings of the Convention, he had been very suspicious of the "bundle of compromises" it had turned out as a Constitution. He thought too much power was being given to a President, who might be re-elected over and over again, and not enough to the people's Representatives. And where was the citizen's protection against the sort of tyranny the Revolution had been fought over? He wrote to Madison suggesting that, after a certain number of States had accepted the Constitution, the others should hold out against adoption until a Bill of Rights had been included. Jefferson wanted the United States Government solemnly to bind itself never to permit certain acts. It should guarantee free speech, free press, freedom of assembly, freedom of religion, and trial by jury in all cases. He also wanted to see standing armies and monopolies, or trusts, forbidden.

Most of these ideas were also being fought for at home by George Mason and others. Eventually Madison got the first session of Congress to pass the first ten amendments to the Constitution as the nation's Bill of Rights. But even before this, Jefferson had been won over to thinking that the Constitutional Convention had done as well as might be expected. What was after all most important was that the constitution of a state had been changed "by assembling the wise men of the state, instead of assembling armies." This would be an example to the world of which the United States could well be proud.

To Jefferson, fresh from a country that was always singing the praises of America's "republican simplicity," the most striking feature of American society was its growing snobbishness. In France they were fond of saying that the American Revolution had opened the walls of the Bastille, and Benjamin Franklin was a patron saint. Luckily they could not hear the talk in New York drawing rooms. They could not see the society about President Washington putting on aristocratic airs and loving to hear itself called "a republican court." Levees were held on exactly the same lines as those of the Court of St. James's in London.

As Secretary of State Jefferson was invited out to homes that were considered the "best society," and these he discovered were the homes of old Tories, people who had entertained the British officers during the Revolution and had drunk toasts to the "confusion of the rebels." This gilded mob, whose greatest distinction in life meant being presented to George III, seemed quite certain that a new aristocracy would be founded here, with themselves at the head of it.

Before Jefferson's arrival, this clique of "best people" had been ridiculously excited over the title to be used in addressing Mr. Washington. All the titles of the princes of Europe were closely examined. Justice McKean had suggested "Your Serene Highness," and Washington himself thought "High Mightiness" not a bad title for the President of the United States.

Even Vice-President John Adams, who had fought so valiantly to have the Declaration of Independence adopted, was horrified that the Chief Executive of this country should be addressed simply as "Mr. President." "Why," he said, "there are presidents of fire companies and of cricket clubs." For days he pondered over this grave problem and conducted weighty discussions in the Senate. Finally he got that body to agree on "His Highness the President of the United States and Protector of the Same." Some of the Senators were highly amused, dubbing each other "Your Highness of the Senate." They were even more amused when Madison, as Speaker of the House of Representatives, sent back Adams's resolution with the dry suggestion that he read the Constitution, where Mr. Washington's title was plainly given—"President of the United States."

Adams, a plain farmer's son and a child of democratic New England, had been impressed, by his sojourn as ambassador to England, with the importance of pomp and splendor in government. Whereas the rude treatment given to himself and Adams by the King in London had turned Jefferson's mind the more decidedly against all forms of aristocracy, it had only succeeded in convincing Adams that no other country would respect the United States unless it, too, could flaunt thrones and high-sounding titles. Jefferson, on the contrary, thought even the word "Mister" unnecessary when two republicans addressed each other.

The feeling of class in those days must not be forgotten. A peppery gentleman of the old school would feel justified in throwing a butcher's boy down the stairs if the latter spoke to him without first removing his cap. The celebrated actor, Harry Hallam, suffered so terribly from the gout that it was sometimes impossible for him to walk. Yet he knew that many people would object to a mere actor keeping a coach, and so on the door of the small one he bought he had painted a crossed pair of crutches as a coat of arms. This was in Philadelphia, to which the government moved in the fall of 1790, and where the new Tory sentiment ran especially high.

Washington, himself, the center of all this excitement about ceremonial and high-sounding names, was really at bottom a plain and simple man without vanity. He had once refused to eat a fish on discovering that his steward had paid an outrageous price for it because it was out of season. All this formality he must have found somewhat tedious.

On the other hand, dignity came quite naturally to Washington. With most persons he was reserved, rather distant, with nothing of the hail-fellow-well-met manner about him. Once at the Continental Congress Robert Morris had expressed the opinion among friends that Washington's aloof air was probably exaggerated. He said that he for one was not afraid to approach the Virginian general with as much familiarity as he would any other man. Morris's friends immediately bet him a dinner that such an attempt would be a failure. The next time, therefore, that Morris met Washington, he laid his hand familiarly on his sleeve. Washington froze Morris with a stare and brushed off his hand. Morris paid his wager, but he said that the joke had probably cost him much more than a dinner for it might have meant Washington's disfavor.

At any rate it was not difficult for Adams and Hamilton, the first Secretary of the Treasury, to persuade Washington that the question of etiquette was an important one. The President was given a coach that matched in splendor that of Botetourt, the old royal Governor of Virginia. It was decorated with cupids and festooned with carved and painted flowers. It was drawn by four horses, which were increased to six when the head of the government rode in pomp to official business.

It was Hamilton's idea to keep the President as inaccessible to the people as was the King of England. Now and then Washington might invite important personages to dinner, but on such occasions he was not to remain long at the table. (As a matter of fact Washington would not have cared to sit very long over the port anyway, for he had recently formed the habit of going to bed at nine o'clock.) Senators, since they were the American substitute for a House of Lords, could speak to the President face to face, but not mere Representatives, and certainly no foreigner with a rank lower than that of Ambassador.

After five years in France, where all the talk was of America's democracy, Jefferson felt almost lost amidst all this royalism. Moreover, he did not like it. A nation based on the Declaration of Independence had no business acting as did the society of New York and Philadelphia. Jefferson showed his distaste for these high and mighty airs, with the result that he was soon being sneered at by some of the "best people." They called him the "leveler from Virginia," the same name he had once received from the rich Southern planters.

By now the French Revolution was going full blast. American society was moved to tears when it heard of the plight of the poor runaway noblemen of France. Some of these counts and marquis began to come to America, where they were petted and made much of. Somehow, Jefferson, who had seen these same aristocrats revel in luxury while the country starved, was not quite so sympathetic over their lot. He felt that, just as in every war some soldiers had to die, so in a great revolution some hitherto privileged persons had to lose their ancient rights. The revolutionists were not to blame for the fact that a rotten system had collapsed, thereby ruining many individuals.

Such opinions were far from popular among America's new would-be aristocrats. The Secretary of State was looked at askance for holding such ideas. They, thank Heaven, would know how to keep the mob in its place. Though they could not have titles, they could still pride themselves on their wealth. It was this early in our history that there began to show itself what others have always accused Americans of having as a religion—the worship of wealth.

The high priest of this vigorous little religion was Alexander Hamilton, Washington's Secretary of the Treasury. Born in the West Indies, as a boy Hamilton had always dreamed of becoming a great general, a dream that never left him though he was to become a great man in an entirely different field. When he was fifteen, a hurricane swept the island of St. Croix. Hamilton wrote such a brilliant account of it for a newspaper that a public subscription was taken up to send this young genius to America to be educated.

Hamilton first attended school at Elizabethtown, New Jersey, where he pursued his studies with an enthusiasm like Jefferson's. When the Revolution broke out, he was a student at King's College, now Columbia University. At seventeen he wrote some very popular pamphlets in favor of the colonies and at nineteen he became a lieutenant-colonel and aide to General Washington. Hamilton was so good at composition that Washington kept him as his secretary, though the boy begged for a command in the field. This was not given to him until the battle of Yorktown.

After the treaty of peace Hamilton served as a member of the first Congress, but his duties soon convinced him that the United States had an unsatisfactory form of government. He became one of the leaders in calling together the Constitutional Convention. Later he worked like a Titan to have the Constitution adopted, though he privately considered it a rather spineless affair.

In the first place he did not think the Federal government centralized enough. He wanted the President and Senators elected for life. The President was to have more powers than even King George was unsuccessfully asking for. He thought the Governors of the various States should be appointed by the President and the Senate. Only men of property should have the vote. Of course, a king and a House of Lords would be even better, but Hamilton knew that unfortunately the Americans would not stand for these improvements.

When Washington offered Robert Morris the post of Secretary of the Treasury (evidently the President bore him no grudge for his little attempt at familiarity), Morris declined it, saying that Hamilton was a better man for the job. Hamilton accepted the position eagerly. He threw himself into the work, took on a great number of tasks, and soon began to consider himself a sort of prime minister.

This was the man—young, energetic, brilliant, and conservative—who met Jefferson on his arrival at New York. As the two faced each other, neither knew, at least Jefferson did not know, that they were in reality bitter enemies. For theirs were two different types of mind that are always in conflict with each other—and this time the prize of the contest would be the future of America. Would the American people be liberal, as Jefferson wished, or conservative, as Hamilton hoped? The radical and the reactionary faced one another—and each liked the other.

Two men with reddish hair; Jefferson seven inches taller and fourteen years older, and by far the less handsome of the two. Both hard workers and all-devouring readers and capable of amazing concentration. There was no reason why two men of such similar intelligence and ability should not like each other at first.

The differences that separated Hamilton and Jefferson as if they were the two poles of the earth were those of temperament. Hamilton saw all glory in the past, Jefferson in the future. Jefferson had at first objected to the Constitution because it had no Bill of Rights protecting the citizen against tyranny; Hamilton's objections were on the ground that the central government did not have enough power. It was enough for an idea to be new and untried for Jefferson to be interested in it and for Hamilton to be suspicious of it.

Where do a man's ideas come from? Why was Jefferson interested in change and progress while Hamilton sought only for stability and security? Why was it that the man who had inherited his wealth, who was a land-owner in an aristocratic society and a slave-owner in the South, had such faith in the common people, while the man who had been practically a pauper in youth had such distrust of the poor, and wished the government to be by and for the wealthy?

A long time ago Jefferson had become convinced that the British form of government was a far from perfect one. Then all the thirteen colonies had been convinced of the same thing, so that they had a revolution to rid themselves of this form of government. Now, it seemed to Jefferson, the air of America had suddenly become filled with praises of the British monarchy. Had we not lived under this monarchy and found it wanting?

In the eighteenth century a new idea was gaining ground throughout the civilized world. Jefferson's mind and temperament were of the kind to be most impressed by this idea. The idea was called "progress." You started out with the thought that nothing done by human beings could be perfect. Swimming records would always be beaten by new records in the end. The British government likewise could be improved upon. Hitherto people had usually been afraid of change, of the future, of the unknown. But science on the one hand, and the American Revolution on the other, had proved that changes could be for the better, that the future was full of changes anyway, that the unknown was like a mine full of gold waiting to be dug up.

Hence you faced the future with optimism and courage, with faith and hope. In other words you tried to keep the attitude of a young man instead of an old one. You were against standing still; you were against falling into the rut of habit. You wanted your mind supple and your muscles limber, so that, if a brand-new problem came up, you were not lost and confused. You had been expecting brand-new problems, you had been waiting for them, and you attacked them with zest.

To Hamilton, all this was nonsense. The world would always remain more or less the same. Human nature would never change. There *were* perfect things, and it was your business to find them and stick by them. For instance, Hamilton would dearly have loved to be a Japanese nobleman. The Japanese had discovered a nearly perfect system of government and stayed by it for hundreds of years. If you were born a Japanese samurai, you knew exactly what were your rights and duties, and what you were expected to do for the rest of your life. Of course, this was before Admiral Perry went to Japan and forced the samurai to believe in progress.

For Hamilton, whatever existed was better than whatever did not yet exist. Once John Adams said that the British form of government would be the best in the world if you took away the corruption that went with it. Hamilton replied at once that without its corruption it would be less perfect. The system was tied up with its corruption, the two went together, and hence it was better not to try to improve it by separating them. Besides, corruption made it possible for the "best people," the wealthy, to run things as they pleased, and whatever the "best people" pleased was best.

Naturally, Hamilton was the darling of the "best people." He was also the leader of the government party, the Federalists, and the strong man of Washington's first Cabinet.

There were only four members in this first Cabinet. Besides Jefferson and Hamilton, there were General Knox, Secretary of War, and Edmund Randolph, Attorney-General. General Knox stood four-square behind Hamilton. His pet ideas were a standing army and the abolition of all State governments. Edmund Randolph was a distant cousin of Jefferson's, the son of the John Randolph who had sold Jefferson his fiddle before quitting the colonies to go to live in England. Edmund Randolph had enlisted with Washington as soon as his father left the country. He had later been a Governor of Virginia. He agreed on policies more or less with Jefferson, but was the sort of man who could not quite make up his mind because he could always see both sides of an argument. The result was that he would go with the side that pushed him hardest. His arguments would support Jefferson and his votes would go to Hamilton—or, as Jefferson put it, he gave the shells to his friends and the oysters to his enemies.

None of these things—Hamilton's background and views, and his own differences from Hamilton—did Jefferson know when, on his arrival in New York, he was met by the Secretary of the Treasury, who walked him up and down in front of Washington's residence for half an hour, earnestly beseeching his help to save the Union from destruction. There was a certain bill before Congress which the members of the Southern States refused to pass. If this bill were not passed into a law, the Northern States threatened to secede. Would Jefferson please speak to the gentlemen from the South and get them to consent to the passage of the law? Otherwise, the Union was doomed.

In order to understand this critical bill, upon which the existence of the Union seemed to depend, we shall have to go back among Hamilton's activities before Jefferson arrived on the scene. As soon as the new government had begun to operate, Hamilton had worked out a complete program of finance. His program had three main points in it. The first was that the United States should promise to pay all the debts it had contracted during the Revolutionary War, dollar for dollar, with interest. This seems at first sight fair enough, but in the meantime this is what had happened.

The Continental Congress and after it the Confederation had very soon run out of money. They had therefore paid their soldiers, and the farmers who had supplied food to the army, with promissory notes. Since, before the adoption of the Constitution, the government could collect very few taxes, it was not able to make good on these promissory notes. They therefore dropped in value, and soldiers and farmers who needed money badly were compelled to sell them for ten or fifteen percent of the amount printed on them. That is, for every dollar of these printed certificates you could get only ten or fifteen cents in cash.

Little by little wealthy men who knew what was coming had been buying up these promissory notes very cheaply. The Senators knew of Hamilton's program and some of them quietly bought up the soldiers' wages. The Senators told a few of their merchant friends in New York, Philadelphia, and Boston, and these cautiously bought up the farmers' claims. These speculators sent couriers on swift horses into the backwoods with bags of money. They sent speedy boats to Southern ports with hard cash. Here the news of Hamilton's program had not yet come, and the speculators made bargains that would bring them in a thousand percent profit.

Thus, when the bill for "the funding of the national debt" came up before Congress, many rich men and Congressmen stood to become richer if the bill were passed. But many poor soldiers and farmers were bound to become angry at hearing how they had been cheated.

Was it fair for Congressmen to vote on a measure that would make them personally rich? Did Hamilton think it was exactly honest? Hamilton was frankly not interested in the morality of the question. He had said something of the sort to Adams when they discussed the corruption in the British government. If the law could be passed only by making certain Senators rich, let them become rich. If the law when passed would make certain rich men richer, why that was one of the purposes of government as Hamilton saw it. Besides, this would have precisely the result for which Hamilton had created his financial program—he would win over the support of the wealthy for his government. Better the support of a hundred wealthy men than that of ten thousand paupers.

For the government was not to redeem these printed certificates with cash. It was to give new promissory notes for the old ones. But these new promissory notes were sure to be paid at full value in time, and they would be bearing interest regularly. This meant that anyone who owned these promissory notes would support the government heart and soul, and would oppose any radical changes in it, for how else would he be sure of getting his money back?

This was the heart of Hamilton's policy. If a man owes you money, you will take an interest in his welfare. You will shudder when he does something foolhardy, risks his life or fortunes for some new-fangled notion. In the same way, you will take an interest in a government if it owes you money and if it promises to make more for you. What about the millions of others whom the government will not owe money and whom it will not try to make rich? Don't you need their support, especially in a democracy? Well, in the first place, Hamilton hoped the country would get over this democracy fad. In the second place, there was one other method of keeping a nation orderly. Interest would hold the "best people"; for the rest there was—force, a strong central government with a standing army.

When the bill for "funding the national debt" came up, a few held out for buying the certificates at the market value only, so that speculators might not amass unearned fortunes. Madison asked for a compromise measure which would be fair to the original holders of the certificates, the soldiers and farmers. But self-interest won the day, and Point One of Hamilton's program was completed.

When the news of his victory finally leaked back to the remote settlements in the South and West, there was a rumbling of protest and revolt. Not only had certain farmers been cheated by speculators, not only had the government rewarded the speculators for cheating them, but—and here was the insult added to injury—the speculators were to be paid out of taxes. Since the people, the farmers, paid the taxes, this meant that they were to pay their own cheaters for cheating them!

Though Hamilton contemptuously brushed such complaints aside, he was thus digging his own political grave. His policies were creating an opposing party which, for lack of a better name, could only be called for the time being Anti-Federalist. This party, as yet unorganized, was based on a detestation of Hamilton's program and a belief in democracy. Some day, under Jefferson's leadership, it would show its power and sweep the Federalists out.

For Hamilton and the Federalists were not the wise politicians they thought themselves. Living in the East they forgot that nine tenths of the country's population lived on farms and

in villages, and did not approve of all these favors to merchants
and business men at their expense. In the East, men without
property could not vote. Of all the New England States, only
Vermont had universal suffrage. In 1790, New York had over
13,000 grown male residents, but only 1300 of them could
vote. But in the new States farther west, democracy in politics
was a fact, and here the embittered veterans of the Revolutionary War and the farmers who felt themselves cheated were a
power that could not be lightly dismissed.

In the meantime Hamilton was going ahead with Point
Two of his three-part financial program, the "assumption of
State debts." The various State governments had also contracted debts, which at this time amounted to about twenty
million dollars. Hamilton's plan was for the Federal government to take over these debts and add them to its own, paying
as before out of taxes.

Again a fair-seeming idea that needs a little explanation.
In the first place, those States, principally in the South, who
had already paid up most of their debts did not gain much by
it. These States, after paying their own debts, would also have
to pay the debts of other States through taxes on farmers. Also
there would be the inevitable speculators who had bought up
the debts cheaply and expected to be enriched for nothing.

Again Hamilton was thinking along the same lines as before. The government would owe more people money, and
these people would support the government, especially his
Federalist government which was doing them such favors.
Also, the central government would thereby become more important than the State governments.

This time Hamilton's policy struck a snag. The Senate
passed his "assumption bill" behind closed doors (just like

the House of Lords!). But in the House of Representatives, which was open to visitors, the bill was defeated by the close vote of 31 to 29. The Federalists were furious. For days the House had to adjourn without doing any business, because the two sides were so angry with each other that they would not discuss anything else.

This was the tangle of affairs in Hamilton's mind as he walked Jefferson, newly arrived at New York, up and down before Washington's house for half an hour, strenuously beseeching him to save the Union. The Northern States, he said, were threatening to secede, and they would surely do it if the "assumption bill" were not passed.

Jefferson was alarmed. From Hamilton's picture of the case, it seemed too unimportant a matter to cause the collapse of so promising an enterprise as the United States of America. Perhaps, too, Jefferson was flattered that Hamilton should appeal to him, a newcomer at the capital and one who had not been in the country for the last five years, as being capable of overcoming the obstinacy of the Southern delegates.

In Paris, when Lafayette had wanted to thresh out a matter of policy with some political friends, he had once invited them to a dinner at Jefferson's house. Jefferson now used the same stratagem, invited several of the leaders of both sides to his rooms, gave them a dinner, and urged them to come to some agreement that would not disrupt the Union.

Now for some time there had been much debate as to where the capital of the United States was to be. So Jefferson brought this question up as one on which some bargaining could be done. Finally, the fellow diners came to a common decision. The North wanted "assumption" more than it did the capital. The Northern delegates, headed by Robert Morris, therefore guaranteed that two of them would vote to build a new capital on the Potomac if two Southerners would vote for the assumption of State debts. Point Two of Hamilton's program was won.

For once Jefferson had stepped out of his character. He had acted as compromiser when his usual rôle was to take a firm stand on a question. In after years he bitterly regretted his part in the compromise, saying that he had been tricked by the Federalists into playing their game for them. For the "danger" to the Union had been mostly in Hamilton's mind.

When Hamilton's third point came up shortly thereafter, Jefferson was prepared for it. Now he knew the purposes of Hamilton's policy. The growing resentment against the Federalists throughout the country made it possible for Jefferson to organize something like an opposition in the House of Representatives. But this opposition was not yet strong enough to defeat the "bank bill."

Hamilton had all along planned a "Bank of the United States" which was to be owned partly by the government but largely by private interests. As before, the Senate at once passed Hamilton's third proposal, but the Anti-Federalists in the House of Representatives, led by Madison, attacked it vigorously.

When the bill finally came up for Washington's signature, he did not know whether to sign it or not. He asked both Hamilton and Jefferson to write out their opinions of it. From the two papers then written comes the great controversy that was to be so often and seriously debated in our government: should the Constitution be strictly or liberally interpreted?

In his report on the "bank bill" Jefferson closed his remarks with a piece of advice to Washington that shows how he was always looking beyond the particular problem into the future. After attacking the "bank bill" as undesirable and unnecessary and unfair to the farmers and the workers; after trying to prove that it was also unconstitutional; and after pointing out the dangers of a loose interpretation of the Constitution, he weakened his own arguments as follows. If, said Jefferson, the President could not decide whether the law was constitutional or not, and if he was not quite sure that Congress had made a very bad mistake, then he should sign the bill anyway. For in such a case the President should always allow the legislature to have its way. *He should use his veto power as little as possible.*

What does this mean? Why does Jefferson prefer to let Congress have its way despite the fact that it has just passed a law which he disapproves of? It is because he looked upon Congress as representing the people more than the President does. He did not feel that any one man should stand in the way of the people's will.

Washington signed the bill, and Hamilton won all the three points of his financial program. But Hamilton did not intend to rest satisfied with having established a strong commercial class in the country. He wanted to make it stronger and to give it more opportunities for growing. It was now his purpose to create a manufacturing industry that would be as great as England's, the home of everything that was great and right.

Unfortunately the United States was a farming country. Whence would come the labor for America's new mills and factories? Again we could learn from England. More than half the workers in English cotton mills were women and children. Though many of the latter were ten, eight, or even six years old, they all worked twelve hours a day, which was one reason why many men like Jefferson were quite content to see America remain a farming country. But Hamilton could see nothing alarming in this. The wealth of the country seemed to him far more important than the possibility that future Americans might grow up stunted in body and mind through lack of schools and fresh air.

So Hamilton tried to soothe the farmers who might be angry at seeing more government favors (which *they* would have to pay for) go to the merchants. In all seriousness he pointed out to the farmers that they would profit, too, because they could then send their wives and their children "of tender age" to work in these factories twelve hours a day and earn extra money.

First, then, Hamilton put through increased import duties to protect the infant industries from foreign competition. Again the farmer had to pay in the form of higher prices for his goods. (This was why Jefferson had advocated free trade in France.)

Then going from words to deeds, the energetic Secretary of the Treasury helped start a factory near the beautiful Passaic Falls of New Jersey, in what became the city of Paterson. But the ungrateful farmers, whose wives and little children were to make so much extra money, protested loudly. They were indignant because the factory owners' charter gave them the right to dig canals on any man's land. Even the other factory owners were outraged when they heard that Hamilton's new factory was not to be taxed for ten years and that its employees were to be excused from military service.

There is no doubt of Hamilton's genius. He was a financial giant, brilliant and forceful. He far outshone any other man in the government in those first years of its existence, including even the President. And, though he helped make many a shady business man and politician rich by his program, he himself seems to have remained honest all the while.

In comparison with Hamilton, Jefferson did not at first make so splendid an impression. Jefferson's duties were not of so important or striking a sort. His opposition to Hamilton, to the sort of country Hamilton wished to make of America, to the type of American Hamilton favored, grew slowly at first.

For a time there was a little confusion among the members of the Cabinet. No one quite knew how far his duties went. Before Jefferson's arrival Hamilton had simply assumed that the Secretary of the Treasury had the most important post in the Cabinet, being the same as the prime minister in England. Even General Knox, who worshiped Hamilton, resented his interference with the War Department when he insisted upon buying all the supplies for it.

The Secretary of State, of course, took charge of all dealings with foreign nations. But Jefferson found that he was also Postmaster General, not so burdensome a duty when mail was carried at the furious pace of one hundred miles a day. Even this was thanks to him, for before he took charge the mails had traveled only fifty miles a day! Then, too, he was made head of the Patent Office, but examining new inventions was a congenial task to a man of Jefferson's scientific leanings.

It was the Secretary of State who decided the question of the Mint, that American coins should be made at home and not abroad. The Mint was set up in Philadelphia, with workmen imported from Europe. Its first big job was to make a large quantity of copper into cents.

Jefferson had had a hand in the adoption of the decimal system for our coinage. One of his dearest dreams now was to introduce the same system into our weights and measures. He drew up a careful plan to show how advantageous such a system would be. Had it been adopted, we might now be learning in our schools:

$$10 \text{ points} = 1 \text{ line}$$
$$10 \text{ lines} = 1 \text{ inch}$$
$$10 \text{ inches} = 1 \text{ foot}$$
$$10 \text{ feet} = 1 \text{ decad}$$
$$10 \text{ decads} = 1 \text{ rood}$$
$$10 \text{ roods} = 1 \text{ furlong}$$
$$10 \text{ furlongs} = 1 \text{ mile}$$

But Congress was afraid to make innovations in business now. The old revolutionary fervor, which makes quick changes possible in everything, was gone, and so we still have the clumsy old British system in measure though not in money.

XIV

LETTERS HOME

JEFFERSON had not been long in New York when he
realized that all the reasons that he had given Madison for
not going back into politics had been well founded. The feverish excitement of the capital, the petty hatreds, the black looks
of society and Federalists made him turn longing looks back
on the peace of Monticello, which he had been permitted to
enjoy with his children for only two months.

Maria was not quite twelve when he had left her. She was
to stay with the newly-wed Martha and Thomas Randolph

part of the time, and the rest with the Eppes family to whom she was so much attached. Before leaving for New York Jefferson had arranged that he would write a letter home every week. The first week Martha would write an answer, the next Randolph, and the third Maria. The hitch in this careful plan was, of course, pretty little Miss Maria.

This was Jefferson's first letter to his younger daughter:

New York, April 11, 1790.

Where are you, my dear Maria? how are you occupied? Write me a letter by the first post, and answer me all these questions. Tell me whether you see the sun rise every day? how many pages you read every day in *Don Quixote?* how far you are advanced in him? whether you repeat a grammar lesson every day; what else you read? how many hours a day you sew? whether you have an opportunity of continuing your music? whether you know how to make a pudding yet, to cut out a beefsteak, to sow spinach? or to set a hen? If your sister is with you, kiss her, and tell her how much I love her also, and present my affections to Mr. Randolph. Love your aunt and uncle, and be dutiful and obliging to them for all their kindness to you. What would you do without them with such a vagrant for a father? Adieu, my dear Maria,

TH. JEFFERSON.

But very soon he was writing this:

New York. May 2d, 1790.

My dear Maria—

I wrote to you three weeks ago, and have not yet received an answer. I hope, however, that one is on the way and that I shall receive it by the first post. I think it very long to have been absent from Virginia, two months, and not to have received a line from yourself, your sister, or Mr. Randolph, and I am very uneasy about it. We had two days of snow the beginning of last week. Let me know if it snowed where you are. I sent you some prints of a new kind for your amusement. I sent you several to enable you to be generous to your friends. Be assured of my tender love to you, and continue yours to your affectionate,

Th. Jefferson.

Then Maria wrote to tell him what a good girl she had been:

Eppington. May 23, 1790.

I thank you for the pictures you were so kind as to send me. I read in *Don Quixote* every day to my aunt, and say my grammar in Spanish and English, and write, and read in Robertson's *America*. After I am done with that, I work till dinner, and a little more after. It did not snow at all last month. My cousin Bolling and myself made a pudding. My aunt has given us a hen and chickens. Adieu, my dear papa,

Maria Jefferson.

But again Jefferson had to complain that his Polly owed him two letters. He will eat a pudding of her making when he comes to Virginia, he promises. Now he wants her to help him keep his notebook records up to date. And so he writes:

My dear Maria—

We had not peas nor strawberries here till the 8th day of this month. On the same day I heard the first whip-poor-will whistle. Swallows and martins appeared here on the 21st of April. When did they appear with you? and when had you peas, strawberries, and whip-poor-wills in Virginia? Take notice hereafter whether the whip-poor-wills always come with the strawberries and peas.

Yours affectionately,

Th. Jefferson.

Maria's reply was meek and dutiful:

Dear Papa—

I have just received your last favor of July 25 and am determined to write to you every day till I have discharged my debt.

When we were in Cumberland we went to church, and heard some singing masters that sang very well. They are to come here to learn my sister to sing, and as I know you have no objections to my learning anything, I am to be a scholar, and hope to give you the pleasure of hearing an anthem. We had peas the 10th of May, and strawberries the 17th of the same month, though not in that abundance we are accustomed to, in consequence of a frost this spring. As for the martins, swallows, and whip-poor-wills, I was so taken up with my chickens that I never attended to them, and therefore cannot tell you when they came, though I was so unfortunate as to lose half of the chickens.

Believe me to be your affectionate daughter,
MARIA JEFFERSON.

In the autumn of Jefferson's first year in the Cabinet, the capital was moved from New York to Philadelphia, where it was to remain for ten years while the new capital city was being built on the Potomac. Jefferson seized this opportunity to take a two months' vacation in Monticello. He offered Madison a lift in his carriage, and they set out together, stopping on the way to visit Washington at Mount Vernon.

When Jefferson left his family again, Maria was living with her sister. Nor was it very long before he was writing her: "I have now been near nine weeks from home, and have never had a scrip of your pen."

Then came the news in January 1792 that Martha had had a baby girl. Jefferson was to be allowed to name his first grand-daughter. He chose Anne as a name common in both the Jefferson and the Randolph families. Maria wrote him all the news about the baby, and Jefferson replied in a jovial mood:

Philadelphia. Feb. 6, 1791.

My dear Poll—

At length I have received a letter from you. I congratulate you, my dear aunt, on your new title. I hope you pay a great deal of attention to your niece, and that you have begun to give her lessons on the harpsichord, in Spanish, etc. I hope your sister and the child are well. Kiss them both for me. Mind your Spanish and your harpsichord well.

But a few months later the mood has changed to the sarcastic. He had been writing his daughter regularly about the flowers and leaves and birds as they first appeared in Philadelphia and had been asking her about the same events in Monticello. Trusting her he had been put to shame.

> Philadelphia. April 24.
> I find I counted too much on you as a botanical and zoological correspondent for I undertook to affirm here that the fruit was not killed in Virginia, because I had a young daughter who was in that kind of correspondence with me, and who I was sure would have mentioned it if it had been so.

However, he continued to send and ask for such information:

> April 5—Apricots in; Cherry leafing.
> April 9—Peach in bloom; Apple leafing; Cherry in blossom.

In one letter he enclosed a sample of striped nankeen to show her the pattern, twelve yards of which he was sending by the same stage. "I am glad you are to learn to ride," he says in the same letter, "but hope that your horse is very gentle and that you never be venturesome. A lady should never ride a horse which she might not safely ride without a bridle. I long to be with you all. Kiss the little one every morning for me, and learn her to run about before I come."

That May, young Jack Eppes, Maria's old playmate, whom she had not wanted to leave in order to go to France, came to Philadelphia to study under Jefferson's supervision. Eppes spent four hours a day studying science at the college and four hours reading law—an educational idea that he must have owed to Jefferson.

Jefferson kept four horses in a stable near his lodgings, and often invited friends to go for a canter with him. One rainy day he wrote a note asking Madison to go "for a wade" with him into the country, and then come back and have dinner at Jefferson's lodging.

Madison and Jefferson discussed many of their political plans on such expeditions. That summer they took a trip to Lake George in New York together. Jefferson sent Maria a letter written on birchbark which she thought very pretty.

When Jefferson went home for his annual vacation that September he only stayed a month. This time he took Maria back with him to Philadelphia. They visited at Mount Vernon on their way up. Because Mrs. Washington insisted on it, Jefferson left Maria with her. She would come up later with the Washington family. Nelly Custis, Mrs. Washington's daughter by her first husband, and Maria Jefferson had become fast friends.

On arriving in Philadelphia Maria was put in a school. She and Jack Eppes again saw a great deal of each other. And the letter-writing problem between her and her father was at least temporarily solved.

CITIZEN GENET

XV

THE DUEL IN THE CABINET

DURING the debates over the bank bill, Hamilton had been very much annoyed by Jefferson's opposition. He was so full of the rightness of his cause that he could see no reason for opposition except a personal one. Had he not after two years in office become the most prominent man in the country? He knew himself to be the idol of the "best people." He therefore put Jefferson's attitude down to personal dislike, perhaps to jealousy. From now on he never went out of his way to avoid irritating Jefferson.

The French question sharpened the animosity of the two men, for in this question their opposite points of view came out clearly.

When France became a republic, Jefferson was extremely anxious that this new government should succeed. Republics should support each other in this king-ridden world, he thought. If the French republic should fail, he said, America's ideas would lose their chief support and the United States might fall back on "that kind of half-way house, the English Constitution."

Hamilton looked with dread and hatred on the French Revolution. He hoped that England would smash the democratic monstrosity. He would very much have liked to aid England personally in this task.

Thus there were growing up two attitudes toward Europe in America: pro-British (Hamilton) and pro-French (Jefferson). It was Hamilton who first took the offensive.

At first England had not deigned to send a minister to the United States. Her business was conducted through an unofficial agent, Colonel George Beckwith. Jefferson naturally refused to have anything to do with him. England must first give up these insulting hole-in-the-corner tactics, and recognize the dignity of the United States by sending a real official minister. The worthy Colonel Beckwith saw at once how things stood in the Cabinet. Instead of trying to do business with the Secretary of State, he always turned to the Secretary of the Treasury when he needed information or help.

Later, when this agent was replaced by a minister, George Hammond, that gentleman followed in the colonel's footsteps. He even wrote to his superiors in London that he preferred to make his communications privately to Hamilton and to have no relations with Jefferson that were not absolutely necessary. Eventually this touching trust in Hamilton was rewarded.

In spite of the terms of the treaty of peace with England, British troops still remained in the Northwest Territory. When this was brought to Hammond's attention, he incautiously remarked that they belonged there by right, since it was in reality English territory. Whereupon Jefferson drew up a reply to the English government that not only demolished any such claims, but that promised to back up the American claims with action. Jefferson had no desire to go to war with England. It was his opinion that a trading nation like England could be brought around to common sense by commercial weapons. America could always boycott the rich British trade, or put an embargo on it. This faith in commercial weapons Jefferson never lost.

The reply to England was, of course, first submitted to President Washington and the Cabinet. With some changes they accepted it and gave it to Hammond to send to his government. Hammond, very much perturbed, turned as usual to his sympathetic friend Hamilton. Hamilton did not fail him. He told the British minister that this report represented only Mr. Jefferson's personal anti-British feeling, not Washington's or the Cabinet's, and that its "violent language" was most deplorable. For Hamilton and the Federalists were not interested in Western expansion, in the growth of a farming population; they considered England's friendship more important. Hammond felt much better. When he sent the report to London, he also included a note giving the opinion of the Secretary of the Treasury. The British government could safely ignore the report, he thought. The British government did.

This little piece of unpatriotic disloyalty of Hamilton's has come to light only in recent years, but it undoubtedly played its part in adding to the bitterness and tension in the Cabinet. Never before had Jefferson's political relations been anything but courteous and pleasant. In the midst of his hottest controversies with "Moderation" Pendleton over the new laws of Virginia, these two gentlemen had been scrupulously polite and fair to each other. One maxim that Jefferson repeated over and over in letters to his daughters was that to get along with one's fellow men was one of the first duties of a civilized human being. Hence, he looked upon Hamilton's deliberate slights with more and more distaste. He resented being placed in what he called a position of two fighting cocks pitted against each other.

In the spring of 1791 occurred an incident which made these feelings flare up violently on both sides. The chief newspaper mouthpiece of the Federalists was the *Gazette of the United States*. It was edited by John Fenno, who was under the impression that he was conducting a "court journal." It frowned on anything democratic and was read by the "best people."

This paper printed all the articles by "Davila," which was John Adams's pen-name, advocating the use of pomp and titles in government. In the winter of 1790 the *Gazette* had hailed with transports of joy the publication of Edmund Burke's *Reflections on the Revolution in France*.

Edmund Burke was a name dear to Americans. He had in England defended their rights against his own King. But he was over sixty now, and one revolution had been quite enough for this respectable Englishman. Besides, when he heard how the Paris mob had attacked Versailles, calling Queen Marie Antoinette vile names, he wept sentimental tears. The high point of his *Reflections* is a description of this Queen's beauty, youth, and splendor. Whatever the French Revolution might claim to do for the people, it could not wipe out its insults to this romantic, glamorous Queen.

Sentiments sweet to the ears of John Fenno, and to the eyes of the readers of the *Gazette!* Fortunately for the Republicans in America, there happened to be living in England at this time Thomas Paine, the man who had played so important a part in the American Revolution. In 1776 his pamphlet *Common Sense* had brought out into the open the movement for American independence that led up to the Declaration. When the Revolutionary War had at first gone against the colonists, his series of tracts called *The Crisis* gave them back their courage.

In 1787 this versatile man—versatility was typical of eighteenth-century genius—returned to Europe to exhibit the model of a new bridge he had designed. When Burke's *Reflections on the Revolution in France* appeared, Tom Paine leaped into the fray with joy. In the spring of 1791 appeared his answer, *The Rights of Man,* a passionate defense of the French Revolution. Before the British government got around to suppressing it, this work had sold in enormous quantities, and of course made its way to America.

A friend of Madison's was the first to receive a copy. Madison borrowed it, read it hurriedly, and passed it on to Jefferson. Jefferson was all enthusiasm for this brilliant defense of democracy. It answered not only Burke, but also the ridiculous aristocratic articles of "Davila" in the *Gazette.*

In the meantime Madison's friend asked to have his copy back, as he had promised to send it to a Philadelphia printer. To save this friend time and trouble Jefferson himself promised to send the work to the printer after he had finished reading it. This Jefferson finally did, sending along with the pamphlet a little note to explain the delay and express his thanks.

"I am extremely pleased to find it will be reprinted here," he wrote, "and that something at length is to be publicly said against the political heresies which have sprung up against us. I have no doubt our citizens will rally a second time around the standard of *Common Sense.*"

When the American edition appeared, Jefferson was as much surprised as were his political enemies to find that his little note, signed with his name and his official title, had been used as a preface to the book. Particularly indignant was the British agent, who asked what the American Secretary of State meant by recommending a pamphlet suppressed by His Majesty. Shocked and indignant were the Philadelphia aristocrats, who were so busy lionizing the cast-off members of French nobility. Hurt and indignant was Vice-President John Adams, who felt that the whole thing was an attack upon himself. So did his son John Quincy Adams in Boston, who at once sat down to write a series of articles that sneered at Tom Paine, Tom Jefferson, and democracy and praised the British government.

Madison pretended not to understand all this indignation of the Federalists. "Surely," he wrote, "if it be innocent and decent for one servant of the public to write against its government, it cannot be very criminal or indecent in another to patronize a written defense of the principles on which the government is founded."

Behind Madison there were the hundreds of thousands who did not write but thought as he did—the farmers of the new West, the veterans of the Revolution, the masses who had taken the Declaration of Independence seriously. These

Indian-fighting pioneers did not care whether Washington rode in state behind four or six horses, nor were they interested in laws that helped the East at the expense of the West, the rich at the expense of the poor.

All over the country Anti-Federalist societies began to spring up, using as their models the French political clubs. They began to call themselves Democrats and Republicans. It is a curious fact that in a republic there should be necessary a political party called Republican. But so it was. Now after the appearance of Paine's pamphlet these Republicans knew who their natural leader was. Was not the Secretary of State also the man who had written the Declaration?

Jefferson keenly enjoyed the results of this happy mistake of the printer. The democratic part of the country was at last aroused. The two political sides were being clearly marked off from each other. To Adams he wrote a note of apology explaining the accident. Adams accepted it with very good grace, for their old friendship was still dear to him. To Paine, who had by now escaped from England into France, Jefferson wrote a letter of thanks. "Our people," he said, "love what you write and read it with delight." The silence of the people hitherto had not meant that they were converted "to the doctrine of kings, lords, and commons." They were now confirmed "in their good old faith."

Now that the Anti-Federalists were beginning to organize themselves into a democratic and republican party, they needed a newspaper that would combat Fenno's "court journal," a paper that would do for Jefferson's friends what the *Gazette of the United States* was doing for Hamilton and his friends. So on October 31, 1791, appeared the first issue of the *National Gazette*. Its editor was Philip Freneau.

Philip Freneau had been a roommate of Madison's at Princeton. There, instead of poring over his Coke and other law books as he was supposed to, he had spent his time writing poetry and political pamphlets, pamphlet writing being one of the great arts of the eighteenth century. Freneau was a born rebel, and the endless shilly-shallying that preceded the Revolution had disgusted him. Expecting nothing to come of all this talk, he had gone for a cruise to Jamaica, on the way studying navigation. His first poems after landing were full of the beauty of nature in Jamaica, but soon there began to appear in them bitter protests against the terrible conditions of slavery on the island.

While a guest of the Governor of Bermuda, to whose daughter he was writing love sonnets, he heard of the Declaration of Independence. He rushed home, spent his whole fortune in fitting out a privateer, and sailed to do battle with the English. In a sea fight his ship was sunk and he was captured. He was thrown into one of the horrible English prison ships of those days, reeking of foulness and disease. When he was exchanged for a British prisoner, he was almost dead of this treatment, and expected to be a chronic invalid the rest of his life. He wrote a poem, "The Prison Ship," about his experiences which was widely read and helped inspire the Revolutionary soldiers in their resistance to the English.

When Madison found him in New York, the former wealthy poet was barely existing by his writings, though he had published in 1787 a book of poems that are now considered the best America had until then produced. Madison secured him a job as translator of foreign languages in the State Department at a salary of five dollars a week.

Freneau was an ideal editor for the *National Gazette*. A poet of freedom, his past experience was not such as to give

him any love for the English government. The first issue of
the journal contained articles in praise of Tom Paine, attacking Burke, and criticizing Hamilton's policies. In later issues
there were references to Senators and Congressmen who had
made huge profits by voting for Hamilton's bills.

Every time Hamilton picked up this newspaper, he grew
more furious. His anger was directed not at Freneau but at
Jefferson, whom he considered the real father of these articles.
As a matter of fact, though Freneau patterned his ideas after
Jefferson, and though Madison occasionally sent a piece to the
journal, the Secretary of State never wrote a line for it.

At last Hamilton could stand these attacks no longer, and
wrote a series of venomous articles for Fenno's paper, signing
them variously "An American," "Amicus," "A Plain, Honest
Man," etc., etc. He claimed that Jefferson was paying out the
government's good money for the support of this rascal
Freneau so that the latter could attack the government that
fed him. He tried to prove by publishing parts of Jefferson's
letters to Madison that Jefferson disapproved of the Constitution. Madison replied to this by publishing the letters entire,
which proved quite the opposite.

Washington was grieved by the personal tone which the
conflict was now taking on. He wrote letters to Hamilton and
Jefferson, reminding them how difficult his own situation was
being made by all this backstairs fighting, and begging them
to be more charitable with each other.

Hamilton's reply admitted that he had written the articles
in Fenno's *Gazette*. But, he said, Mr. Jefferson had never
ceased opposing him from the moment he came to New York.
Had not Mr. Jefferson created the *National Gazette* with the
principal idea of making the Secretary of the Treasury hateful
to the people?

Jefferson's letter explained again that he differed with Mr. Hamilton's system not because it was Mr. Hamilton's but because such a system would undermine the republic by putting a certain department (the Treasury) over the people's elected legislature (Congress). Furthermore, Jefferson complained, since they were on the subject, he might mention that Mr. Hamilton was constantly interfering in *his* department, particularly in relation to England and France.

As to the charge that he had foisted Freneau upon the government so that he could run a paper against it, Jefferson said sharply:

I have never inquired what number of sons, relations, and friends of Senators, Representatives, printers, or other useful partisans, Colonel Hamilton has provided for among the hundred clerks of his department, the thousand excisemen, custom-house officers, loan-officers, appointed by him, or at his nod, and spread over the Union; nor could ever have imagined that the man who has the shuffling of millions backwards and forwards from paper into money and from money into paper, from Europe to America, and America to Europe, the dealing out of Treasury secrets among his friends in what time and measure he pleases, and who never slips an occasion of making friends with his means—that such a one, I say, would have brought forward a charge against me for having appointed the poet Freneau, translating clerk to my office, with a salary of two hundred and fifty dollars a year.

Though a little more thick-skinned against criticism and censure than when he was Governor of Virginia, Jefferson was still a sensitive man. All this bickering in the Cabinet, all this abuse from Hamilton's party, all these disapproving frowns of the "best people," were beginning to get on his nerves. He who had been looked up to as the prophet of a new order in the drawing rooms of France was reviled as a "filthy democrat" by the judges, in the colleges, from the pulpits, and in the drawing rooms of Philadelphia.

In March 1792, with Washington's first term only one more year to run, Jefferson wrote Martha that he expected this year to be the longest in his life. "The next we will sow our cabbages together," he told her. March 4, 1793, was going to be for him what land was to Columbus, he wrote another friend. He was now actively preparing for his retirement to Monticello. He sent to Scotland for one of the new threshing machines. He had workmen building over his house again according to plans he had conceived while in France; there was going to be a dome over Monticello. He was already packing his books and was making plans for Jack Eppes to enter William and Mary.

Jefferson was having private as well as political troubles. He was not satisfied with the way the overseers were running his estate. Though he owned ten thousand acres of land, 154 slaves, 34 horses, 5 mules, 249 heads of cattle, 390 hogs, and 3 sheep, he was far from being as wealthy as he seemed. Only two thousand acres were under cultivation, and these were burdened under debts.

When his wife's father died, he had left the Jeffersons an estate worth $40,000 but carrying a debt of $13,000 to some British creditors. Impatient to pay off this debt, Jefferson had sold a fine farm, but by the time he received the money for it the War had broken out. The State of Virginia called upon all patriotic citizens who owed money to Englishmen to deposit it in the State Treasury at Williamsburg so that it could be used for equipping revolutionary troops. Jefferson deposited his $13,000. When finally Virginia gave this money back to Jefferson after the War it was in currency that was worth much less than what he had given it. This currency became worthless so rapidly, that for his original $13,000 Jefferson was able to buy only a single article of clothing. Whenever he passed the farm he had sold, he used to remark laughingly to his companion: "There is the land that I sold for an overcoat."

So Jefferson had had to pay this debt all over again. During the War, Cornwallis had destroyed several thousand dollars' worth of Jefferson's property. In a similar case many Americans refused to pay their debts to British creditors, but Jefferson thought that the private English gentlemen to whom he owed money should not be made to suffer for Cornwallis's crimes. There were other debts, too, for Jefferson's salaries, both in France and in Philadelphia, had never been large enough to pay his expenses.

When in 1792 Washington was elected for a second term, the President asked Jefferson not to resign. This plea was seconded by Madison, Monroe, Page, and Edmund Randolph. His private business could wait. He must do this for the country, save it from the Federalists, and not allow people to say that Hamilton had driven him out of office. At last Jefferson gave in. He would remain in the Cabinet a while longer. But so sure was he of going home soon that he sent his library to Monticello, sold his bulkier furniture, and moved into three furnished rooms.

No sooner had Jefferson agreed to stay in Philadelphia, than the struggle between the Federalists and the new party of Democratic Republicans burst out with more fury than ever before. Again the question was, what shall be our attitude toward France and toward England? This conflict was brought to a head by the Genêt affair.

When the French formally declared themselves a republic,

there had been some pretty wild excitement in America. In Boston there was a parade, boys shouting from the roofs, and women waving American and French flags from the windows. Later all the paraders took part in the barbecuing of an ox. Similar celebrations were held all over the country.

But when the news came that the French had beheaded their King, half of the nation seemed to become monarchist overnight. This was very curious, since hundreds had already lost their heads under the guillotine without rousing anything like the same protest. But there is something extra about a king, a something that makes the daily newspapers fill columns with the birthday of a princess or the bright sayings of a prince.

Jefferson, who had many personal friends among the exiled nobles, thought that they should be looked upon as soldiers who had fallen in battle. He could sympathize with their loss and yet not hate the Revolution that brought it on. For a revolution is a vast house-cleaning carried out suddenly. It has no time to ask whether a particular individual is a villain, whether he is personally guilty of crimes against the people. It can only ask whether he is for or against the new order. Hence many innocent people must suffer. In our own Revolution thousands of Americans who remained loyal to the King had to leave their homes and emigrate to Canada.

Besides, France was not only in revolution. It was at war with the combined armies of all the kings of Europe. The crime Louis XVI and Marie Antoinette were accused of was sympathizing with and helping the enemies of France, which happened to be true. Madison was one of those who looked coolly upon the King's execution. "If he were a traitor," he wrote, "he ought to be punished like any other man." Jefferson wrote Mr. Short, who had been his secretary in France: "My own affections have been wounded by some of the martyrs to this cause." But he went on to say that he thought the attempt to wipe out so much injustice and set up something better to be worth the sacrifice. No one should be allowed to stand in the way of France's success in founding a true democracy.

Jefferson considered this success to be important for America as well as for France. If the French experiment failed, people here would say that a democratic form of government was impractical, that it could not work, and they would allow the Federalists to set up a British form of government here. If the French succeeded in their aims, the idea would spread to the rest of Europe, and any republic was safer if it was not surrounded by jealous kings.

Needless to say, the Federalists felt quite differently. Their chief city, Philadelphia, had been accustomed to celebrate the birthday of the King of France. His execution was a great calamity. Hamilton told Randolph that he held the French Revolution "in abhorrence." Ternant, the French minister, went into mourning for his prince, and ceased his visits to Jefferson, becoming more intimate with Hamilton.

Gouverneur Morris, Jefferson's successor in Paris and an ultra-aristocrat, was naturally enough not very popular in France. He had been shocked when the Parisians had not cheered the Queen as she passed. He had even acted as financial agent in a romantic plot to rescue the King and Queen out of prison. Washington felt that Morris should be replaced and offered his old post back to Jefferson. But Jefferson, bent on retiring, now declined the position. He wished only to stay long enough to greet the new minister that the revolutionary government of France was sending to replace Ternant.

The new minister, Edmond Charles Genêt, was a person of more enthusiasm than tact, not a very good combination for a man whose job was supposed to be diplomacy. He landed at Charleston on the frigate *Embuscade*. From there he sent the frigate on ahead to Philadelphia while he made the journey by land, in order to become acquainted with this sister-republic. The five weeks' trip from Charleston to Philadelphia was a triumphal tour. He was wined and dined. People flocked in from everywhere to cheer the emissary of revolutionary France.

The *Embuscade* arrived in Philadelphia first, making a brave show. On her stern was carved a liberty cap. Her mizzen-top bore the strange device: "We are armed to defend the rights of man"; her main-top: "Freemen, we are your brothers and friends"; her fore-top: "Enemies of equality, relinquish your principles or tremble." As the frigate came into harbor, it gave a thundering salute of fifteen guns, one for each State in the Union. As everyone in the city rushed down to the wharves, the sailors of the *Embuscade* scrambled into the rigging and cheered. All day the Philadelphians swarmed over the ship, where they were given a hearty welcome.

In the meantime matters had grown very tense in the Cabinet. How should the American government treat this "upstart" Genêt, as Gouverneur Morris called him? This was the problem bothering Hamilton. Hamilton had written out a set of questions for Washington to ask his Cabinet. Though Washington asked the questions, Jefferson at once recognized their author.

First question: Should Genêt be received at all?

"Yes, with qualifications," said Hamilton.

"Yes, unqualifiedly," said Jefferson.

General Knox dutifully echoed Hamilton and then ("like

the fool that he is," Jefferson said later) admitted that he knew nothing about it.

Secondly: Should we treat with Genêt if we receive him?

There is no proof, said Hamilton, that the execution of the King was just. None of the courts of Europe think so. Why should we throw in our lot with a new republic that so many respectable governments are opposed to? (Hamilton here had his eyes on England.) Therefore, let us receive him, but not treat him like a regular minister.

Jefferson said: If we receive the minister at all, we recognize his government. How can we recognize this government by receiving its minister and then, by refusing to treat with him, refuse to recognize his government? This is nonsense.

Thirdly: What is now the condition of our old treaties with France?

Said Hamilton: We made these treaties with the King. There is no longer any king. Hence the treaties are annulled.

Jefferson answered: It is the nation, the people, of France with whom we made the treaties. They used to carry on their affairs with a king, now they do without one. This is none of our business but is the private affair of France. For that matter, *both* of us have changed our government since signing the treaties. Do you forget that we adopted our Constitution afterward? Both nations, however, still exist, and the treaties are still good.

These opinions of Jefferson became the guiding principles of our State Department in settling most problems of recognition ever since.

Washington decided to receive Genêt, but to remain neutral in France's war with England and the other kingdoms of Europe. On this last point Hamilton, who would have preferred joining England, and Jefferson, who would have liked to help

France, had to agree. After all England was still mistress of the seas, and Spain, which had joined the coalition of kings, held Florida and the mouth of the Mississippi. This territory contained the Creek Indians, among the most warlike tribes of North America.

Genêt wound up his triumphal tour in Philadelphia, two weeks behind the *Embuscade.* The Republicans of that city, afraid that the Federalist officials would try to prevent a warm welcome for the Frenchman, appointed seven distinguished members of their party to meet him at Greys Ferry. But Genêt, arriving early, managed to slip into the city unnoticed and went to the City Tavern. On to the tavern marched the seven Republicans, followed by an immense crowd. At the tavern they read Genêt an address of welcome, which he replied to in excellent English. The crowd hurrahed and huzzaed and then went peacefully home.

That night Genêt was given a banquet in the best hostelry in town. The Ambassador sang the new French fighting song, *La Marseillaise,* and all the diners put on liberty caps, and toasts were drunk to the French and American Republics.

Genêt was greeted cordially by Secretary Jefferson, but when he called on the President he got a rather frigid reception. He was especially aggrieved to see on the wall of the room in which he was received portraits of Louis XVI and Marie Antoinette. He could not understand why the President, his Cabinet, and the majority of Congress were not in sympathy with republican France. Had he not seen with his own eyes that three fourths of the people were enthusiastically behind him? Did not girls and boys throng the streets of Philadelphia wearing the French red-white-and-blue cockade and singing the *Marseillaise?* In Gerard Street (then an open square) had there not been erected a liberty pole crowned with a liberty cap? Around it danced staid old gentlemen hand in hand with schoolboys and all singing revolutionary songs. Everywhere people were beginning to address each other as Citizen Brown and Citizeness Smith just as they did in France. In Boston they had renamed Royal Exchange Alley into Equality Lane, and in New York, King Street was now Liberty Street.

Genêt did not understand why the Federalists should be so mortally afraid of offending England. When he asked if he might take provisions out of the country as part payment for the debt America owed France, he was bluntly refused. The New England merchants were not going to have the British navy on their necks even if, all the way up from Charleston, the farmers had come to Genêt offering to sell France their foodstuffs at less than market price.

From amazement at the difference between the American people and the American government, Genêt began to go over into irritation. He claimed that the treaties between France and the United States permitted him to fit out privateers to capture British ships, as he had already done at Charleston. Jefferson explained to him that Washington had decided to remain neutral in France's wars and would not permit him to fit out privateers in America. But the American people was *not* neutral! Genêt indignantly pointed out. That may be true, said Jefferson, but the President has decided . . . The President! exclaimed Genêt, but isn't this a *republic,* don't the people do the deciding here through their Congress? Yes, Jefferson patiently explained, Congress makes the laws but the President enforces them, and no one can force the President to enforce them. . . . Genêt stood up and bowed to Mr. Jefferson. He could not, he said, make him his compliments upon such a Constitution.

American historians sometimes treat Genêt as if he were stupid not to have understood this. He was by no means stupid. He came from a country that had just got rid of its King, so that the people could make their own laws. Now this country, during its Revolution, had always looked upon America as an older sister who had also done this and had shown France the way. And the first thing Genêt finds in the United States is another king, a man who can do as he pleases despite the people's will!

From this time on Genêt's actions became slightly insane. He was still under the delusion that he could appeal to the people over the head of the government, and in this delusion he was encouraged by many Americans. He outfitted more privateers; he formed a Jacobin revolutionary club; he organized a troop of mounted Frenchmen in the United States.

Among the prizes captured by the *Embuscade* was the British vessel *Little Sarah*. Genêt rechristened her *Le Petit Démocrate* (The Little Democrat), outfitted her, and prepared her to sail from the mouth of the Delaware, which was within a mile or two of the President's Philadelphia house. Washington was then away at Mount Vernon, and Jefferson made Genêt promise that he would not let "The Little Democrat" sail until Washington returned. For it was suspected that she had American arms and citizens on board, and Jefferson wanted the President to decide what to do about her.

Hamilton was all for erecting a battery on Mud Island to fire on the *Petit Démocrate* if she should attempt to sail before the President came back from Mount Vernon. Considering the politeness with which Hamilton swallowed every insult from England, this foolish plan made Jefferson lose his temper. "The erection of a battery," he pointed out, "might stimulate the ship to leave. A French fleet of twenty men-of-war and a hundred and fifty merchant vessels were hourly expected in the Delaware and might arrive at the scene of blood in order to join in. Suppose there *are* fifteen or twenty Americans on board her: are there not ten times as many Americans on board English vessels impressed in foreign ports? Are we as ready and disposed to sink British ships in our harbor as we are to fire upon this French vessel for a breach of neutrality far less atrocious? How inconsistent for a nation, which has been patiently bearing for ten years the grossest insults and injuries from their late enemies to rise at a feather against their friends and benefactors.

"I would not gratify the combination of kings with the spectacle of the only two republics on earth destroying each other for two cannon." And he added that even for an infinitely greater cause he would not permit his country to give the "last stab" to the only other country that held out any hopes for mankind.

How Hamilton must have wished then that he was Secretary of State! Indeed, if the *Petit Démocrate* had been fired upon, there is little doubt that many Americans would have rushed to her rescue. This might have meant revolution. So soon after the first Revolution, the country not yet properly settled down, this might have got us into the habit of revolution. We should have become like so many South American nations, deciding all our disputes by one revolution after another, with each really meaning less than the last.

The battery was not erected. When Washington returned, sick of the squabbles in his Cabinet, he determined to let the Supreme Court settle all such questions in the future. Within three days the *Petit Démocrate* put out to sea.

But what to do with Genêt? The Federalists wished simply

to deport him out of the country. Jefferson's plan finally prevailed in the Cabinet, however. A list of Genêt's undiplomatic acts was sent to France with a copy of Jefferson's letters of remonstrance. France was asked to recall her minister. Jefferson's last act as Secretary of State was to send one of these letters of remonstrance to Genêt. For, in spite of Washington's pleas, Jefferson had now finally made up his mind to resign.

Genêt was recalled, France at the same time asking the United States to take back her Gouverneur Morris, whose activities were certainly equally undiplomatic. But Genêt, having fallen in love with the daughter of George Clinton, the stanch Republican Governor of New York, married her, became an American citizen, and lived here for the rest of his life. Strangely enough, Morris, having fallen in love with Paris, also refused to leave it for several years after he had lost his post.

XVI

FRANCE OR ENGLAND?

JEFFERSON resigned his position in the Cabinet on the last day of the year 1793. For two and a half years he was allowed to devote himself to his old love—Monticello. He rebuilt the house, he farmed, he entertained visitors, he wrote letters. He was quite happy. He was over fifty now and expected to live out his days as the private gentleman farmer—the perfect life. He refused Washington's offers to come back to his job in Philadelphia.

Perhaps Jefferson wrote too many letters and read too many

of them. More and more he was being considered everywhere as the real leader of the Democratic Republican party, in spite of his retirement. He could not keep from sending his congratulations to the writer of a successful Republican article. In friendly letters to Madison he often had something to say about the irrepressible Mr. Hamilton's latest activities.

Hamilton resigned two years after Jefferson, to practice law in New York. Fenno's *Gazette* had given two lines to the news of Jefferson's retirement. When Colonel Hamilton left the same Cabinet, Fenno outdid himself. A great spread of double columns mourned the nation's loss. The reader had the impression that now nothing was left of the American government but an empty shell. But Hamilton, too, still remained the leader of his party.

Now, when it became known that Washington declined to serve a third term as President, the Republicans at once insisted on nominating Jefferson for the office. He himself wanted Madison nominated, but Madison joined the others in urging Jefferson to accept the honor. Jefferson had written too many letters, had shown too much interest and concern in politics. He must end his pleasant vacation.

The Federalists nominated John Adams. This was not according to Hamilton's plans at all. Adams was a good Federalist, but he did not take orders easily, and he was one of the few Federalists who did not think that the sun rose and set by Mr. Hamilton's commands. So Hamilton worked hard to defeat Adams and have another Federalist, Thomas Pinckney, elected.

The result of this little conspiracy was very sad for Hamilton, for not only was Adams elected, but Jefferson became Vice-President. Adams received 71 votes from the electors, Jefferson 68. In those days the candidate who received the second highest vote for the Presidency was made Vice-President. Adams, however, kept Washington's old Cabinet, all the members of which were under Hamilton's thumb, so that all was not yet lost for the old-guard Federalists.

When Washington and Adams had first been elected, an imposing embassy had been sent to notify them. But the new democratic Vice-President begged that there should be no pomp and ceremony in this case as far as he was concerned. Just drop a note in the post office, was his suggestion.

When the note came, Jefferson got into his carriage and had himself driven to Alexandria. The greater part of his luggage was, not new court costumes, but the bones of a mastodon. These relics of an extinct animal had been sent to him by someone who knew he was interested in all such scientific curiosities. Jefferson was taking them along because, a few weeks before, he had been elected President of the American Philosophical Society, founded long ago in Philadelphia by Ben Franklin. This was the chief scientific academy and museum in America, and Jefferson wanted it to have these fossil bones of an animal that had ranged over America hundreds of thousands of years ago.

At Alexandria, Jefferson took the public stagecoach. Arriving in Philadelphia, he came upon the sort of surprise party he had begged his friends not to provide. A company of artillery met him with sixteen salutes. It carried a banner reading:

T. JEFFERSON, THE FRIEND OF THE PEOPLE

On March 4, 1797, Jefferson was sworn into office in the chamber of the Senate, of which he was now President. He gave a brief address and, at the head of his Senators, marched into the Hall of Representatives to hear Adams take the oath

as President of the United States of America. After the ceremony, as they were all leaving the hall, Jefferson and Washington met at the door. Jefferson fell back a step to let the ex-
President go first. But Washington, a private citizen since
the last few minutes, made the new Vice-President go before
him.

This was the only public office of the many Jefferson held
that paid its own expenses. Nor were his duties very heavy.
Every year there were almost eight months of recess in which
Jefferson could continue to look after his beloved Monticello
if he wished, or carry on scientific studies, or make some money
out of his plantation.

Presiding over the Senate was not as arduous as dealing
with foreign nations, but just as, when he was Secretary of
State, he had laid down many rules that are followed to this
day, so too he was responsible for many of the present Senate
rules. His was still, and always would be, the kind of mind
that never touches a task without changing it in some way.
He was still the revolutionary of 1776.

When Jefferson was a young lawyer about to enter the
House of Burgesses, it was like him to make a thorough study
of parliamentary procedure. It was like him to jot down in a
leather notebook the various rules he discovered. It was like
him, too, to have kept the notebook.

Before leaving for Philadelpha he dug up this old notebook,
but now he did not find it complete enough. So he wrote to
his old friend, George Wythe, the man who had taught him
law, asking for help. Wythe had stored in his mind all kinds
of legal treasures, but his seventy-odd years made it difficult
for him to write. Jefferson therefore wrote out all the rules he
thought were right, leaving large margins in which Wythe
could simply write "Yes" or "No." Wythe needed only to draw

a line through passages he disapproved of or to add a word
here and there, and thus give his old pupil the benefits of his
vast knowledge with the least effort to himself.

The result of these studies was a book entitled *A Manual
of Parliamentary Practice*. It furnished the rules by which
the Senate is still run today, and after it was published in 1801
it was translated into several languages.

In June, Maria became engaged to her half-cousin Jack
Eppes. When Jefferson received the announcement he wrote
Martha that he could not have found Maria a husband more
to his wishes "if I had had the whole earth free to have chosen
a partner for her." Jack was a charming young man of an
agreeable disposition and a finished education. The young
couple was married in October. Although Jefferson begged
them to stay at Monticello, they went to Jack's home, Eppington, to live.

Then suddenly, in the midst of these peaceful reforms and
domestic joys, Jefferson found himself the best-hated man in
America. The French situation was again to blame.

After Gouverneur Morris's recall from Paris, James Monroe
had been sent in his stead to represent the United States.
Monroe was enthusiastically received. He was publicly introduced to the National Convention, the President of which embraced him. He presented the American colors and received
those of France.

The popularity in France of this friend of Jefferson's was
not pleasing to the Federalist Cabinet at home, and the
Cabinet did not deal frankly with its representative. When
Monroe told the French that there was no danger of America
allying herself with England, this was precisely what he had

himself been told. Then when rumors came that John Jay had signed a treaty in London favorable to England, he was as surprised and indignant as the French. But the French could not believe that the American government had duped its own minister. Monroe became unpopular and Washington had to recall him.

Jay's treaty was a Federalist triumph. It seemed to bring America and England closer together. Yet in a sense it was an American defeat, for it made no mention of the British practice of boarding American ships and impressing American seamen. Now, too, the French felt doubly justified in sending out privateers against American ships that traded with her enemy England.

When Monroe's ship reached America, his irritation at the way his government had made a victim of him was only increased by further petty annoyances from Federalist officials. As Mr. and Mrs. Monroe started to leave ship, they were rudely ordered back by Federalist health officers and examined with the rest of the immigrants. On the other hand, the Republicans gave Monroe a banquet, when he was finally allowed to land; and at the advice of Jefferson, he wrote a five-hundred-page defense of his conduct in France.

Washington had then sent General C. C. Pinckney, a stanch Federalist, to France. The infuriated French refused to receive him. This was the situation that confronted Adams as the new President.

With large sections of the country clamoring to go to war with King George again, on account of Jay's "humiliating" treaty, the Federalists thought this a poor time to start trouble with the French. So Hamilton proposed that a commission be sent over to reconcile the difference with France. In order that the commission have a united country behind it, one of its members should be a Republican. Through his mouth-piece, General Knox, Hamilton suggested Jefferson as the Republican member, perhaps to get him out of the country.

Adams wrote Knox in answer: "What would have been thought in Europe if the King of France had sent Monsieur, his eldest brother, as an envoy? What if the King of England had sent the Prince of Wales? Mr. Jefferson is in a sense in the same situation. He is the first prince of the country, and heir apparent to the sovereign authority." (Adams was lucky indeed that no Republican newspaper got hold of these phrases, these "first princes" and "heir apparents." They would have had some lovely fun at his expense.)

Adams did, however, decide to consult Jefferson about the problem. Of course, this was not to the Federalists' liking. But Adams could see no reason why politics and parties should keep him from asking the advice of a man "whom I knew to be attached to the interests of the country and whose experience, genius, learning, and travels had eminently qualified him to give advice."

Adams asked Jefferson if he thought Madison would consent to go to France. Jefferson doubted it, but promised to ask Madison. They chatted amiably for a while—after all they were old friends though they saw so little of each other nowadays—and then parted.

Madison refused to go to France. The next time Adams and Jefferson met was as they were both leaving a banquet. When Jefferson brought up the subject of Madison, Adams seemed perturbed, hemmed and hawed, and departed as quickly as possible. Jefferson suspected what had really happened in the meantime. At the mention of Madison's name,

Adams's whole Cabinet had threatened to resign if that ardent Republican were sent to France. That was the last time Adams ever consulted with Jefferson over a matter of policy.

The three men Adams finally sent were General Pinckney (the same faithful Federalist), John Marshall (another Federalist), and Elbridge Gerry. Gerry, the only Republican, was a signer of the Declaration of Independence, and would later become Vice-President under Madison. He and Jefferson had met and become friends when Jefferson, aged twenty-one, came North to be inoculated against the smallpox in Philadelphia.

Talleyrand was then Minister for Foreign Affairs in the French government. He kept the three American commissioners waiting just as Jefferson and Adams had once been kept waiting in London. The commissioners, growing more exasperated each day, lingered on in hopes of an interview. Finally they were approached "after candlelight" by three men who have come down in history as Mr. X, Mr. Y, and Mr. Z. These last three letters of the alphabet suggested that the way to get action was to cross with silver the palms of the leaders of the French government.

When the American commissioners, hardly able to believe their ears, cried out their astonishment, these alphabetical gentlemen simply shrugged their shoulders. They saw nothing to get excited about. Had not the United States bribed the Algerian pirates, and the Indians? Why this prejudice against bribing the French?

The commissioners had several more interviews with Messrs. X, Y, and Z. The French Revolution was now in a sad moral state. It had lost its first idealistic fervor, and was now going rapidly downhill toward Napoleon, by whom it would shortly be conquered. The very fact that a man like Talleyrand could hold so high a position proved that such underhand dealings were quite possible.

The news of this reception of American ministers raised a storm at home. Even pro-French Republicans joined in the cry: "Millions for defense, but not one cent for tribute." Madison was stunned by this piece of dishonest stupidity. It would surely drive America into the arms of England.

Of course, Pinckney's and Marshall's report of the interviews was not entirely uncolored by Federalist prejudices. Monroe, indeed, declared the whole thing a swindle. As a matter of fact, Messrs. X, Y, and Z had no credentials to show they were really acting for the French government, and the French government disclaimed all knowledge of the affair, saying that Messrs. Pinckney and Marshall were too willing to believe anything evil of France. But the Jefferson party had received a bad blow. For some time now it would be at the mercy of the Federalists.

Federalist newspapers worked themselves up into a frenzy of hatred against France. Every day saw new French plots against America in their columns and headlines. French troops land in Charleston! French sailors plunder American farms! Negro slaves incited by Jacobin spies to rise against the whites! Masters murdered in their beds, children kidnaped, churches burned—all because of Democracy!

President Adams set aside May 9th as a day of fast and prayer. He received three anonymous letters saying that on that night Philadelphia would be put to the torch. He took these seriously and had servants carry arms and munitions into his house by the back way. On that fateful night a few apprentices did collect in the government yard and yell until some soldiers dispersed them. On this day of fast and prayer Fed-

eralist mobs smashed the windows of Benjamin Franklin
Bache, editor of the Republican newspaper, *Aurora.* Then
they went and smeared mud from the gutter over the statue of
his grandfather, that dead but none the less "filthy democrat,"
Benjamin Franklin.

Congress created a Secretaryship of the Navy.

Hamilton, who just a few months before had recommended
sending Jefferson on a peace commission to France, now suddenly became as war-mad as the most rabid of his followers.
But the reason was not the X Y Z affair.

There was a Venezuelan named Francisco Miranda, a
soldier of fortune, a patriot, who had served with the French
in the American Revolution. Then he had fought in the
French Revolution. Now he dreamed of a South American
Revolution against Spain. In London he had met Rufus King,
the American Ambassador, and had interested him in the
scheme. King wrote Hamilton about it. The idea was to get
Spain to join France; then have the United States declare
war against France, which would also mean against Spain;
then America and England together would wrest from Spain
her South American colonies. What was there in this for the
United States? Why, Florida and Cuba, for instance; and England could be depended on to take all she could hold.

The brightest part of it all for Hamilton was the visions
he had of himself commanding the American expeditionary
forces in South America. His boyhood ambition come true, he
would be like Hannibal crossing the Alps. That is why he suddenly became intensely passionate in urging America to
avenge this French insult. He began to write vicious attacks
upon France.

"For heaven's sake, take up your pen," Jefferson wrote

Madison. It was the party leader giving orders to the only man who could stand up as a writer against Hamilton's powerful pen.

Jefferson, as acknowledged head of the Republican party, received his share of abuse. Many a night he heard Federalist revelers sing and play the *Rogue's March* under his window. No toast of the war party was complete without an insult to "T. Jefferson, the friend of the people." One popular toast was: "John Adams—may he like Samson slay thousands of Frenchmen with the jawbone of Jefferson." Another milder one: "The Vice-President—may his heart be purged of Gallicism in the pure fire of Federalism or be lost in the furnace." There were even spies at Jefferson's dinner table who twisted his most innocent statements into libels that could be used against him in the Federalist papers. He began to seal all the letters he sent to Madison in such a way that it could be told whether they had been tampered with.

The slanders against Jefferson grew incredibly wild. For instance, there was the Logan affair. Dr. Logan was a friend of Jefferson who could not bring himself to believe that the republican government of France should want to go to war with her sister-republic. He therefore decided to go to Europe and look over the situation with his own eyes. Naturally, he asked the Vice-President for a certificate of character and citizenship which would make it easier for him to meet people and at the same time protect him as an American citizen who was not a spy or an Anti-Republican.

This courtesy Jefferson extended to him as he had to hundreds of others, especially since Dr. Logan told him he was going on purely private business. Unfortunately, Dr. Logan began to make something of a mystery of his going and thus attracted the attention of Federalists. Their newspapers raised a hue and cry. Dr. Logan was being sent by the leader of the American Jacobins (Jefferson, of course) to betray our army secrets to the French Jacobins! He was to instruct the French army how to land here and ravage our coast!

This war-fever in America, this spy-hunting, Jacobin-hating madness was the ideal moment for striking one good sharp blow at the Republicans and wiping them out once for all. The Federalists felt they could not miss this golden opportunity while the Republican leaders were all so dismayed and disorganized by events. So, in spite of the warnings of their best minds, including Hamilton, the Federalists rushed through two laws, which began what has been called "the American Reign of Terror."

The Republicans in their confusion were not strong enough to stay this storm. In Congress the Anti-Federalist battle had to be waged almost single-handed by Albert Gallatin, and against him much of the anti-French fury was directed.

Albert Gallatin, born in Geneva, Switzerland, of a wealthy and noble family, had come to Massachusetts in 1780. His relatives had wanted him to become an officer in the Hessian army, but Gallatin had been reading Rousseau. He refused to serve a "tyrant" and came instead to throw in his lot with the new republic across the Atlantic. His fine, clear mind, the iron control of his temper, and his native gifts of leadership soon made him one of the chiefs of the Anti-Federalist party. He was a man upon whom Jefferson could depend as he would on Madison.

Now the fact that Gallatin had been born a Swiss was a fine weapon in the hands of the Federalists. A Swiss was the next thing to a Frenchman, and Gallatin *must* be "pro-

French." His own friends were afraid to stand by him, and an excited Congress passed the Alien Bill. It provided that foreigners would have to reside here fourteen years before they could become citizens and that the President could order out of the country any foreigner he thought dangerous. This bill was aimed directly at Frenchmen, of course, and at critics of the Federalist party.

This bill was never enforced, though because of it two boatloads of French immigrants left our shores. One reason for its not being enforced was that there were in this country many runaway or exiled French royalists, of whom the Federalists were rather fond. Most of the other aliens at this time happened to be Englishmen, whom the Federalists would not have hurt for the world.

The law did affect one type of immigration, however. The prisons of Ireland were at this time filled with Irishmen who had fought to free their country from England. Many of these were sentenced to exile, and they usually chose to be sent to America. When Rufus King, the American Ambassador at London, heard of this, he was scandalized. Pointing to the Alien Law he bitterly protested at having such undesirable aliens sent to America. Why, they were revolutionists! England stopped sending them to America for a while.

The celebrated Irish patriot, Archibald Hamilton Rowan, wrote to ask Jefferson whether he thought it would be safe for an Irish rebel to stay in the United States. Jefferson invited him to come to Virginia, where he would surely be protected against unconstitutional laws. Later Rowan was a guest at Monticello.

The Republicans hated the Alien Law intensely. They liked to think of America as a haven of refuge for oppressed people, for enemies of tyranny, from all over the world. It was they who gave America the character of "the home of the free, and the land of the brave." Naturally the Irish who came here became Democratic Republicans, and this explains why to this day they are usually Democrats in the Eastern cities.

If the Alien Law could not be enforced, the Sedition Law, which was aimed directly at Americans and not foreigners, was very vigorously enforced. The Sedition Law punished with fines and imprisonment any persons who combined to oppose any measure of the government. This was intended to wipe out the Democratic clubs. More important, you could not even publish a criticism of an American law or official. All a Federalist judge had to believe was that such a criticism tended "to bring the government of the United States or its officers into disrepute or to excite the hatred of the people," and he could clap the Republican writer or editor into jail.

One of the first victims of the Sedition Law was Matthew Lyon, a Republican member of Congress from Vermont. In a letter he had once referred to President Adams's "unbounded thirst for ridiculous pomp," to his "foolish adulation and selfish avarice." A Federalist judge sentenced him to four months in jail and a fine of $1000. There was a jail at Rutland, Vermont, where Lyon was tried, but it was too good a jail for a filthy Democrat, and so he was taken to a dirty hole in a village forty miles away.

Matthew Lyon had been one of Ethan Allen's Green Mountain Boys. His old comrades threatened to smash the little jail and rescue him, but Lyon wrote and begged them not to break the law. When a mob of sympathizers gathered in front of the jail, Lyon came to the bars and pleaded with them to do nothing here but to go home and vote out the Federalists. President Adams turned down a petition signed by thousands of Vermonters asking for Lyon's release. At the polls, this convict still behind bars was elected to Congress by an overwhelming majority.

The Federalists, however, still had hopes of never seeing him in Philadelphia, for Lyon was not rich. Where would he get the $1000 to pay the fine? Jefferson, Madison, and other Virginia Republicans were seeing to that. Senator Mason, his saddlebags stuffed with a thousand dollars in gold, arrived in Vermont just in time to meet Mr. Austen, a wealthy Vermont Republican carrying a strongbox full of silver. They were both on their way to pay Lyon's fine. So Congressman Lyon went to Philadelphia after all, and he received ovations in every State he passed through.

For, though Republican editor after editor was being thrown into jail, the Republican party had *not* been crushed by the Sedition Law. On the contrary, the Federalists had by this act of tyranny turned the country against them, as Hamilton had feared. Gone was the fever of war against France. More and more people lost their fear of being called "filthy Democrat," or "Jacobin," which had once been terrible names to call a man. The Democratic Republican clubs, which the Sedition Law was supposed to make illegal, began to make their appearance everywhere.

These clubs had been modeled on the French political clubs. In Paris, one of these clubs, the Jacobins, had become the leading revolutionary party. The Federalists did not forget this. Nor did they forget that the revolutionary Committees of Correspondence before the American War of Independence had started the same way. One of these early clubs, the Tammany Society, is still famous today in New York, though it has changed its character considerably since the eighteenth century.

Jefferson had kept informed of the growth of these clubs, and increasingly these clubs looked to Jefferson as their real leader, as the man who most truly represented American ideals. Thus it was that among other of Jefferson's achievements can be counted the beginning of American party organizations. For the Federalists were not really a well-organized party based on the mass of the people. They depended too much on the "best people," on outstanding names, to pay much attention to the rank and file of Americans, to whom they did not want to give the vote anyway.

Meanwhile, Jefferson, with the Democratic clubs behind him, was waging a fight against the Alien and Sedition Laws. Of course, these laws were unconstitutional since they denied the right of free speech and free assembly. They were just the sort of laws that would act as protection for people who wanted to destroy the rest of the Constitution, who wanted to introduce life terms for the President and the Senate and other such fond ideas of the Federalists. Petitions began to pour into Congress for the repeal of the Alien and Sedition Laws.

In 1798, during an adjournment of Congress, Jefferson was in Virginia. There came to visit him at Monticello two men with a plan for attacking the unpopular laws. They were Wilson Cary Nicholas, a leading Jeffersonian of Virginia, and John Breckenridge, a young man who had become imbued with Jefferson's ideas. Their plan was to get various State legislatures to pass resolutions declaring that the Alien and Sedition Laws violated the Constitution and were therefore null and void and could not be enforced. Jefferson wrote out the resolutions they wanted. Breckenridge copied them with some changes of his own and took them to the Kentucky legislature, where they were passed. Madison drew up the resolutions for Virginia, which were also passed.

Jefferson and his followers knew that these resolutions could never be passed in Federalist States, but they also knew that a lot of comment would be caused. In the debates that would follow, both favorable and unfavorable, the facts would come out before the people, and the people as a whole, they knew, would oppose the two tyrannical laws.

In the meantime the Federalists seemed quite blind to the fact that the war spirit in America was rapidly evaporating. Federalist talk was all of armies and rank. Intrigues for high commands went on merrily, though war had not yet been declared. Hamilton, who almost looked upon this war, especially the South American part of it, as his own private property, was the busiest intriguer of all.

General Washington, of course, would be commander-in-chief, but, as he was now too old to see active service, the real leader of the American forces would be the second-in-command. Hamilton was determined that this should be no one but himself. Unfortunately, Adams was the man who would do the naming of the second-in-command, and Adams was having less and less love for Mr. Hamilton, who was always trying to tell him what a President should do.

One day Adams asked his Secretary of State, Pickering: "Who do you think should be in command of the army?"

"Hamilton," answered Pickering at once.

Stony silence from the President. Three different times he asked the question, and three times he had the same reply. The third time the President broke out: "It is not his turn by a great deal." After all, the Constitution made the President the commander-in-chief of the armies.

Hamilton did not politely wait for Adams to make up his mind. First he got Washington to support him. Then he wrote letters and articles to prove that all good Federalists preferred him above Generals Knox and Pinckney, both of whom out-ranked him. Then he had his friends in the Senate tell Adams that in confirming his choices they had understood that Hamilton would be put at the top of the list. Finally, when Washington sent Adams a curt little note, Hamilton was appointed acting head of the army.

This was to be something of the very best in armies, quite aristocratic, with only Federalists in command. When Adams suggested Aaron Burr, known to be a brave and capable officer, for a command, he was reminded with lifted eyebrows that Mr. Burr was a Democrat!

Soon the country began to have a taste of what all this jingling of spurs meant for ordinary people. Militaristic nations have a way of encouraging their professional soldiers to look down on civilians as less than nothing. This was precisely why Jefferson opposed the use of a standing army. He thought that militia was just as good a protection against others as a regular army. Militia, also, is not always craving an excuse for a war in which to show off its training. Moreover, if every able man belonged to the militia, then there could be no differences of feeling between civilians and soldiers, since every civilian was a soldier and yet not a professional soldier.

Soon the newspapers began to publish reports of military outrages against the population. In Reading, Pennsylvania, some mounted troops had ill-used some citizens. The editor of the local paper complained. The same troops came to his office, stripped him, and started to lash his bare back when they were stopped by other troops.

William Duane, editor of the *Aurora,* denounced such offenses. One day thirty petty officers, armed and in uniform, came to his office. While some of them cornered the printers, others dragged Duane downstairs and beat him in the yard. He was saved from death by his sixteen-year-old son, who threw himself across his father's body until civilians from the neighborhood came to his rescue.

Adams himself later said that the army was as unpopular "as if it had been a ferocious wild beast let loose on the country."

Aside from American civilians and Republicans, where was the enemy all this time? There did not seem to be any.

When Marshall and Pinckney had left France with the X Y Z papers, Gerry had stayed behind. At length he got into touch with Talleyrand, who told him that the French government had had nothing to do with the unsavory affair, and that France absolutely did *not* want war with America. France would be glad to receive a minister who was not Anti-Republican and pro-British. She had not sent a minister herself only because it was feared he would not be received at Philadelphia. Finally, as a sign of his good faith, Talleyrand sent Gerry a new decree just issued by the French government. It required all French privateers to put up a bond in money guaranteeing that there would be no unauthorized attacks on American shipping.

Gerry hastened home with what he thought was good news. But his report only proved to the saber-rattling Federalists that France was now so frightened that she should be easy to defeat. Otherwise, they had no use for Gerry's report of Talleyrand's peaceful overtures. Gerry expected his country's thanks for bringing her an honorable peace. He discovered instead that all the time he had been serving as his country's emissary, his family at home had been constantly terrorized. His poor wife and children at home had been awakened at night by savage yells and blazing fires outside their windows. One morning they found that a little guillotine had been put up in their yard.

Gerry's news *was* good news—for Jefferson, who felt that more people must be made to know the truth of the French situation. For this purpose, Jefferson now turned in a surprising direction. One would think that two men could not have less in common than Jefferson and Edmund "Moderation" Pendleton. Yet they did have in common: sincerity, a love of justice, and a desire for peace. Jefferson now asked Pendleton to take Gerry's voluminous report, which very few people would read, and boil it down to a short summary of facts. Coming from Pendleton, who was by no means a "Jacobin," Gerry's report would close the mouths of the Federalist warriors. Everyone could and would read it.

The case for war began to seem weaker and weaker. Following Gerry's report there came a flood of letters from Americans in France assuring the government that the French did not want war. Lafayette wrote imploring letters to his hero Washington. He offered to come to America and explain everything if Washington thought it would be wise and that it would aid the cause of peace. Talleyrand, who knew Adams personally and had spent pleasant hours at his house in America, sent the President a personal message asking that bygones be bygones.

Dr. Logan, too, had finally talked to Talleyrand. Every important personage in France assured him that war with America was unthinkable. This news only made the Federalists more furious at him. Congress went so far as to pass what was popularly known as the "Logan Bill." It forbade any

American citizen to communicate by word or in writing with
any official of a foreign government about matters of dispute
between the two governments. In other words, an ordinary
American citizen could not even talk about American foreign
problems if there was a foreign official present.

There is no doubt that all this fuss about the Logan affair
was really being aimed at Jefferson. No one was less fooled
about this than Jefferson himself. Sitting at the head of the
Senate and seeing it pass laws that were aimed against himself
required a cool nerve on Jefferson's part. He became more
cautious about his correspondence. He knew that Federalist
postmasters scrutinized his mail. His friends expected any
moment that he would be brought to trial under the Sedition
Law. "I know not which mortifies me most," Jefferson wrote
sadly, "that I should fear to write what I think, or that my
country should bear such a state of things."

Some of his letters he dared no longer sign. To Elbridge
Gerry he ended one letter with: "And did we ever expect to
see the day when, breathing nothing but sentiments of love
to our country and its freedom and happiness, our correspondence must be as secret as if we were hatching its destruction!
Adieu, my friend, and accept my sincere and affectionate
salutations. *I need not add my signature.*"

On the envelope of a letter to James Monroe, he wrote:
"P.S. Always examine the seal before you open my letters."
Undoubtedly, Jefferson expected Federalist officials to spot
this little message. Perhaps he hoped to make them blush at
their petty spying and prying.

Then, in the darkest days for democracy, the blow fell, not
on the Republicans, but on the Federalists. Adams had been
thinking things over. First Gerry's report, then Logan's, and
now reports from William Murray, American minister to

Holland, all showed that there was no longer cause for war, and that the French were apologizing handsomely. Adams was an honest man with no Napoleonic ambitions. He decided not to declare war, and in February 1799 he named Murray as ambassador to the French Republic.

The Federalists in their newspapers screamed themselves hoarse at Adams's "treachery." The Republicans sighed with relief. Now their turn had come. They knew that the people were becoming wearied of the aristocratic manners and military ambitions of the Federalists. The forces of democracy, the clubs in the cities, the farmers in the backwoods, began to gather up their strength. Next year there would be elections for the Presidency.

There were two ways in which Jefferson could take much credit for this rising tide of Republican feeling. First, he always tried to keep the facts before the people's minds. Secondly, he gave the people a program to fight for. These two things are enough to create a political party, and it is for these reasons that Thomas Jefferson has come down in history as the father of the Democratic Party. For the Democratic Republicans, who first called themselves Republicans, later called themselves Democrats.

As a matter of fact, in a sense Jefferson was also the father of the Republican Party. For, when Abraham Lincoln's party was born, fifty years later, as a party of the common people and the farmers, of idealism and anti-slavery, it chose the name Republican because that was what Jefferson had called himself. Lincoln took some of his attacks upon slavery from Jefferson's *Notes on Virginia*. By then the Democratic Party had lost some of its Jeffersonian ideals. Then, after the Civil War, it was the Republican Party that lost its Jeffersonian ideals.

The first part of Jefferson's task was to have the people know and be excited about the facts. Here he employed the same methods that had turned the colonies against George III. He encouraged Republican newspapers and pamphlets everywhere. If money was needed for a new journal or a pamphlet, Jefferson, without an apology, made out a list of his many, many friends who must subscribe to it. The Federalists were ready to explode with indignation when that scoundrel and jailbird Matthew Lyon established four different newspapers. It was Jefferson's plan to publish tens of thousands of copies of Pendleton's little pamphlet on Gerry's report. They were to be circulated by Congressmen returning to their homes. Jefferson not only wrote an unceasing stream of letters himself; he constantly urged his friends, especially Madison, to write and to talk.

The one fact that the Republican journals harped on all the time was the terrific expense of a war—an unnecessary expense when it was an unnecessary war. The best medicine for the war-fever, Jefferson was never tired of saying, is the tax-collector. Gerry's report, the pamphlets repeated, proved that France did *not* want war, did *not* intend to invade America, and that, therefore, war with France *was* unnecessary.

As for Jefferson's program: He opposed the Alien and Sedition Laws as dangerous to the people's liberty. He opposed a professional standing army. Why have recruiting officers lounging at every courthouse and luring the laborer from his plow? A laborer made a country's wealth; a soldier either destroyed it in war, or wasted it in idleness. For national defense Jefferson preferred the militia.

The government should be as frugal and simple as possible, with no taint of monarchy or aristocracy. He was against taking away the power of the States to give to the Federal government or of taking away the power of Congress to give to the President.

"I am for free commerce with all nations," he wrote, "political connection with none." Free trade was the advice he had given his French friends, because a country made up of farmers needed low prices for manufactured goods. In advising against foreign entanglements he was following Washington's Farewell Address.

"I am for freedom of religion, for freedom of the press, and against all violations of the Constitution [which try] to silence by force and not by reason the complaints or criticisms, just or unjust, of our citizens" against the conduct of their officials. He was against going "backwards instead of forwards to look for improvement." Finally, "I am for encouraging the progress of science in all its branches."

On these principles Jefferson hoped to see laid the foundations of a political party. But, as Federalist spies began to annoy him more, Jefferson began to think of his quiet home in Virginia, where his mail, at any rate, would be less likely to be tampered with by officials looking for treasonable statements. So in the summer and autumn of the year 1800, feeling his work well done, Jefferson retired to Monticello. He rode his plantation and cultivated his crops. A new pianoforte had arrived for Maria, and he must tune it himself.

XVII

MR. PRESIDENT

MRS. MARGARET SMITH was the daughter of a die-hard Federalist. She was a young bride, having just married a cousin who was unfortunately the editor of a Republican paper in the new capital of Washington. One morning she was sitting alone in her parlor when a servant came in to announce a gentleman to see Mr. Smith. The young wife's frank greeting was at first checked by the dignified and reserved air of her visitor. This feeling lasted but a moment, however, for the middle-aged gentleman accepted a chair and was soon deep in conversation with her. In a remarkably soft and gentle voice he talked interestingly of this and that. Be-

fore she knew it, she was telling him what she liked and disliked about her new home. The attention and kindness with
which he listened made Mrs. Smith think he must be an intimate acquaintance of her husband's. Indeed, he put her so
much at her ease that she forgot she was not talking to a
friend of her own but to a stranger, until her husband came
into the room and introduced the stranger to her as "Mr. Jefferson." The Vice-President had come to see Mr. Smith about
publishing his *Manual of Parliamentary Practice.*

Poor Mrs. Smith! She felt her cheeks burn and her heart
throb and could not utter another word. For that lady in her
father's house had always heard and in her father's newspapers
had always read of Thomas Jefferson as a man of the coarsest
looks and the rudest manners, a man utterly loose in his
morals—"the violent democrat, the vulgar demagogue, the
bold atheist and profligate man." "Can this man," she asked
herself, "so meek and mild, yet dignified in his manners, with
a voice so soft and low, with a countenance so benignant and
intelligent, can he be that daring leader of a faction, that dis-
turber of the peace, that enemy of all rank and order?" He
was, and from that time on Mrs. Smith was as ardent a
Republican as her husband.

This incident shows how far the Federalists had gone in
painting the black picture of the writer of the Declaration
of Independence and how much this picture was believed to
be the true one. For the Federalists were now attacking him
with a fury that made their past efforts along this line seem
pale and unconvincing. The reason for this was that Jefferson
was his party's choice for President, and it looked as if he
might be elected.

The charge against Jefferson that was most drummed upon
was that he was an atheist, a man who did not believe in God

and who would burn all the Bibles in the land if he were elected. This was especially malicious since Jefferson's views on religion were exactly the same as Adams's. They were both Deists, who were in the eighteenth century what might be called Unitarians today. These religious attacks went back to the days when Jefferson, with Madison and Wythe, had successfully fought for the separation of church and state in Virginia.

Many of Jefferson's friends urged him to publish his religious beliefs so that these slanders could be scotched. But Jefferson had learned that the best way to treat such charges was to ignore them. He never answered his detractors, except once, when the Reverend Cotton Smith had made the ridiculous charge from his pulpit that Jefferson had got his property by robbing a widow and her fatherless children. Jefferson believed that religion was something for friends to discuss in quiet conversations and not to be dragged into the heat of politics.

While Jefferson had been taking his last vacation at Monticello, the capital had finally been moved to the new city of Washington in June 1800. This was the "capital city on the Potomac" for which Jefferson had bargained his support of Hamilton's first financial bills. It was to this crude, raw, brand-new city, and not to fine old Philadelphia, that Jefferson returned from his vacation in November. Crude and raw as it was, it was Jefferson's own capital as aristocratic Philadelphia could never have been. For that November Thomas Jefferson had been elected President of the United States. Or so it seemed.

His election had been fought tooth and nail, by fair means and foul. When Hamilton had seen his own State, New York, go Republican, he had suggested a little plan to his friend Governor Jay for reversing the people's choice. Fortunately, Governor Jay thought there were some things an honest and fair man could not do, even to beat Democrats. In some of the other Northern States various unconstitutional plans for ignoring the people's vote were discussed.

Then Hamilton in desperation began to flounder from one intrigue into another. Not only did he wish to see the Republicans defeated; he also did not want to see Adams made President again. For he despised Adams, this man who had "traitorously" allowed peace with France, who had disbanded the temporary army that was to have borne Hamilton to glory. First he tried to get Washington to run again. But before a letter could reach Mount Vernon, the "father of his country" died. Then Hamilton published a criticism of Adams, and appeals to all Federalists to vote for C. C. Pinckney instead. These criticisms by Republican editors would have landed them in jail, but Hamilton always felt himself a little above the law. The only effect of these attacks, however, was that more people voted for the Republican candidates.

Twist and turn as he might, Hamilton's cause was lost. The result of the elections Jefferson called the "Revolution of 1800." For the second time the American people turned to the principles of the Declaration of Independence and against the principles of old Europe. Adams and Pinckney were both defeated. Jefferson and Aaron Burr were elected.

But Jefferson and Burr each had the same number of votes! Here was something the Constitution had overlooked. The Constitution stated that the candidate with the second highest number of votes should be Vice-President, and it was really as Vice-President that the Republicans had nominated and voted for Burr. The Constitution also stated that, in the case of a tie between the highest candidates, the House of Representatives should decide which was to be President and which Vice-President. And the House of Representatives was still Federalist when counted by States, which was the way it was to vote!

If the Federalists went about it right, they might make Burr the President and thus defeat Jefferson as well as all the Republicans who had naturally thought they were voting for Jefferson. Some of the Federalists actually came to Burr with this plan. If he would promise to do thus and thus for the Federalists, why then . . . But Burr refused to deal with them. It would mean betraying his party. Hamilton, too, opposed this deal. He hated Burr perhaps more than he did anyone else in the world. It was Burr who had won New York State away from him.

Aaron Burr was an ambitious man, very much like Hamilton in character, which is perhaps why they hated each other so heartily. Though he could not bring himself to plot for the Presidency, neither could he bring himself to renounce it openly. He kept quiet. If fate were to make him head of his country, even by a sort of accident, well, he might . . . or he might not . . . No one knows what was in his mind. This unclearness in Burr's actions earned him the distrust of many Republicans, including Jefferson.

Jefferson, for his part, expressed himself as quite willing to abide by the decision of Congress. But the Federalists had a better plan on foot even than the election of Burr. Suppose Congress came to *no* decision by the time Adams's term was up. Then the country would be without a President. Then the Senate might take over the country and run it for the Federalists. A plot not unworthy of Napoleon, and so Jefferson considered it. He let it be known that, if this were tried, the Senate could expect armed troops to come into Washington from Pennsylvania and Virginia and save the Constitution from that sort of revolution.

So the House of Representatives assembled behind closed doors, with the Senate as witnesses, to choose the President. Each of the sixteen States had one vote. On the first ballot Jefferson received only eight votes, Burr six, and two States could not make up their minds. The winner needed nine votes. The House voted again. Same result. Again the House voted. The vote remained unchanged.

Joseph Nicholson was a Representative from Maryland, one of the States that would go neither one way nor the other. He was seriously ill with fever, but insisted on being carried through the February snowstorm to the House of Representatives. He must cast his vote for Jefferson, or the Federalists from his State would throw the Maryland vote to Burr. His doctor protested, but his wife upheld him. In a room off the side of the hall in which the Representatives were voting, Nicholson lay on a bed. At each balloting his wife held his hand and helped him form the words: Thomas Jefferson.

Again and again and again, all that night, the Representatives voted. Pillows and blankets were brought in so that some of them could sleep between ballots. The next morning nothing had been settled. Days passed, and the vote was still the same. Gouverneur Morris met Jefferson on the steps of the Capitol and suggested that a bargain might be struck with the Federalists. Jefferson refused to have any dealings with them. A week passed, and on the thirty-sixth balloting, Maryland and Vermont swung over to Jefferson, giving him ten votes.

The tension throughout the country suddenly relaxed. Monroe, then Governor of Virginia, had had dispatch riders galloping in every day with the news from Washington. Virginia was jubilant. Republicans everywhere set up a triumphant cheer. And Representative Nicholson of Maryland grew well.

The Federalists faced a future in which the country was no longer to be theirs to rule. But they still had a card up their sleeves. Until the inauguration on March 4th, Adams was still President, Congress was still Federalist. Congress hastily set about providing for the future of many faithful Federalists. Following a plan of Hamilton's, they passed a law creating many new Federal courts. The judges were to be appointed for life, so that they could not be removed by the incoming Republican administration. As Jefferson, still sitting at the head of the Senate, pointed out, there were at that time already more Federal courts than the country needed, but that had nothing to do with the plan.

The law was hurriedly passed, the judges were appointed, the Senate consented to the appointments. Time was passing swiftly and, by the evening of March 3rd, several of the commissions had not yet been signed. Late into the night Chief Justice John Marshall, acting as Secretary of State, sat at his desk filling out the commissions and signing them.

Jefferson knew quite well what was going on, and disapproved of the whole business as unfair and unconstitutional. He had already chosen Levi Lincoln as his Attorney-General. The story, as it came down in his family, is that Jefferson called on Mr. Lincoln, gave him his watch, and ordered him to take possession of the State Department on the stroke of midnight. After that magic hour he was to let no one take anything out of the building.

At the moment when ghosts are supposed to walk abroad Lincoln dramatically entered Judge Marshall's office. "I have been ordered by Mr. Jefferson," he said solemnly, "to take possession of this office and its papers."

"Why, Mr. Jefferson has not yet qualified," exclaimed the startled Chief Justice and acting Secretary of State. "It is not yet twelve o'clock," and he drew out his watch.

Whereupon Lincoln drew out his, and showed it to Marshall. "This is the President's watch," he said, "and rules the hour."

Judge Marshall looked longingly at the unfinished commissions on his desk. Later he used to say laughingly that he had been allowed to pick up nothing but his hat. But in his pocket he had a few of the commissions, and the men who finally received them were thereafter called "John Adams's midnight judges."

On the morning of his inauguration Jefferson came down for breakfast to the dining room of the boarding house where he had been living. Mrs. Brown, the wife of the Senator from Kentucky, impulsively got up from her seat at the head of the table and offered it to the new President. The new President declined it with a bow and took his usual place at the foot. This was no John Adams, worrying about how the President should be addressed, and about who should precede whom in rank.

Jefferson had, however, written his son-in-law Jack Eppes to buy him four carriage horses for the occasion. Jack had been so particular in choosing the horses that they did not arrive in time for the inauguration. Jefferson was not in the least upset. He walked the short distance to the Capitol.

Burr had already taken his oath when Jefferson entered the Senate chamber. Jefferson gave his inaugural address, was sworn in by Chief Justice Marshall, one of his bitterest foes, and became President of the United States of America.

John Adams was not there to congratulate his successor. On that same famous midnight of March 3rd, he had ordered his carriage and left.

The city of Washington had been twelve years in the planning and building, and it was by no means a finished city yet. All Washington lacked, wrote the witty Mr. Gouverneur Morris to a French princess, was but "houses, cellars, kitchens, well-informed men, amiable women, and other little trifles of this kind to make our city perfect. . . . For we can walk here as if in the fields or woods."

There were other natural beauties, too. For instance, between the White House and the Capitol there was an almost impassable swamp. The few scattered houses in the town were separated by waste-lands, woods, and gravel pits. For those Representatives who enjoyed hunting it was not necessary to go more than a few hundred yards from the Capitol to bag some partridge.

As for the White House itself, the condition it was in just before Jefferson moved into it has been described by Mrs. Adams in a letter to her daughter—the same one for whom Jefferson had once been commissioned to buy corsets in France.

The river, which runs up to Alexandria [wrote Abigail Adams], is in full view of my window, and I see the vessels as they pass and repass. The house is on a grand and superb scale, requiring about thirty servants to attend and keep the apartments in proper order, and perform the ordinary business of the house and stables; an establishment very well proportioned to the President's salary. [A wry little joke that Jefferson was soon to appreciate.] The lighting of the apartments from the kitchen to parlors and chambers is a tax indeed, and the fires we are obliged to keep to secure us from daily agues is another very cheerful comfort. To assist us in this great castle, and render less attendance necessary, bells are wholly wanting, not one single one being hung through the whole house. I could content myself almost anywhere three months; but, surrounded with forests, can you believe that wood is not to be had, because people cannot be found to cut and cart it! We have not the least fence, yard, or other convenience, without; and the great unfinished audience room I make a drying room of, to hang up the clothes in. The principal stairs are not up, and will not be this winter.

Mrs. Adams then cautioned her daughter that she must keep all this to herself, and, if anyone asked her how her mother liked it in the White House, she was to say that it was beautifully situated, which it was.

No doubt, in time, after Jefferson came to the White House, the staircase was finished and bells were ringing. As for the forests in the city, the inhabitants gave them short shrift. Destroying forests was for a long time one of the favorite occupations of the American people. In one single night as many as seventy tulip poplars in Washington were killed by girdling, to be cut up later at leisure.

Jefferson always felt badly over this wanton destruction. To see a tree felled unnecessarily, when it had taken perhaps centuries to grow, seemed to him little short of murder. Once his friends at a dinner party were startled by hearing him say that he wished he had the power of a despot. "Yes," Jefferson replied to their stares, "I wish I was a despot that I might save the trees."

Jefferson's first task as President was the selection of his Cabinet. The two outstanding members of Jefferson's party were James Madison, the natural choice for Secretary of State, and Albert Gallatin, who received Hamilton's old position of Secretary of the Treasury.

Jefferson and his Cabinet immediately set about cleaning up Federalist abuses. They pardoned all those in prison for violating the Sedition Law. They gave back the fines collected. They canceled the offices of the "midnight judges." To those who had suffered under the Alien and Sedition Laws Jefferson wrote personal letters of cheer and good will.

Dr. Joseph Priestley, the chemist who first discovered oxygen, had come to America to escape persecution. In England his religious views were not liked nor was the fact that he had supported America during her Revolution and later France during hers. For free minds like his the Federalists had neither gratitude nor admiration. They, too, had tried to persecute him under the Alien Law. Now he was among the first to receive an official letter from Jefferson.

Jefferson felt it a public duty to atone for the inhospitality his country had shown to the first eminent scientist who had come to live among us. He invited Priestley to Washington, and offered him the White House as a home during his visit. America's laws, he wrote, "were made for the good and wise like you."

During the Federalists' baiting of Republicans they had not spared even that old democratic patriot, Samuel Adams. Him, too, Jefferson sent a letter full of affection and loyalty. He told the eighty-year-old revolutionist that he had been thinking of Sam Adams when he delivered his inaugural address. Did Mr. Adams approve of it? He asked for Adams's counsel and blessing on the new Republican government.

Thomas Paine was still in France, now living unhappily in a dirty little hovel, seemingly forgotten by the nation he had done so much to create. Then one day he received a letter from the new President of the United States. Jefferson wrote that now America was more like what it had been just after the Revolution, when men had believed in liberty and the rights of man. Would Paine, who had all his life labored to make the world like this, care to come back to America? The President offered him passage in a naval vessel then visiting France. For Paine did not dare cross the ocean in an ordinary merchant ship. The English navy might easily have picked him up during a search at sea and clapped him in irons. The British government was one at least that had not forgotten Tom Paine.

Paine read the letter with joy, and showed it to his friends. Wouldn't it be fun, said the old trouble-maker, if Jefferson should send me to the English Court that has outlawed me! Tom Paine presented at the King's levee! All the bishops and ladies would faint away!

Now Jefferson was doing a rather audacious thing in bringing Paine back to America in a naval ship. For, while in a French prison, Paine had written his last great work, *The Age of Reason,* in which he had said some very outspoken things about religion. So again the hue and cry broke out in the newspapers, and this had its effect even in the home of the Republican President himself.

Once when Jefferson was home in Monticello he received a letter from Paine saying that he was coming to pay the President a short visit. When Jefferson mentioned this to his daughter Martha, she let him know, more by looks than by words, that she would be just as happy if Mr. Paine stayed away from Monticello. Jefferson's reply to this unspoken appeal was: "I see Mr. Paine is no favorite of the ladies. But he has earned the hospitality of every American home, and certainly of mine." Paine came to Monticello.

In December 1801, Congress assembled again. Instead of appearing before it to deliver his annual address, Jefferson sent it a written message—a practice which has been followed by all the Presidents ever since except Woodrow Wilson. The Federalist journals sneered. Some more of Mr. Jefferson's Republican novelties? Was not a procedure that was good enough for the King of England good enough for Mr. Jefferson? As a matter of fact Jefferson had sent in a written message simply because he wrote better than he spoke. If he had thought of the King of England, he certainly would not have changed his plans. The last thing Jefferson was interested in was giving an aristocratic impression.

He forbade the use of the President's image on coins. He made it a practice to refuse all presents. He did not allow his birthday to be celebrated as Washington's and Adams's had been. He avoided anything that aped royal customs. The custom of holding levees like the King of England's, for instance, was abolished.

Once each week Washington and Adams had stood stiffly at one end of the reception room and greeted the selected individuals who were introduced to them. The Federalist dames still in Washington would not give up their "republican court" without a struggle, however. On the usual day, and at the usual time, two o'clock, a party of ladies and gentlemen presented themselves at the White House. Mr. President was out. He had gone for his daily two-hour horseback ride, an exercise he never neglected. When he returned at three, he was told that the reception room was full of ladies who had been waiting an hour. Realizing at once what was up, he stalked into the reception room just as he was—booted, spurred, riding crop in hand, and dust all over his clothes. He pretended that it was only a happy accident that had brought so much company together. He greeted them with easy, charming affability. The joke was on the ladies. This was the last time the "courtiers" of Washington tried to force their manners on Jefferson.

Two days only were set aside for public receptions—New Year's Day and July 4th. On matters of business Jefferson was to be seen any day. Specially proclaimed days of thanksgiving or of fast, Jefferson also abolished. These were church matters, he said, and the Constitution had definitely separated church and state.

The Governor of a State once wrote to Jefferson to ask him what should be the etiquette when they met. "My dear Sir," Jefferson replied, "there will be no etiquette." Gradually these democratic manners began to seep down from the President through the Cabinet to all branches of the government. Residents should pay the first visit to new arrivals, with no questions of rank. After the first visit, they were to be considered no longer strangers and were expected to act like other residents. When in company all were to feel as equals, with titles or without, government officials or private citizens. Going into dinner or passing from one room to another, there was to be no other rule of correct order than that ladies preceded gentlemen.

These may not seem serious enough questions to have been worth discussing, but in 1801 they were considered very important indeed. Mr. Merry, for one, was outraged. Mr. Merry was the minister from England, and he felt perfectly lost without his accustomed ceremony. His troubles began with his very first introduction to the President.

In full-dress uniform, with gold brocade and sword, Mr. Merry was conducted by Mr. Madison to the White House. The President was not to be found in the audience chamber, so Madison promptly guided Mr. Merry to a small hall leading to Jefferson's study. Just then the President stepped into the narrow hall. The three men were crowded, and so His Majesty George III's official representative (who knew what was what) backed himself out. When finally the formal introduction took place, Mr. Merry was astounded to see that Jefferson had on down-at-the-heel slippers, cotton stockings, and a careless lounging coat.

If Mr. Merry showed his indignation, he could only have given Jefferson a little impish pleasure. Maybe he thought of the time he and Adams had cooled their heels at the Court of St. James's, waiting on the grand lords who had taken the hint of cold-shouldering the two Americans from their royal master. Even now, Mr. Merry was not a full ambassador, because the British government did not consider the United States important enough to rate one.

Jefferson's dinner rules—the President himself humorously referred to them as "the pell-mell system"—were Mr. Merry's last straw. One day the Merrys were invited to a dinner for foreign ministers, members of the Cabinet, and their wives. When dinner was announced, Jefferson took the arm of Dolly Madison to lead her in. Mrs. Madison caught Mrs. Merry's black look, nudged her partner, and tried to move him over to Mrs. Merry's side. Jefferson serenely held on to Dolly Madison and escorted her to the dining room. What was the use of being President if you couldn't rag a self-important British diplomat and his aristocratic airs?

Eventually, Mr. Merry lived in a perpetual state of social confusion. If he received an invitation to family supper from Jefferson, he wanted to know from Madison whether he was being invited as a private person or as a minister. When Martha came to visit her father in the White House, Mrs. Merry wished to know whether she was in Washington as the President's daughter or as the wife of a Virginia gentleman.

You see, it was extremely important, for in the first case she would call on Mrs. Randolph and in the other Mrs. Randolph should call on her. These questions were raised partly out of spite, and Mrs. Merry never visited Jefferson again. All in all, Washington was not a happy place just then for "correctly formal" people.

Ordinarily Dolly Madison served as hostess for the White House except during the short visit paid Jefferson by his daughters in the winter of 1802. Martha Randolph and Maria Eppes were both charming first ladies of the land, Martha earning praise for her wit and Maria delighting by the beauty she had inherited from her mother. Maria would rather have been like the tall plain Martha, with her father's mind, than like herself. She always felt, when people admired her looks, that they only did it to avoid mentioning the fact that she was not as clever as Martha. Neither of the women, by the way, adopted their father's thoroughgoing simplicity, especially in the matter of dress. There is one letter to their father in which they tell him to ask Mrs. Madison to get them "two wigs of the color of the hair enclosed and of the most fashionable shapes" to be ready in Washington when they arrived. American ladies were still not wearing their own hair in public, though the French court had done so when Martha was a girl in Paris.

Jefferson's interest in democratic simplicity must not be confused with frugality. Cotton stockings and all, Jefferson's was still the lavish hospitality of the Virginia planter. Indeed, it was in the White House that he finally wrecked his fortune for good. Jefferson's steward would frequently spend fifty dollars on food alone in a day's shopping. The long dining-room table was usually crowded with guests. Jefferson, remembering the custom that had made Paris such a gay, hospitable

place when he was there, was always urging people to drop in.
The Reverend Mr. Cutler, a New England clergyman, once
attended a dinner at the White House, and the bill of fare as
he reported it was something as follows:

Rice soup
Round of beef
Turkey
Mutton or veal
Fried eggs
Fried beef
A pie called macaroni, filled with onions or shallots
(very strong and not very agreeable—Italian dish)
Ice cream (very good)
Dish somewhat like pudding (very fine)
Many other gimcracks
Great variety of fruit
Plenty of wines (and good).

Fifty dollars went pretty far in those days. Dinner often began
at four and lasted with talk till night.

Jefferson had brought his French steward Petit back with
him from Paris, along with waffle irons and notebooks full of
French and Italian cooking recipes. He made his former Paris
secretary, Short, get him a spaghetti mold while in Naples,
and besides macaroni he also brought vanilla into the United
States. Ice cream, a fairly rare delicacy, appeared almost every
day at the four o'clock dinners in the White House. In a
political speech Patrick Henry once stirringly denounced Jefferson as a man who had "abjured his native victuals," and
been unfaithful to good old-fashioned roast beef.

When he was Vice-President, Jefferson had thought the
President's salary much too high. Now he knew better, and
he must have smiled wryly when he read a Federalist paper
that wrote about him: "He always thought $25,000 a great

salary when Mr. Adams had it. Now he will undoubtedly think $12,500 enough. Monticello is not far away; he can easily send home his clothes to be washed and mended. His servants he owns [the slaves], and his vegetables he can bring from his estate."

When Jefferson became President, he found on the country's hands a large navy that had been got together during the fever of war against France. The Republican Congress at once set about scrapping this unnecessary expense. For what was left of the navy Jefferson found a very good use. When he had been ambassador to France, he had thought it disgraceful that civilized nations should pay tribute to the Barbary pirates. He had thought so as Secretary of State. Now he sent America's little navy against Tripoli. In the naval war that followed, Stephen Decatur made a name for himself by his bravery, and the Tripoli pirates were for the first time given a taste of force instead of tribute. The older countries eventually followed this infant nation's example, but America's is the honor of first having brought the pirates to terms in 1805.

The most important event to happen during Jefferson's eight years in the Presidency was the Louisiana Purchase. Most historians consider it the most important event in the history of the United States next to the Revolution and the Civil War.

When the United States extended only to the Mississippi, it made a great difference which nation controlled New Orleans. If the farmers of the West, of Kentucky and Ohio, could not float their produce down the Mississippi into the Gulf of Mexico, they were lost. The overland roads were nothing but muddy trails. New Orleans was therefore the back gate to the United States. As long as Spain, a weak country, held this key

city, there was no trouble, but when Napoleon took it from
Spain, the farmers of the West grew uneasy. They had a right
to be, for in 1802 Napoleon canceled the treaties that Jefferson
had signed with Spain and closed New Orleans to American
produce.

Immediately a new clamor for war broke out in the West.
This time it was the Federalists in the East who were all for
peace. But Jefferson was consistent. He refused to plunge the
country into war. Instead he sent Robert Livingston, American minister to France, instructions to arrange some sort of
treaty. The West was full of rumors that Napoleon was coming
over to conquer America, but Jefferson sent messages pleading
for patience.

Livingston began to negotiate with Napoleon. He offered to
buy New Orleans for six million dollars. He seemed to get
nowhere and wrote back that the whole matter might as well
be dropped. Meanwhile, Jefferson was corresponding with a
friend in France. This was Dupont de Nemours, a philosopher,
who had the ear of the French government. He was doing for
Jefferson what Lafayette had once done. He wrote Jefferson
that something very important for America was about to happen. Jefferson at once sent James Monroe to help Livingston
with the negotiations.

Before Monroe could reach Paris, however, Napoleon had
come to a sudden decision. He was about to embark on a new
war with England, and England's fleet was the strongest in
the world. How could Napoleon hope to protect the Louisiana
Territory so far away? Besides, he needed money for his wars.
Give him fifteen million dollars, he said, and the United States
could have, not only New Orleans, but the whole of Louisiana.

Livingston was dazed. Buy a whole empire as big as the
United States? Those had not been his instructions, but, taking

his courage in his hands, he seized the bargain. Monroe arrived and agreed with him. They signed the treaty in April 1803.

When the news came out, Spain was indignant, the French journals even more so, and America was astounded. Perhaps no one was more surprised than Jefferson that the French should give up an empire as easily as this. He was overjoyed, too—ever since he had been Secretary of State he had been afraid that England might some day acquire this territory.

On the other hand his conscience bothered him. Did the Constitution give him the power to take over land like this? Now it would be the Federalists' turn to cry "Unconstitutional," and he who had always fought for a strict interpretation of the Constitution would not know what to answer. He played with the idea of rushing through an amendment to the Constitution. But there was no time. Suppose it failed; suppose Napoleon changed his mind in the meantime! The treaty was adopted.

How the Federalists in the Senate stormed! "The Constitution!" they cried. "The Constitution!" For what did Boston merchants and Philadelphia manufacturers know or care about Kentucky's needs? They knew more about Shanghai and Liverpool than they did about the West. Louisiana could only mean more Democrats, more pioneer farmers with Jeffersonian ideas.

They were right, of course. Jefferson himself said that an empire had been won for liberty. From then on the pioneer mind became the typical American mind. And this mind always faced West until finally the Pacific had been reached. Out of the Louisiana Purchase were finally carved the States of Louisiana, Arkansas, Missouri, Iowa, South Dakota, Nebraska, Kansas, and Oklahoma, with great portions of Colorado, Montana, Wyoming, North Dakota, and Minnesota. This great empire at four cents an acre!

A great deal of this territory was practically unknown. Even before the signing of the Louisiana Purchase, Jefferson had busied himself with a plan for opening up the northern part of this country. This plan is so very much the sort of thing Jefferson would do that no account of his life would be complete without the story of the Lewis and Clark Expedition. Also, forty years later, this expedition started by Jefferson would be important in the westward march of America across the continent. For it became the basis of America's claims to the Oregon country.

The author of the *Notes on Virginia* had often thought with greed of the wealth of knowledge that a trained observer could find in the great Northwest. He had tried to inspire the explorer Ledyard with this enthusiasm while in France. When, in 1792, Captain Gray discovered the Columbia River on the Pacific coast, Jefferson's interest was fired anew. That year he suggested to the American Philosophical Society that it send an exploring expedition across the continent. He and some others would contribute the money.

Such an expedition was actually started. It was put in charge of Meriwether Lewis, a young man of nineteen who had grown up not ten miles from Monticello. Meriwether's mother used to make very good hams and every year she sent a few to Jefferson. Lewis was a fine woodsman. Even at the age of eight he used to go out in the night alone, except for his dogs, to hunt possum and raccoon. But the other leader of the expedition, a French scientist, was ordered elsewhere by his government, and that plan also fell through.

Meriwether Lewis volunteered with the Virginia troops to put down the Whisky Rebellion, joined the regular army, fought Indians under "Mad Anthony" Wayne, became a captain. Now he, too, shared Jefferson's dream of a voyage of

exploration into unknown America. In 1801 he became
private secretary to the President and they must have discussed
the idea again and again.

Their chance came in January 1803. Congress was debating
an act to establish trading houses with the Indian tribes. The
President sent Congress a confidential message in which he
urged that the Indians of the Missouri Valley should not be
overlooked. To lay out trade routes and look the possibilities
over it might be a good idea to send an expedition first. The
message had to be secret, of course, because this territory was
owned by France.

Congress fell in with the idea and voted the President a
modest sum of money for such an expedition. Jefferson added
some from his own pocket. You can imagine the excitement of
the two men. Jefferson thought, who knows, one might find
mammoths still ranging the plains!

Captain Lewis would, of course, be in charge. Jefferson now
knew him, after two years of working together, to be the ideal
man for the job. He was a good leader of men, expert in wood-
craft, knew the character of the Indians as well as their customs
and beliefs, was a careful observer of nature, and, most important of all, knew just what Jefferson expected of the expedition.

These were Jefferson's instructions: Go up the Missouri
River to its source, cross the Rocky Mountains, and find a
river, like the Columbia, which will take you to the Pacific.
First see how much of this continent can be crossed by water.
Make a careful study of the Indians; find the names of the
nations and their numbers, the boundaries of their possessions,
their relations to other tribes, their languages, traditions,
monuments; note how they carry on agriculture, hunting, fishing, war, arts, and what tools they use; describe their food,
clothing, houses; the diseases they are subject to and the reme-

dies they use. Is there anything peculiar about their laws; what articles do they need that we could send them? Always be as friendly with the Indians as possible. Tell them that the United States is looking for peaceful trade. Take them some cowpox for vaccination. Invite their chiefs to come to Washington at government expense. Tell them that we shall gladly educate their children if they wish.

Other objects to notice are soil, character of the land, plant life, animals (especially those not found in the United States), fossil bones of extinct animals, mineral resources, climate, etc. In other words Captain Lewis was to do for the West what Jefferson's *Notes* had done for Virginia.

Lewis then asked if he might have go with him his old comrade-in-arms, William Clark. Lieutenant William Clark was the youngest brother of the George Rogers Clark who had captured the Northwest Territory for the United States just before Jefferson was made Governor of Virginia. Like his brother, William Clark was a veteran Indian fighter and woodsman.

While the preparations for the expedition were being secretly carried out, Lewis went to Philadelphia to study more science and to learn the use of geographical instruments. Jefferson personally supervised the purchase of all the instruments to be used on the trip.

Late in 1803 Lewis and Clark took their little party into winter quarters in St. Louis, at the mouth of the Missouri. Here they trained their men thoroughly until they were ready to start in the spring. Meanwhile, the great news came that Napoleon had sold Louisiana and that the exploration was therefore to be made in United States territory after all. There would be no interference from France or Spain.

On the 14th of May, 1804, the expedition finally set out in

three boats. It consisted of fourteen army soldiers, nine volunteers, an interpreter and his Indian wife, and Clark's Negro valet. Part of the way they were accompanied by sixteen additional men. That winter they spent in North Dakota among the Mandan Indians. They continued up the Missouri until they came to three forks of the river which Lewis named the Jefferson, the Madison, and the Gallatin. Then they followed the Jefferson into southwestern Montana, where the Shoshone Indians gave them horses to cross the Rockies. They paddled down the Columbia River in canoes and reached its mouth on November 15, 1805.

In a year and a half the expedition had traveled about four thousand miles. It had met Indian tribes never before seen by white men. It had discovered new animals like the grizzly bear, the mule deer, and the mountain goat. It had collected many specimens of earths, salts, minerals, and plants. It had been the first party of explorers to reach the Pacific by crossing the continent north of Mexico. And it had thereby established America's most important claim to the Oregon Territory. In everything that Jefferson had wished, it was a success.

After spending the winter on the coast the party started back on March 23, 1806, and reached St. Louis exactly six months later, one third the time it had taken them to go, though they stopped to explore the Yellowstone on the way. Lewis and Clark came back to Washington as men who had successfully carried out the most romantic exploration of modern times. The leaders were rewarded with large grants of land. Captain Lewis was made governor of the northern part of the Louisiana Territory, while Clark became brigadier-general of the territorial militia, and later Indian agent.

When Lewis died shortly after, in 1809, the President himself supervised the publication of the report of the expedition.

thus giving still more proofs of how important he considered the encouragement of scientific discovery. The explorations of Lieutenant Pike were also set afoot by him. Pike was the first American to explore the northernmost reaches of the Mississippi and the valley of the Arkansas River, and his name still lives as that of the famous peak he discovered in Colorado.

Jefferson's administration has been called "the most memorable in the history of American science." Not only did he try to give official encouragement to every scientific labor; he also tried to make personal contributions to knowledge. In the basement of the White House he had sorted out a great many of the fossil bones of extinct animals brought back by Lewis and Clark, another subject for jeers by his political opponents. Even the thirteen-year-old Federalist poet, William Cullen Bryant, had something to say about these activities, of course in verse:

> Go, wretch, resign the Presidential chair,
> Disclose thy secret measures, foul or fair,
> Go, search with curious eyes for hornèd frogs,
> 'Mid the wild wastes of Louisiana's bogs,
> Or, where the Ohio rolls his turbid stream,
> Dig for huge bones, thy glory and thy theme.

Encouraged by the Louisiana Purchase Jefferson tried many times to buy Florida from the Spaniards but without success.

One of the great glories of the Federalist administrations had been Hamilton's financial policies. The result is that people always think of Hamilton as the inventor of our Treasury system. As a matter of fact it was Jefferson's Secretary, Albert Gallatin, who gave us the Treasury system we have today.

Jefferson had always accused Hamilton of purposely making the nation's financial affairs mysterious so that most of the people could not understand what was being done with their money. Gallatin at once brought the country's money affairs out in the open.

It had been Hamilton's idea to keep the government constantly in debt to the rich. This would give people with money a chance to make more out of the government; and it would also mean that the wealthy classes would always support the government, since their money was invested in it. During Jefferson's campaign the Federalists tried to scare people away from voting for him by saying that, if Jefferson were elected, he would refuse to pay back the debts that the government owed. But the man who had practically paid the same debt twice to British moneylenders after the war was not likely to do such a thing. Instead he started to pay back the government's debt as fast as possible. He hoped to have it all paid back by 1817, even including the cost of the Louisiana Purchase.

For Jefferson had the curious idea, which no government has ever followed, of making each generation pay back its own debts. He did not think it fair for people to make debts that their children would have to pay.

So Jefferson and Gallatin sold the government's share of the United States Bank. They paid for the Louisiana Purchase by selling the land cheaply. They economized expenses, abolishing many unnecessary government offices that had been filled with place-hunting Federalists. They reduced the number of ministers sent to foreign countries and cut down the size of the navy. This made it possible for Congress to reduce the taxes of the country.

Jefferson's first term of office was ending with the country as a whole very well satisfied with the Republican Party's administration. Jefferson himself was immensely popular. He should now have been one of the happiest men in the world. But now, at the height of his public triumph, he was overwhelmed by private tragedy.

Every year during his Presidency, Jefferson made two trips to Monticello, for a short stay in early spring to see things bloom, and for a longer vacation at the end of summer. He always stopped off at Edgehill, near Shadwell, where his son-in-law Randolph lived. Here he picked up Martha and her whole family and took them with him to Monticello, four miles away.

Maria often stayed at Edgehill with Martha, especially in winter when both their husbands were in Philadelphia. For both John Eppes and Thomas Randolph were Congressmen. The children were thus together also, for Thomas Jefferson was now seven times a grandfather. Martha had six children, and Maria had just had a boy baby whom she named Francis.

Early in April 1804 Jefferson arrived at Edgehill full of anxiety. Maria was seriously ill. The whole family packed up and went to Monticello, Maria being brought up the mountain in a litter carried by men. When the weather permitted she would be taken round the lawn in a carriage. Nothing seemed to do her any good, however. Her strength steadily declined. On the morning of April 17, she died.

"I have lost the half of all I had," Jefferson wrote to his old school friend Page, then Governor of Virginia.

Abigail Adams saw an account of Maria's death in the newspaper. She had cut off all relations with Jefferson, angry at him for freeing some of the scoundrels who had been imprisoned for reviling her husband in their newspapers. But she remembered the charming child who had once said to her in London: "Oh, now that I have learned to love you, why will they take you from me?" She wrote Jefferson a letter of sympathy.

That winter Martha's family moved into the White House

to help her father bear his loneliness. He had loved his way-
ward Polly, so different from himself and looking so much like
her mother, in a special way.

In the election of 1804, Jefferson received 162 electoral
votes while C. C. Pinckney, the Federalist candidate, got only
14. This Republican landslide spelled the finish of the Federalist party. Its spirit had already been broken with the death
of Alexander Hamilton in July 1804. The enmity between
Aaron Burr and Hamilton had reached such a pitch that Burr
sent the Federalist leader a challenge, fought a duel with him,
and killed him.

Burr's political career seemed ended by this deed. Jefferson's
Vice-President for his second term was George Clinton, former
Governor of New York. The Twelfth Amendment to the Constitution was passed so that never again would there arise the
question as to which of two men had been elected President
and which Vice-President. From now on Vice-Presidents were
voted for only as Vice-Presidents.

Jefferson hoped in his second term to devote himself to
making public improvements and to encouraging the growth
of education and science. With the national debt being rapidly
paid off, and Gallatin insisting on simplicity and economy in
government, this should have been easy. But these grand
schemes for prosperity and public happiness were ended by
events in Europe.

England and France were at death grips for the control of
Europe. England with her great fleet decided to starve France
into submission. In 1806 she declared the western coast of
Europe under blockade. Any ships trying to deliver goods on
the west coast would be captured. Napoleon immediately

struck back by declaring the British Isles blockaded. Any ships trying to deliver goods to England would be captured.

Now Napoleon's blockade meant practically nothing, for he had not the ships to enforce it, but England's blockade was disastrous for American commerce. Soon the American coast had warships from France and England hovering around, capturing American vessels and violating all the rights of neutral powers. England was the worse offender simply because she had the larger navy, and also because she searched American ships for runaway British sailors. Conditions on British ships were so vile that undoubtedly many sailors did run away to America. They usually also became American citizens, but the British followed the rule, "Once an Englishman, always an Englishman." This practically denied that America had ever won a War of Independence.

A great many Americans began to shout for war against England. A great many others, whose experiences were different, raised an equal shout for war on Napoleon. Now, whichever side America joined, she would help the other. And both were acting like enemies. This gave Jefferson a chance to keep America out of the war altogether, in spite of the treatment of American ships and seamen. For one thing, Jefferson did not like this particular war. As between Napoleon and George III he could see nothing to choose. Both were the sort of tyrants Jefferson detested. Their wars only added to the corruption and tyranny over Europe. Why should America help either, especially when what America needed most just then was a peaceful chance to grow.

So, assailed on both sides, by his anti-English friends and by the anti-French Federalists, he nevertheless managed to keep his country out of war. But the arrogant high-handedness of the British and French navies in the Atlantic grew so great that Jefferson had to do something. What he did amounted to declaring a war on both countries that was yet not a war. Like Mercutio in *Romeo and Juliet,* he said: "A plague on both your houses!" He resorted once again to his favorite commercial weapon. He got Congress to pass an Embargo Act in December 1807. From then on American ships were forbidden to leave America for any European port whatsoever.

For a year this law held good. Then the vigorous American shipping industry began to languish and die. Next came the turn of the farmers whose produce piled up in the warehouses till it decayed, because it could not be sold abroad. Complaints began to rise higher and higher until in March 1809, during Jefferson's last few days in office, the bill had to be repealed. In its place was passed the Non-Intercourse Act, which merely forbade trading with England and France. In little more than a year Jefferson had lost almost all the popularity he had enjoyed for more than six years of his Presidency. But Jefferson never once regretted having kept his country out of this war, nor his having refused to sign the humiliating treaties that England offered him. It certainly cannot be proved that America would have been better off in the long run to have gone to war with either France or England or with both.

The only satisfaction that the year 1808 had brought the President was the opportunity to put his signature to an act of Congress forbidding the future importation of slaves. This was the earliest opportunity for such an act under the Constitution.

When candidates for the next election were being chosen, eight State legislatures passed resolutions endorsing Jefferson for a third term. This, in spite of the unpopularity of the

Embargo Act, must have made him feel much better. More States would have followed, but Jefferson stopped the talk of a third term at once. He said: "That I should lay down my charge at a proper period is as much a duty as to have borne it faithfully." He pointed out that, though the Constitution said nothing about restricting the number of terms any one man might serve, such a restriction would be the best way to keep the office from becoming a position for life and possibly even hereditary. Short terms were safer for democracy. Washington had set the precedent for serving no more than two terms. Jefferson referred to Washington's refusal and actually made it part of the unwritten Constitution.

So Madison was chosen to be the next President, to Jefferson's intense joy, for he loved the faithful Madison as he would a son. The country would be in good hands. It would follow in the direction pointed by the Declaration of Independence.

For forty years Jefferson had been in public service, as a young Burgess, as a member of the Continental Congress, as wartime Governor of Virginia, as ambassador to France, as first Secretary of State, as second Vice-President, as third President, and always as a leader of democracy. He had seen thirteen colonies become a nation, a new kind of nation that would perhaps continue to serve as a model for the rest of the world. He had played as great a part in this great work as any man. He had done more than his share. He could retire now, at the age of sixty-six, to cultivate his Monticello. And he could permit himself a sigh of relief. "Never," he groaned, "did a prisoner released from his chains feel such relief as I shall on shaking off the shackles of power. *Nature intended me for the more tranquil pursuits of science by rendering them my supreme delight.*"

XVIII

THE GARDEN

AT the end of the famous novel *Candide,* by the great French writer Voltaire, the hero, after hair-raising adventures all over the globe, decides that the only true and good life is that of the man who stays home and "cultivates his garden." These were now the sentiments of Thomas Jefferson in his last and final retirement. At the age of sixty-six he would devote himself to his home on the little mountain and "cultivate his garden."

Safely home at Monticello, never more to leave it for more

than a hundred miles, Jefferson's first delight was to lay out new flower beds on the lawn and under the windows. Soon he was stalking about with a measuring rod, followed by a gardener with spade and hoe. A troop of Jefferson's grandchildren surrounded them and watched them plant hyacinth and tulip bulbs. Each bulb had a lovely name—"Marcus Aurelius," "King of the Gold Mine," "Roman Empress," "Queen of the Amazons." Next to each kind of flower was planted a bit of stick with a label telling the name.

Every day the children came to the garden to see which of the new flowers had arrived. They would raise a shout and run to Jefferson. "Grandpa, the Queen of the Amazons is up!" He would come to see if it were so, and praise the children for their watchfulness. Then, when all the rich purple, crimson, delicate lilac, or pale yellow blossoms were up, he and his daughter and her children would discuss transplanting them and arranging them in different groups.

Thomas Jefferson came naturally by his love for flowers, from his botanist grandfather Isham Randolph. From the time that young Jefferson, about to bring home his bride, had first begun to draw up grand plans for Monticello he had imagined it beautified by flowers. But he had never found the time to put his ideas seriously to work until he was President. In the meantime he had never let a hint or a lesson go to waste. Even during his short stay in England he had taken the opportunity of studying the famous English gardens and storing away his impressions for future use.

Long ago Jefferson had started to gather together works on plant life until his library now held one of the best collections of botanical books in America. This library was always at the disposal of his friends. It also meant that Jefferson's knowledge was thoroughly scientific, as can be seen from the *Notes on*

Virginia. While he was ambassador to France Jefferson was looked upon as an authority on American botany and was continually having to answer the questions of French scientists and garden-lovers.

Sometimes his eagerness to praise American plants made difficulties for him. Once he described with such vividness the sweet richness of a certain soft-shelled nut that grew in the west of his country, that his French friends begged him to get them some. So back went a letter to a friend in Virginia asking him to send two or three hundred "paccan" nuts, packed in sand against injury. The friend was not certain which nut Jefferson meant, and so there was more correspondence, and a whole year passed before Jefferson's French friends could gratify their appetite for the pecan.

When Jefferson returned to America, he saw to it that his French friends continued to receive American plants, sending them himself. For twenty-three years the superintendent of the Paris Garden of Plants regularly sent Jefferson boxes of seeds of plants that did not grow in the United States. Just as regularly Jefferson sent these to the public and private gardens of the various States.

Many of Jefferson's letters are about flowers, for his interest in them was well known to his friends. Thus, for instance, we have him writing to Madison asking him please to bring some seeds of the Kentucky coffee tree, as another good friend wanted them. On the excursions Madison and Jefferson took together when the latter was Secretary of State, they would take as much interest in viewing and discussing plants as they did in monuments and battlefields. Once they made a find which Jefferson described to his son-in-law in a letter. It was a kind of azalea, but very different, with large pink clusters of flowers, more thickly set on branches of a deeper red and high pink, very fragrant. This plant was not classified scientifically until some twelve years later.

So it is no wonder that Monticello was beautifully ornamented with shrubs and flowers. While Jefferson was still President, his overseer used to send cartloads of fruit, vegetables, and poultry to Washington, and Jefferson would send the cart back loaded with shrubbery from a nursery in Washington. The result of this intense care was that Jefferson personally knew almost every tree on his estate. After some absence from home he could tell where one was missing. In the tract about the house he enclosed three hundred acres from which he never let a tree be cut down alive.

The garden that Jefferson retired to cultivate was not simply one of fruits and flowers. Nature, as he said, had rendered science his "supreme delight," and science is the fruit of the garden of the mind. The thirst for scientific knowledge which had been aroused in the boy Jefferson by Professor Small had not been quenched in these fifty years. The scientific adventure had not lost its thrill.

In fifty years of reading Jefferson had acquired a more or less scholarly knowledge of physics, mechanics, aeronautics (balloons), engineering, surveying, mathematics, astronomy, meteorology (climate and weather), geology, zoology, entomology (insect life), surgical anatomy, paleontology (fossil remains), and economics. His knowledge was too wide and varied for him to be a real authority in any of these sciences, with the possible exception of botany. But in all of them his point of view was soundly scientific.

Of course, in the eighteenth century it was vastly easier than it is today to read all the important works of science, since it was in the nineteenth century that the body of science had its greatest growth. But Jefferson also tried to *be* the scientist. He was the only American of his day to be elected a foreign member of the Institute of France.

The *Notes on Virginia* was for many years a popular handbook on geography and natural science. So much so that it is the fault of Jefferson's book that even today the American wapiti is mistakenly called an elk. Jefferson and Agassiz are the two men who gave nature study its real start in America, and Jefferson has been referred to as the "great patriarch of American natural science."

Still another science in which Jefferson attempted to make some practical contribution to knowledge was what we now call anthropology, the science of primitive man. For thirty years Jefferson had been collecting vocabularies of American Indian languages. Some of these dialects were all but extinct, and others were being lost by mingling with those of other tribes. When Jefferson was about to leave the Presidency, he had amassed those of about fifty tribes. The manuscripts of these Indian dictionaries he packed in a trunk and sent on to Monticello from Washington by water. But the trunk was noticed by some thieves who discovered that it belonged to the President. Thinking that it must surely contain valuables or gold, they broke into it and found—papers written in some incomprehensible language. Thereupon they threw the papers overboard, and the James River swallowed up thirty years of work and a valuable contribution to the science of primitive man.

The study that gave Jefferson the keenest sense of mental satisfaction was mathematics; and he was forever figuring and computing. He could find latitude and longitude as well as any sea captain, and in 1778 he predicted an eclipse with great exactness. He used to amuse himself by sitting atop his own mountain and measuring the height of the ranges all about him. For these purposes he owned a complete surveying outfit, as well as astronomical instruments.

All in all, there was not a single field of serious study into which he had not delved, of which he could not talk with intelligence, and on which he did not have an opinion. Even in spelling, for instance, he advocated dropping the *u* from words like "labour" and "honour," and this we have since done. Whenever he met a new acquaintance, he made that man talk "shop," his *own* "shop," whether he was a carpenter or an astronomer.

In short, Jefferson was the sort of person to whom his friends and neighbors would send any new and interesting information they might pick up, and to whom people would in turn go for information. Now in his retirement, the country began to think and speak of him as the "Sage of Monticello." The circle of friends and acquaintances who had scientific and political questions to ask him seemed to grow larger every day. Was there anyone left in the land who did not write to Jefferson in search of information, as they might have thumbed through an encyclopedia?

More and more of the time that Jefferson had hoped to spend in the cultivation of his various gardens went to the writing of answers to inquisitive admirers. He had always been a great letter-writer. The organization of the Democratic Republican party had been accomplished by this method; whenever he was away from home he had deluged his children with educational advice by this means. Some years he had written as many as fifteen hundred letters, all in his own clear and legible hand, with a quill pen that he sharpened himself. Ever since he had broken his right wrist in France, he had used either hand for writing, but he would now have needed six or eight hands, like some Indian idol, to keep the time spent in writing letters within decent limits.

This work was doubled when he made copies of his letters, as he often did when they dealt with important matters. He had finally overcome this difficulty by using a polygraph. This was a device in which two pens were so connected that when you wrote with one the other made a perfect copy at the same time.

John Adams was perhaps the one correspondent to whom he did not begrudge this slavery to the pen.

Ever since March 4, 1801, when Adams had left the White House in a huff after appointing the "midnight judges," the two men had not spoken or written to each other. This coolness lasted for more than ten years. Gradually, however, these two patriots began to find themselves almost the last survivors of the signers of the Declaration. As they grew older, too, memories of those heroic days began to occupy more of their thoughts. Then one day Jefferson in Monticello heard from a mutual friend that Adams had said at his home in Braintree, Massachusetts: "I always loved Jefferson and still love him." This was enough; the two old comrades were really hungry for each other; and in 1812 began a correspondence that lasted to their death.

Such letters as they wrote! They discussed everything without reserve. What did Jefferson think of the hereafter? Would Adams live his life over again if he had the chance? Did Jefferson remember that time at the Continental Congress . . . ? Wasn't it in London that Adams had said . . . ? And so on, for more than ten years.

Adams, who had more free time, sometimes wrote two or three letters to Jefferson's one. This Jefferson explains in a letter in which he envies Adams the time he has for reading. He himself could only read at night, by candlelight, and then only by stealing long hours from his sleep; for from sunrise to one or two o'clock, and often from dinner to dark, he was drudging away at his writing table. "And all this to answer letters in which neither interest nor inclination on my part enters, and often from persons whose names I have never heard. Yet, writing civilly, it is hard to refuse them civil answers. This is the burden of my life."

Here he was wrong; this was only half the burden of his life. To cultivate one's garden, the first requirement is privacy, but how was Jefferson to know that, in retiring from Washington, he was stepping out of almost no privacy to even less? There was no one to tell him that Monticello would become a public place of pilgrimage.

Visitors, visitors, visitors. Did a distinguished foreigner arrive at these shores? Of course, he had to visit Jefferson at Monticello. How else could he write a complete book of his travels? Did a leading Democrat from Vermont happen to find himself in Virginia? Of course, he had to consult the oracle of his party. How else could he quote the Sage's exact words when he next spoke in the Vermont legislature? Artists came to paint his picture, journalists to interview him, historians to find out the facts, scientists and politicians to enlist his support, tourists and sightseers to gape at him, acquaintances to greet him, strangers to make his acquaintance.

Some came from affection and respect, some to give or receive advice, some from curiosity. Many of the guests were neither invited nor bore letters of introduction. They were merely people who wanted to be able to tell their neighbors or their children or their grandchildren that they had spoken to the great man. Having heard stories of his punctuality they would plant themselves in the corridor between his study and the dining room and, watch in hand, wait for him to come through. They hunted him out on his walks and rides. If he sat in the shade of his portico, parties of men and women would come up and stare at him as though he were a lion in a cage. One woman punched a hole in a windowpane with her parasol in order to get a better view of him.

There were no taverns near by, and so visitors who had come all the way out to Monticello, invited or not, expected to be put up by Jefferson. They came with carriages, horses, and servants. One friend from abroad arrived with a family of six and stayed ten months.

Of the thirty-six stalls in the Monticello stables, only ten were occupied by Jefferson's horses, but the others were always filled to overflowing. Bacon, the overseer, often sent a wagon-load of hay up to the stable, only to find the very next morning that there was not enough left to make a hen's nest. In desperation he told the servants to put the visitors' horses on a half-allowance of hay, but Jefferson got wind of this and counter-manded the order.

No inn in that part of the country had so much company. A fine beef would be eaten up in a day or two, and all the produce of the farm was not sufficient to entertain the hordes of strangers. Martha, who had charge of accommodating visitors, once had to find beds and meals for fifty guests in one night.

Not that Jefferson disliked seeing new faces, making new friends, and entertaining on a grand scale. He really liked it very much, but one of the worst results of this swollen stream of outsiders was that it kept friends and neighbors from coming. Jefferson himself, in the pleasant months of the year, was forced to flee ninety miles away to Poplar Forest, the estate left him by his wife.

Another evil result was, of course, the expense. "If I live long enough," Jefferson ruefully said, "I will beggar my family." For the estate that his entertainment was slowly devouring was his only source of income. It was a large estate, and Jefferson was proud and happy to be a farmer, but it must be admitted that he was not altogether a successful one.

In the first place Jefferson had had very little opportunity for being a practical farmer. As a student, as a lawyer and statesman, he had had to put everything into the hands of his overseer. While he was in France his farms had been taken care of by William Bacon, the son of an old schoolmate of his. When Jefferson became President, this job was taken over by William's young brother Edmund Bacon. Edmund Bacon remained Jefferson's overseer for twenty years.

It was not until he was President that Jefferson could take any uninterrupted concern in the details of running his plantation. His vacations at Monticello were supplemented by long letters to Bacon from Washington. From then on Jefferson became his own chief overseer. But he always remained a "book" farmer. That is, the things that actually interested him were the things that would advance the progress of agriculture in general rather than the things that would save him money personally.

This had been the interest behind his efforts to introduce Italian rice, French olives, and Spanish cork into his country. So also, he and Madison were the first to import full-blooded Merino sheep for improving the native wool. Of course, he distributed the lambs among his neighbors. He did the same with broad-tailed sheep from Barbary.

No sooner did he hear of an improvement in farm machinery than he had to have one. He had a corn-cob crusher, a sheller, and a drilling machine. His was the first threshing-machine from Scotland, and the first thing he did with it was to make an improvement of his own. All the planters round about, when they saw how useful this invention was, followed his example. Tinkering with new machinery must have been more fascinating to him than using it. For making an improvement in the plow while in France, he had been awarded a gold medal.

When the planters of Albemarle decided they needed a flour mill, they naturally thought that Jefferson should be the one to construct it. Since it would be a real benefit to the community Jefferson was nothing loath. So, at a great expenditure of money, the dam was built and the mill erected. It had not been grinding flour for very long when a big freshet came along and swept the dam away. Jefferson calmly built another.

More fortunate was the nailery that Jefferson established on his plantation. Ten boys, under the supervision of a blacksmith, forged nails at two fires. Monroe was among those neighbors who bought some of these nails for building houses. There were also three spinning machines for making all the servants' clothes on the plantation and some of the family's. A plantation was something more than a farm.

Jefferson's land consisted of ten thousand acres, but most of it was on uneven ground and hard to work. It was divided into four plantations—Tufton, Lego, Shadwell, and Pantops —each with a white overseer and a separate Negro quarter. The Monticello overseer was a Negro.

Every plantation was a self-sustaining community. Underneath the big house at Monticello, and the terraces around it, were the cisterns, ice houses, wine-cellars, and kitchen. At one time Jefferson also owned forty beehives.

The stables held mostly bay horses, for that was the color Jefferson preferred in his mounts. All his horses were broken in for both saddle and carriage use, and one of Jefferson's first tasks as ex-President was the making of a model of a carriage. All the woodwork, blacksmithing, and painting for it were done on the plantation.

What is it one sees first when one thinks of a Southern colonial home? Piazzas with tall columns before them. These classical Roman porticoes owed much of their popularity to Jefferson's influence on American architecture. It was Jefferson's enthusiasm for the Roman style that helped make the classical revival so powerful a movement here and dotted the country with so many private and public buildings of classical form.

In America architecture had not been considered a regular profession, but the sort of thing an educated gentlemen might learn, along with playing the flute and writing sonnets. But Jefferson went into the designing of buildings with such passion, making of it a lifelong study, that it may be considered one of his many professions.

One of the attractions that architecture first had on Jefferson's mind lay in the fact that it was, among other things, a mathematical science. It combined in one fascinating whole the two different matters of taste and formulas. Jefferson did not make any great novel departures in this art. Nor did he experiment with other forms than the classical Roman. But he was very ingenious in adapting to his own needs the ideas he borrowed from antiquity. Though he had never received any regular training, his drawings were always beautifully clear.

In building Monticello, as part of the plantation idea, he had to have slaves on his own estate trained as bricklayers, stone-cutters, carpenters, cabinet-makers, and iron-workers. Jefferson probably did not regret the time this took, for Monticello was a plaything that in his heart of hearts he never wanted to see really finished. "And so I hope it will remain during all my life," he said, "as architecture is my delight, and putting up and pulling down one of my favorite amusements." So Monticello was thirty-five years in the building.

He had come back from France determined to put a dome on his home as well as several other alterations. But as Secretary of State he could only spend one month out of the year at Monticello and this had to be given over to farming matters and repairs. It was only as President, with longer vacations, that he was finally able to finish the rebuilding of what he hoped to make the most beautiful home in Virginia, that State of beautiful homes.

From the point of view of an architect solving problems Monticello is a splendid achievement for two reasons. With one stroke Jefferson solved both problems. First, he united all the outbuildings to the "big house" in such a way that they make up a single symmetrical whole. Secondly, he built *for* the top of a mountain; Monticello is a mountain house—to build it anywhere else you would have to tear up the countryside.

Monticello is laid out in the shape of the capital letter E (see the endpapers at the front or back of the book): The main building (the small tongue of the E) is connected by underground passages to the slave quarters on the lower bar of the E, and to the row of outhouses on the upper bar. Embraced between these bars lies the lawn, which is really the flattened mountain top. The slave quarters are cut into the slope of the hill, and the lawn behind them comes almost up to their roofs. But the servants had plenty of light and air through the doors and windows that face away from the E. They, too, had a portico with brick columns before their doors, giving them shade in summer. At the lower outside corner of the E, is the "honeymoon lodge," to which Jefferson brought his bride. The little building opposite was his law office.

The outbuildings included the carriage house, ice house, toolhouse, and workshop, where Jefferson could often be found discussing the making of novel contrivances with his Negro carpenter Heming. For the lord of this aristocratic manor was something of a Connecticut Yankee when it came to making ingenious devices. He was forever designing little household gadgets and instructing a skilled Negro workman in their making.

On the same side as the servants' colonnade was a smoke-house and the summer kitchen. In winter the cooking was done in the basement of the big house.

If you came into the house by the east or "private" portico, you entered the hall. This room was two stories high, with a gallery running round it. The first thing to catch your attention would be two busts facing each other from opposite walls, and both done by the artist Ceracchi. One was of Jefferson and the other of Hamilton!

Also in this hall there hung a curious collection of Indian relics, many of them found by Lewis and Clark on their expedition. There were bows, arrows, poisoned lances, stone pipes of peace, wampum belts, beaded moccasins, dressed buffalo hides with maps and pictures drawn on them by Indians. Considering that other walls held the head and horns of an elk, a deer, and a buffalo, and the skeleton head of the extinct mastodon, this great room must have given the impression of a museum of natural history.

As you entered the hall, there was, facing you in the opposite wall, a long double glass door. Pull one panel of this door and the other also swings open (a little contrivance of Mr. Jefferson's that is now sometimes used in trolley cars). You are now in the drawing room, which is also two stories high, and is under the part of the roof with the dome on it. The drawing room was also the picture gallery of Monticello. Jefferson had brought from Europe one of the best private art collections in America. Besides copies of famous paintings, there were placed all along the walls the busts of men important in American history—the navigators, Columbus, Amerigo Vespucci, and Magellan; Madison in the plain Quakerish dress of his youth; Lafayette in his revolutionary uniform; Franklin and Washington.

Still walking straight forward, you came out on the west veranda, the "stately" portico. All the other main rooms had been in the wings to either side of you as you passed through the house: the dining room, the tea room, Jefferson's bedroom and library, Martha Randolph's room, and the two guest rooms, which were called Mr. Madison's and Mr. Monroe's rooms because they were reserved for these friends when they came to the house.

The second stories of the two wings were connected together by the galleries running across the hall. On this second floor were more bedrooms and nurseries.

To get up to the second floor there were narrow stairways on each side of the house, no grand curving balustrade from the hall or drawing room. Just like a philosopher, people used to say laughingly: Jefferson builds himself a grand home and only remembers to put in stairs for the second floor at the last minute, and has to content himself with furtive little ship's companionways! As a matter of fact Jefferson did not consider grand staircases things of beauty. As ornaments they took up too much room, and they took away half the privacy of the interior. In others of his buildings he has the same sort of stairways.

Directly under the new dome Jefferson had built a billiard room with a spherical ceiling. Before he was finished with it, however, what does the State of Virginia do but pass a prohibition law against all billiard playing! So there was the billiard room like the empty skull of the house until Jefferson found some other use for it.

Jefferson had landed from France with eighty-six large cartons of household furnishings for Monticello, including forty-four gold chairs and six gold sofas, the drawing-room mirrors, and the lamp to be hung in the hall. But all the little things that made his home one of the most comfortable in America, Jefferson had thought up on the spot. On the inside of each door he put automatic catches that held it in place when it was swung open. The sides of the fireplace in the dining room opened out to reveal two tiny dumbwaiters by which bottles could travel one at a time to and from the wine-cellar directly beneath.

Jefferson would have been an enthusiast for all the modern conveniences. But he had the advantage of most people of his time, because he was able to invent his own. He had a chaise-longue built in which he could lie or sit at any angle he wished; for a person who spends as many hours as he did in reading, writing, or drawing must change his position frequently to keep his body from becoming tired. The leg rest of this chaise-longue was detachable; and the seat itself was a swivel-chair, one of his little inventions that the Federalists sneeringly called, "Mr. Jefferson's whirligig." He had a table that fitted nicely over his legs as he sat in this chair. The top of the table spun around on a pivot so that he did not have to reach over it for anything. When Mrs. Franklin D. Roosevelt, on a visit to Monticello, saw the three-piece combination couch, chair, and table, she thought it so ingenious that she had it copied and installed in the White House for her husband's use.

Jefferson built still another table with hollow legs that telescoped, so that he could work at it sitting or standing. He could adjust two of the legs shorter than the others, thus tilting the table top like a drawing board. He had a passion for things that folded up compactly when not in use. In later years he always took with him when he went out a camp-stool made of three pieces of wood and a piece of cloth that folded up into a neat little bundle.

In all the many rooms of Monticello there was not a single bedstead. In each bedroom there was a sleeping alcove with iron hooks sunk in the wall. From these hooks could be slung a bedspring made of laced cord, on which were laid mattress and sheets. So the problem of carrying bedsteads down those narrow stairs never had to arise. Thus every guest could close the curtains of his alcove, and have a decent sitting room or study with no bed in sight.

Jefferson's own bed was snugly set in a little alcove between his bedroom and his study. Thus he had air on both sides; and he was one man who could answer the question, "On which side did you get up this morning?" by saying, "On the bedroom side," or, "On the study side."

Living at Monticello were Louis Leschot, a Swiss clockmaker, and his wife. It was he who installed the eight-day clock under the east portico. This clock had one face in the hall and another outside. For weights it had cannonballs which marked the day of the week as they slowly descended. To wind it Jefferson must of course have a ladder that could fold up into a small, slender pole when not wanted. In the ceiling of this same veranda was a compass connected up with a weathervane on the roof, so that he could tell the direction of the wind without leaving his seat.

Jefferson had also had a hand in the ornamenting of his home. The spread-eagle decoration for the ceiling of the hall, from which hung the lamp, was of his own design, as was also the pedestal on which the artist Ceracchi had placed Jefferson's bust. This pedestal made use of the leaf, stalk, and bud of the tobacco plant as decorative elements, just as the Greeks had used acanthus leaves, and the Egyptians lotus blossoms.

The chief impression one gets from standing anywhere in Monticello is of light. Architects now marvel at the ingenuity by which Jefferson achieved this effect of seeming to be in a glass house. Everywhere were great windows and skylights. From all sides, on the porches or inside the house, there was a magnificent view of the countryside, the red hills of Albemarle, the valleys below, and the gardens around the house.

Yet with all this exposure went the last degree of privacy. In the first place Monticello was on a hilltop. Blinds could shut in every room, and every room was built to be soundproof and, as it were, detachable from the rest of the house.

Jefferson's success as designer of the Capitol at Richmond and as architect of his own home brought him much fame in his State. Friends and neighbors frequently asked him for designs or assistance in the building of their homes. His skill may therefore still be seen in several of the beautiful "colonial" mansions of Virginia. Lower Brandon, the home of the Harrisons on the James River, is a fine example among these. But, next to Monticello, Jefferson's greatest achievement as an architect—and otherwise—is the University of Virginia.

XIX

HE STILL LIVES

SOON after Jefferson's retirement from Washington some young men came to seek his advice about their studies. They took lodgings in Charlottesville and used Jefferson's fine library, reading under his direction. In supervising the course of their reading Jefferson's aim was, he said, to keep their attention fixed on the main object of all science—the freedom and happiness of man.

As Jefferson discussed their problems with his young disciples, there grew sharper and more insistent in his mind a pet scheme that he had cherished for many years. Even as a young Virginian lawmaker he had fought vigorously for a well-rounded plan of free public education, embracing everything from grade school to university. Despite Madison's able help, these plans had not made much headway against the conservative leaders of the State. Now Jefferson fastened on the university part of the plan as something he *must* see accomplished. Old as he was, he was prepared to fight for years; he would yet see Virginia with the sort of university she should have.

It never failed; whenever Jefferson went into a battle of this sort he always found a passionate, capable lieutenant to back him up. This time his young champion was Joseph Carrington Cabell who, after several years' sojourn in Europe for his health, had come back to America in 1806, with bad lungs and a letter of introduction to President Jefferson. Jefferson was at once charmed by the young man and struck with his brilliance. He offered Cabell his choice of diplomatic posts, but Cabell had made up his mind to stay in America, and he refused them.

Cabell had always been interested in education, and during his search for health in Europe he had made a fairly close study of the different methods practiced there and had attended most of the leading schools. One of the services he wished to do his old alma mater, William and Mary, was to install a natural history museum there. Since he knew Jefferson's weakness for natural history museums, and that Jefferson was also a graduate of William and Mary, he wrote the President about his project.

Jefferson had given up all hope of William and Mary. For some time now the old college had been going into a decline. With the charter she has, Jefferson told Cabell, it's a waste of time to worry about her. We must start fresh. What you should do, he urged Cabell, is to enter the State legislature and help pass laws that will give our children primary schools and our young men a worthy university.

Cabell did just that. He ran for the House of Delegates and was elected. In 1810 he ran for the State Senate, was elected, and stayed there nineteen years. He refused appointments to Madison's and to Monroe's Cabinet, preferring to stay in Virginia where he could keep an eye upon what he considered his trust—the educational laws of his State.

In waging his grand fight for what he called "the holy cause of the University," Cabell discovered many enemies. First and most important was the indifference of the people, which is one of the heaviest burdens that a believer in democracy must learn to bear and understand. Then there was the opposition of William and Mary, loath to see another university in the State. Finally there was the intolerance of many to the idea of an "infidel college," for Jefferson's unconcealed purpose was the creation of a non-sectarian school.

As the years went by seemingly without result, Jefferson finally seized an opportunity to found the sort of university he wanted even without the help of the State. One morning in 1814 as he was cantering down a hillside, he passed a little academy not far from his home. This academy was in difficulties and the board of directors happened to be sitting to solve its problems when Jefferson rode by. The president of the board was Peter Carr, Jefferson's nephew and the son of Dabney Carr, Jefferson's old friend. "Let's call in Mr. Jefferson," said Carr; "he's always been interested in education."

Jefferson alighted from his horse; he was glad to be of help; what seemed to be the trouble? After Jefferson had heard their explanations and had told them his theories of education, he was struck by a new idea. Why not reorganize this little academy into the university he dreamed of?

Not long after, Jefferson had convinced the board of the wisdom of such a plan, and they all set about founding Central College. Jefferson himself, burdened as he was by debts, contributed a thousand dollars. Three years later Central College was well on its way to being finished.

Then at last, Cabell and his friends, by a great effort, pushed through a bill for the founding of a State university. Jefferson immediately offered the partly completed Central College to the State. Not only would this save the State money but it would keep the State college where Jefferson wanted it—at his own doorstep.

Long ago, as Secretary of State he had been approached by the faculty of the University of Geneva in Switzerland. The faculty was dissatisfied with conditions in Geneva and suggested that it might like to come over to America as a body. Jefferson was tremendously excited over the prospect of transplanting an entire university. Nothing came of it, but one of the reasons Jefferson had pushed the idea so hard was that he could thus have ready to hand a group of scientists in whose congenial company he could spend his time.

Jefferson was prepared for any argument against accepting his offer of Central College. The State university must not slip out of Albemarle County! He had all the reasons for this location down on cards that he could produce at a moment's notice. Did anyone dare say that other counties were more healthful than Albemarle? Out would come a card with the names of all the men in the neighborhood over eighty years of age. But a university supported by the State should be centrally located? Indeed it should. Here was a card cut in the shape of the State of Virginia. The dot here represented the proposed site of the school. Place a pencil point under this dot, and twirl the card. It does not fall off, because this is the exact center of the State. But a third gentleman might argue that a site might be geographically central without being the center of population. Jefferson had a third piece of board with the population of every district in Virginia written into it. Again Albemarle was central!

Jefferson's friends may have smiled at the old man's wiles, but they knew he was right and they worked to get him his way. Who else would supervise the fledgling college with such loving care? Who else would take so many pains and who deserved greater credit for the success of the bill? This seventy-four-year-old man had fought forty years for this university, and now that it existed it should be his to run. So the State accepted Jefferson's offer, and at the first meeting of the Board of Visitors, Madison got up and said: "This is Mr. Jefferson's scheme. The responsibility is his, and it is but fair that he should carry it out in his own way." All agreed.

So, though Jefferson never lived to see popular education as well grounded in Virginia as it was in Northern States, he did finally have his university. At least he had a university to build, for the whole fight was not yet over. For the next nine years the old man and the younger consumptive one in the Senate, Joseph Cabell, would have to struggle against the enemies of their infant college.

One of the men with whom Jefferson had been in constant correspondence about his university and who had given him some ideas for running it was Thomas Cooper, a son-in-law of Dr. Joseph Priestley. Dr. Cooper was democratic in politics, and for a rather innocent paragraph in the papers about President Adams had been sentenced to six months' imprisonment and a four-hundred-dollar fine. He was well versed in the sciences of chemistry, physics, and physiology, and was in addition accomplished in the law, on which he had written some books.

Cooper was therefore from every point of view the sort of man Jefferson admired, and so Jefferson offered him the combined professorships of chemistry and law. But Cooper had also brought the wrath of the clergy down on his head by publishing and editing his father-in-law Priestley's unpopular works on religion. When the news of Cooper's appointment came out, such a clamor was raised by influential Virginians that the very existence of the university seemed threatened.

Rather than make trouble, Cooper sent in his resignation, which was accepted by the Board of Visitors. Jefferson was bitter. Was this man's Unitarianism something for which he should be burned, he asked. He had counted on Cooper as the cornerstone of his faculty, and his going was an irreparable loss.

Cooper went instead to the University of South Carolina. And Jefferson promptly sent Francis Eppes, Maria's son, there. The University of Virginia was not yet ready for students.

We have many founders of universities, but by them we usually mean men who have donated sums of money for other men to build with. Jefferson was a true founder, not only in fathering the whole idea, but in having a hand in every detail of its planning and building.

First Jefferson was concerned with the physical appearance of the University. This was to be no rude pile or haphazard jumble of buildings. This school was to have a sound mind in a healthy body. It was to delight the eye as well as stimulate the intellect. Thus would the university gain prestige, attract famous teachers from all over the world, and give the students real examples of beautiful classical art. So Jefferson turned again to Palladio, his architectural Bible. He had five editions of Palladio in his library, three translations in English and two in French.

Two tracts of land were bought, one containing a lot of fine timber and stone that could be used in the construction of the university. Then Jefferson set to work with his overseer Bacon and another helper to mark out the foundation. Jefferson would study the ground and then drive into the earth a peg cut from a shingle. To this peg was tied a ball of twine which Bacon unwound as he went this way or that, following Jefferson's directions. Jefferson would measure off the distance and drive in another peg.

Finally the ground was ready for the digging of the foundations. President Monroe himself laid the cornerstone when the time came. While the building progressed, Jefferson came down nearly every day to supervise the work. He came on horseback over rough and mountainous roads early in the morning. He would sit on the little three-legged camp-stool he had invented and watch the masons and carpenters making his last dream come true. If the weather was too stormy for the old man to ride in, he would watch the progress of the work five miles away through a telescope.

For Jefferson was the contractor of the enterprise as well as the architect. He had estimated the amount of bricks and timber needed; he had himself explained to the workmen precisely how he wanted each little job done; he had even trained some of the laborers and designed some of their tools for them. He had all the wood for the interiors weathered for three years before allowing it to be used. He had sent to Philadelphia for his hasps, hinges, and locks; to Staunton for the best roofers in Virginia; and from Italy he had imported two marble workers.

The rest of the time Jefferson pored over his designs, read in Palladio's book, corresponded with other architects. His granddaughter Cornelia showed considerable skill in draftsmanship, and he used her talent a great deal.

Jefferson's plan was that the university should be, not a single building, but a sort of well-thought-out academic village. There was to be a small and separate lodge for each professor with one or two large halls below for his class and two chambers above for his living quarters. Connecting these lodges would be one-story dormitories where the students were to have their rooms. A covered way made it possible for students to go from one school to the next in any weather without getting wet. Of course, the students of any particular professor were to have those dormitories nearest his lodge. Jefferson remembered how much his personal contact with Professor Small had meant to him in his own college days.

There were to be ten of these lodges, ranged, with their accompanying dormitories, on two facing sides of the quadrangle. It can at once be seen that this arrangement resembles the one at Monticello. There, too, the servants' quarters and outhouses flank the two sides of a great lawn. But the lodges and dormitories faced inward on the quadrangle and not outward. At the head or northern end of the quadrangle was the Rotunda, in which was housed the library. The Rotunda was to be for the campus what "the big house" was to Monticello.

Each professor's lodge had a backyard which ended with another row of buildings parallel to the dormitories. These extra two rows were called the Ranges; they also were one-story dormitories for students. The doors of the Ranges faced away from the quadrangle and not toward the backyards, so that the professors' gardens gave them real privacy. The Ranges, too, had colonnades, but of brick arches instead of stone pillars. Interspersed among the dormitories of the Range were "hotels," where the boys were to eat.

The Rotunda was modeled on the Roman Pantheon, the ancient Temple of All the Gods. Each of the ten lodges, too, was adapted from some different famous building of ancient times—the Theater of Marcellus, the Baths of the Emperor Diocletian, the Temple of Fortune, and so on. Studying Greek and Latin, ancient history, and classic art inside such buildings might make what the students read more alive to them.

A taste in architecture runs to expense, and again and again in the years after 1817 the work had to stop for lack of money. Then Jefferson would urge Cabell to push the legislature into providing some, and Cabell would beg the "Grand Sachem," as he always called Jefferson, to use his influence by writing to important people. But this was no longer an easy task for the man who had written so many letters all his life. His stiff right wrist was now, in his old age, beginning to cause him much pain. He told Cabell that now "a letter of a page or two costs me a day of labor and of painful labor."

Other difficulties cropped up. The Italian marble workers, for instance, found that Virginia stone could not be used as had been hoped, because it crumbled away rapidly, and so Italian marble had to be imported for the pillars. After the pavilions were up, one of the professors said that Jefferson should have consulted Martha about interior conveniences, for there were no closets in the rooms.

Meanwhile, Jefferson was expending just as much energy and care over the *true* interior furnishings of his university as he had over its physical appearance. He wanted as teachers men who were not only eminent in their own fields but who were educated in the sciences generally. He wanted the professors to enjoy each other's company and to stimulate each other's work. After having his offers of appointment to two particular posts turned down by American scholars he sent a friend to find professors from among the great universities of England. Naturally the older and established men would not come, but young and brilliant men might be induced to take a chance in America.

There were to be many novel features in the University of Virginia. For one thing there was to be no president. Every year the professors were to elect one of their own number to act as chairman. The professors were also to remain free to choose their own textbooks. Their lodges were assigned to them by drawing lots.

Though Jefferson had planned on ten schools or faculties, there was money enough for only seven when the university formally opened in March 1825. These seven independent schools taught Ancient Languages, Modern Languages, Mathematics, Natural Philosophy (physics), Moral Philosophy, Chemistry, and Medicine. An eighth school, that of Law, was opened the next year. Only two degrees were to be granted: "Graduate" to any student who completed the course in any one school, and "Doctor" to a graduate of more than one school who also showed that he would continue his studies and would probably do something for science. The 116 students with whom the University opened were free to enter any of the schools they wished, and to take any of the courses they were prepared for. This is the elective system that Jefferson had

observed in Europe but which was a new idea in the United
States.

One of Jefferson's novelties that aroused the most ill-feeling
was the fact that the University was not under the guidance of
any particular church. It was non-sectarian. Every college in
those days was expected to have a clergyman at its head. At the
University of Virginia clergymen of different denominations
were asked to preach each Sunday, but the students were not
forced to attend chapel if they did not wish.

Some people reasoned that, if Jefferson's college was not to
teach religion, then it must be going to teach irreligion. Why
else this unusual emphasis on science? Jefferson was only
building a horrid trap in which he undoubtedly hoped to
destroy his students' religious beliefs! When one clergyman
heard that a favorite pupil of his was being sent there, he exclaimed to the boy's father: "Much as I love your son, I would
rather, this day, follow him to his grave than see him enter
the University!"

Another typical Jeffersonian idea was student self-government. He felt that minor offenses at least should be left to a
board of trustworthy students to punish. He also advocated
the honor system in examinations, but this plan did not go
into effect until sixteen years after his death. An incident
very shortly after the opening of the University almost brought
all such liberal ideas to grief.

Fourteen students, who had taken a little more wine than
they should, thought it would be fun to put on masks and make
an uproar on the quadrangle. Two professors came out and
tried to quell the riot only to be driven back, first by insults
and then by brickbats. The next day the faculty insisted that
it was the students' duty to tell who the fourteen in masks had
been, whereupon fifty more students joined the rioters and

pledged themselves to resist the faculty to the bitter end. A meeting of the trustees of the University was being held at Monticello. Hearing of the disorders, the trustees came down in a body and called the students together in the Rotunda. First Jefferson got up to speak to them, but his emotions overcame him after a few words and he had to sit down. His whole belief in the honor system of student government depended on his faith in the honesty of students, and these events were terribly shocking to the old man.

Another of the trustees then gave them such a tongue-lashing for the way they were abusing Jefferson's faith that with one accord the fourteen guilty students stepped up and gave their names. Now Jefferson could not restrain himself; among the fourteen who had so carelessly almost destroyed the work of years was his own grandnephew!

Just as he had formerly known and spoken with every mason and carpenter on the University grounds, so now Jefferson tried to keep in touch with every professor and student. Members of the faculty were frequent guests at Monticello. Once a week he invited students to his house in groups of four or five. Before and after dinner he spoke with each boy individually, but he let them dine by themselves. At this time his hearing was becoming difficult so that he could not understand very well when more than one person was speaking at once. So as not to disturb the boys' fun he therefore sat by himself in a little recess near the dining room.

Jefferson had by no means stopped designing things for the University. Over eighty, he drew up plans for an astronomical observatory and for an anatomy laboratory, though money was lacking to build them. For the University was his plaything, now that Monticello was so long finished, and he felt that it was a much nobler plaything than his own private home.

Why was the University a nobler creation than Monticello?
Not merely because it was made for others instead of for
himself, not only because it served his passion for education,
which was greater than his passion for beauty; but because in
the University he had created something that lived. No matter how many centuries Monticello stood, people would always
regard it with a backward-looking eye; no matter who inhabited it hereafter, it would always seem that its grandest period
must have been when its maker lived in it. Its greatest interest
would always be that of a monument, something grand and
beautiful, but dead as soon as Jefferson had died.

The University on the other hand had a *future,* and contemplation of the future had never failed to give Jefferson a
thrill. This thing that he had made would live its own life,
would *grow,* even after he was dead. The world might forget
the name of Thomas Jefferson, and yet he himself would be
alive in this child of his, shaping the minds of thousands of
young men of the future, some of them perhaps geniuses that
America would always be proud of.

That was why Jefferson had been so anxious that his University should not copy all the hoary customs of the older universities. He wanted it to be young, for unless it was young
to start with it would never grow. And that was why he had
insisted so much on the importance of science, for he knew
that science, too, was young, and that the future would belong
to it.

When Jefferson was dying, one of the few really deep satis-
factions of his life was the University of Virginia. If he could
have lived on, he would not have been disappointed. He
would have seen the young University of Michigan take over
the main ideas from his University, and then other young universities do the same, and then older universities become young

again by doing the same. He would have seen young men with
names like Edgar Allan Poe and Woodrow Wilson sleeping in
his dormitories and studying in his Rotunda.

It must not be thought that in the midst of all this building
and planning for the future Jefferson had forgotten the hopes
with which he had retired from the White House. He still
"cultivated his garden." The University itself was merely
the most splendid growth of that garden—a sort of sturdy oak
planted in the midst of homely vegetables and pretty flowers.
The prettiest of all the flowers were his grandchildren.

Jefferson adored his grandchildren and was adored by them.
Martha Jefferson Randolph had eleven children, six daughters
and five sons. The names of the boys show that Martha and
her husband always had Grandfather's pleasure in mind. They
were Thomas Jefferson Randolph, James Madison Randolph,
Benjamin Franklin Randolph, Meriwether Lewis Randolph,
and George Wythe Randolph. The girls were named Anne,
Ellen, Virginia, Cornelia, Mary, and Septimia.

When Grandfather came home to live for good, the children
formed the habit of following him all over the house and
garden. He supervised their games and invented new ones
for them and gave out the prizes to the winners. He asked them
questions on their schooling and answered theirs. As soon as
each child could read, he had begun to send it letters, and,
as soon as it could write, he expected letters from it. When
away, he was always sending them clippings and poems he
thought would interest them.

He liked to buy the children novels and to distribute them
in a manner all his own. He would show them the closed book
with a number of strings, like bookmarks, hanging out from
between the pages. Each of the grandchildren would draw out

a string, and the one who had picked the shortest would read
the book first. The next shortest string meant the second
chance to read, and so on. But the child that had pulled the
longest string and had to wait to the last was allowed to keep
the book for good.

Jefferson was forever giving the children presents as soon as
they were old enough to appreciate them. One granddaughter
remembered that it was he who had given her her first Bible,
her volume of Shakespeare, her first writing-table, later her
handsome writing-desk, her first Leghorn hat, her bridle and
saddle, her gold watch.

The oldest boy, Thomas Jefferson Randolph, went to school
in Charlottesville, and almost every Friday evening he brought
several schoolmates home with him to play. They often stayed
all night. Jefferson would also have over Francis Eppes, his
daughter Maria's only child, as often as the boy's father would
permit it. So there never was a lack of children at Monticello,
and the larger the troop of them that followed him about,
the better Jefferson seemed to like it.

The older Jefferson grew, the more of a miser he became
of his time. As if he had not accomplished enough for one
man, he wanted to squeeze the last drops of wisdom and activity out of the few years that remained to him. Once he said
to his daughter: "It is surprising how much you can do if
you are always up and doing." So he was always up and doing.

No matter what time he had gone to bed the night before,
he always rose with the sun. While the rest of the household
still slept, he wrote and read letters until breakfast, which he
took early. After breakfast he usually read for another half-
hour. Then he visited his garden and rode over the plantation
or, in later years, to the University. When he came back, he

either studied or amused himself at his work bench, where he always had some new model in progress. From one to three he was sure to be on horseback. In the evening he dined, and conversed with friends or played with the children. He went to his room at about nine, where he read for another hour or two before going to bed.

The twilight hour on winter evenings, when it was too dark to read and the candles had not yet been brought in, was the children's favorite time for playing with Grandfather. The quiet games were played then: "Cross Questions" and "I Love My Love with an A." Jefferson, always curious, might even learn some game that had not been played in his childhood. When the candles finally came, he took up a book, and the children, quiet as mice, would also read. These, of course, were the rare quiet days when there did not happen to be all sorts of distinguished visitors to see Grandfather, whom everybody was now calling the Sage of Monticello.

In the summertime, if visitors became too numerous, Jefferson would run away to his estate at Poplar Forest, taking along a couple of his granddaughters for company. He lifted the children into the seat of his carriage, tucked them in comfortably with one of his long capes, and drove away, stopping to picnic by some roadside spot on the light lunch he had put up himself. At Poplar Forest, Jefferson kept the miniature library that he had collected while in Washington. It contained the tiniest editions he could find of his favorite authors in English, Italian, French, Greek, and Latin.

Fortunate for Jefferson that he had the building of the University to take his mind off his big Southern household sometimes, for he would have gone distracted at the great burden of debt it was piling up on his shoulders. Little by little, pieces of his various estates began to slip away to pay these debts. He found that he was what is sometimes called "land poor." That is, he owned lots of land that was only making him poorer every year. His Embargo Act in 1808 had hit his own farms as badly as anyone else's, and the War of 1812 had made his crops of cotton and tobacco almost worthless, for they could not be sold.

During the War, the British had burned down the Library of Congress, and Jefferson saw a chance both to do his country a good turn and to satisfy his own creditors somewhat. He offered to sell his own library—one of the best and largest in the country, one that he had lovingly collected for fifty years— to the government. The government bought it at just about half the price he had paid for it. It was a gloomy day when Jefferson watched his Negro carpenter making many boxes and the overseer Bacon filling them with books while Ellen and Virginia and Cornelia helped. The boxes of books filled ten wagons and they made a curious caravan as they set out for Washington.

Jefferson could never have brought himself to do this if it had meant hundreds of empty shelves at Monticello. But some years before he had inherited George Wythe's library, almost as big as his own. Jefferson now moved this into Monticello, and, as for the empty shelves remaining over, why, he was very soon ordering things from the booksellers again. He wrote Adams at the time: "I cannot live without books."

All the money from the sale of his library went to pay debts. It did not pay all the debts but it helped considerably, and Jefferson was beginning to look up again from under his burden when another financial blow suddenly threatened to crush him. Former Governor Wilson Nicholas of Virginia, an old political friend, whose daughter Thomas Jefferson Randolph had married, went bankrupt. Jefferson had endorsed a note of his for $20,000, and now Jefferson was expected to pay this, too. It was the finishing touch to the ruin of Jefferson's fortune.

In desperation Jefferson tried to sell his estates, even in the end offering up Monticello itself. But he could find no rich buyer. Then he asked Cabell to see if the legislature would allow him to sell the estates by raffle or lottery. This permission was finally granted, but, when his friends throughout the United States heard that the Sage of Monticello was about to lose his home, they began to rally behind him in the newspapers. Subscriptions were at once taken up. New York City sent him $8500; $5000 came from Philadelphia, and $3000 from Baltimore. And this seemed but the beginning.

Jefferson was deeply touched. "No cent of this," he exulted, "is wrung from the taxpayer—it is the pure and unsolicited offering of love." It seemed to him, in this last year of his life, that all his financial difficulties would be solved. Martha and the grandchildren would still have Monticello to live in after he was gone.

These closing years were made happy by still another event. In 1824 Lafayette came back to visit America. His march through the cities was one triumph after another. "I hope we shall close his visit with something more solid for him than dinners and balls," said Jefferson, and it was he who proposed that Congress pay Lafayette part of the debt the country owed him but which he had never claimed. Congress did vote Lafayette $200,000 and a township of land.

Lafayette did not fail to visit Monticello. The two old friends had last seen each other thirty-six years ago at the dawn of the French Revolution. They had both been young men then, and it had been quite a different world from the one they lived in now. Lafayette was now sixty-seven and permanently lamed from his hardships in prison; Jefferson was eighty-one and almost on the threshold of death. But they had always written each other, and their friendship had not changed nor had their attitude toward the things they had done altered.

For it was no secret to Jefferson that he had not much longer to live. When Adams asked him in a letter whether he would live his life over again, he had answered that he would, that he thought his life had been worthwhile and happy, and that he was a natural optimist. Jefferson had never suffered from boredom because he had early learnt never to be without an interesting occupation. Though he had been sensitive to criticism, and had received plenty of it, he had learned to bear that, too, so that it had never made him give up his faith in free speech for all men.

He had had only one fear, Jefferson said, and that was that he might live too long, leading in his extreme dotage the life of a cabbage and boring others by telling the same old tale four times over. But now even that fear was gone, for Jefferson had discovered that he was afflicted by an ailment that would soon carry him off. The darling of his old age, the University, was not only finished but actually working; he felt he was ready to go.

One day, as Jefferson was walking off the veranda, a rotten step gave way under him and he fell. His left arm was broken, a serious thing for a man over eighty. For a long time the hand and fingers of his left arm were quite useless, and writing was now almost out of the question. The ailment he had been keeping from his family, which was dysentery complicated by other signs of old age, at last began to sap his great strength, making it difficult for him even to walk, except for a few steps in the garden. But he still insisted on riding.

A day without horseback exercise was for Jefferson like a day without sun. His long lean form on horseback had now for many years become one of the things that people in the neighborhood expected to see daily. He cut a curious figure, too.

Though a dandy in youth, Jefferson had grown more and more careless about clothing the older he grew. In Monticello he paid almost no attention to the fashions, considering himself old enough to wear what was most comfortable or what he liked best. When everyone wore short waistcoats, his was long. He still continued to wear a white cambric stock fastened with a buckle behind when the cravat had replaced it with every one else. The one change in fashion that he fastened on immediately was the pantaloon or long trousers, instead of knee-breeches. He considered it a real improvement in convenience and wished it had come in sooner. As a matter of fact, when riding he had always worn overalls over his own knee-breeches. Perhaps, too, he was glad to see knee-breeches go because they had become the mark of the aristocrat. The same reasons, too, made him cut off his pigtail when queues went out of style.

A visitor to Monticello after Jefferson's retirement from politics has left an amusing account of the ex-President's appearance on horseback. "I was well aware by the cut of his jib who it was. His costume was very singular—his coat was checkered gingham, manufactured in Virginia, I suppose. The buttons on it were of white metal, and nearly the size of a dollar. His pantaloons were of the same fabric. He was mounted on an elegant bay horse going at great speed, and he had no hat on, but a lady's parasol, stuck in his coat behind, spread its canopy over his head. This was Thomas Jefferson."

That "elegant bay horse" may have been old Eagle whom Jefferson rode to the last. Though grown old in years Eagle was still a spirited animal. Waiting for Jefferson to come out for his daily ride, Eagle would paw and stamp the ground before the door, but he would at once quiet down when his master appeared. His one serious fault had always been the suddenness with which he would turn when startled. No one could keep his seat when this happened, and Jefferson remembered occasions in his best riding days when he had been thrown by Eagle.

Just recently, with his left arm in a sling and his right hand without strength, Jefferson had been tumbled into a creek by Eagle. The water was fairly high, and he would surely have drowned had he not clung with one arm to the bridle and thus been dragged ashore by the frightened horse. Now Mrs. Randolph worried over her father when he went riding alone. "Do at least let Burwell ride with you," she begged. Burwell was one of the most trusted servants on the estate.

Jefferson would not hear of it. Since childhood he had always been at home in a saddle, and he liked to ride alone without having his thoughts interrupted by a companion. Rather than take a nursemaid with him, he would give up riding altogether if his family insisted. His family would not deprive him of his daily ride; so in his eighty-fourth year, up to three weeks before his final illness, Jefferson still rambled alone over the plantation on Eagle's back.

But the end was approaching fast, and Jefferson knew it. His last letter was to a committee declining their invitation to come to Washington as an honored guest in the festivities celebrating the fiftieth anniversary of the Day of Independence. He was too ill and feeble, he said.

He had already drawn up his will, leaving Monticello to

Martha. To all the children who had so far received none, he left gold watches, and to Thomas Jefferson Randolph, the oldest, he left his silver watch because it had a better movement than the gold. To James Madison he left his gold-headed walking stick. He gave their freedom to three of his slaves— Heming the carpenter, Burwell, and Fosset. He would have freed them all but they belonged to his creditors.

He had even written the epitaph to be carved on his tombstone. It is curious what this man, who had accomplished so much and who had held so many honors, omitted from the simple list of his life's achievements. His greatest pride is not in having been President of his country, but in having given it those things by which it would grow great and admirable. His Presidency was of the past, but these three things pointed into the future:

HERE WAS BURIED
THOMAS JEFFERSON
AUTHOR OF
THE DECLARATION OF AMERICAN INDEPENDENCE
OF THE STATUTE OF VIRGINIA FOR RELIGIOUS FREEDOM
AND FATHER OF THE UNIVERSITY OF VIRGINIA

The third of July 1826 found Jefferson in bed ill and dying. The problem troubling him was: Who would take his place as rector of the University of Virginia? He hoped it would be Madison, and felt better at the thought. Then he became delirious. Fifty years were swept aside. The American colonies were about to declare their Revolution to the world. He went through the motions of writing. He spoke of the Committee of Safety. He said: "Warn the Committee to be on the alert."

Jefferson became conscious again in the night. "This is

the Fourth?" he asked the people at his bedside. No one answered, for they could not bear to tell him it was not, knowing what he wanted.

"This is the Fourth?" Jefferson repeated. His son-in-law nodded. "Oh," said Jefferson and seemed pleased. Up in Washington they would be celebrating the fiftieth anniversary of the Day of Independence. He had declined the invitation to be an honored guest. He had had his own accounts to settle with history on that day. He lay back, satisfied, and history did not cheat him, for it was not until one o'clock in the afternoon of July 4th, 1826, that he breathed his last.

Up in Braintree, Massachusetts, that same day, John Adams lay dying in his ninety-first year. As the sun sank on the fiftieth anniversary of the Day of Independence, John Adams died. His last words were:

"Thomas Jefferson still lives."

NOTE ON MONTICELLO
AND
ACKNOWLEDGMENTS

Jefferson died content that Monticello would go to his daughter Martha and her children. But the gifts that had come pouring in stopped soon after his death, and the estate had to be sold to pay off debts. The house on the mountain top went through several hands: one owner tried to cultivate silkworms there; another stored grain in it and used to drive his teams up the front steps. For a long while Monticello was altogether abandoned and would have crumbled away if it had not been so sturdily built. The furniture was scattered over the country.

In 1923, almost a hundred years after its master's death, the Thomas Jefferson Memorial Foundation was organized for the purpose of buying Monticello and making of it a national shrine. Not only has the Foundation accomplished this; it has also restored the mansion and outbuildings to their original beauty and collected together again many of the furnishings. The money was raised by public subscription, much of it coming from schoolchildren.

It is to the officers of the Foundation that I owe most gratitude for assistance in writing this book:

First and foremost, to the late Anna Dauer Mann, assistant to the President, who for ten years, until her early death in the summer of 1933, devoted herself to the cause of Jefferson's

memory and the restoration of Monticello, and at whose suggestion I began the work;

To Mr. Stuart G. Gibboney, President of the Thomas Jefferson Memorial Foundation, for continuous co-operation in
extending to me the use of the Foundation's books and pictures and the facilities of its offices;

To Mr. Theodore Fred Kuper, National Director of the
Foundation, for patiently reading the book, for many criticisms and improvements, and for a host of courtesies;

To Mr. Thomas L. Rhodes, superintendent of Monticello
for the last forty-five years, for his kindness in showing me
over his domain and for anecdotes and reminiscences.

Equally kind and helpful have been officers of the University of Virginia: Dean Ivey Foreman Lewis, Professor of
Biology and Agriculture, who read my first chapter; Dean
Walter S. Rodman, Professor of Electrical Engineering, and
J. Malcolm Luck, Secretary of the Alumni Association, who
made suggestions in the last two chapters; and William H.
Wranek, Jr., Editor of the University News Service, who for
two days guided my every step through the grounds of Monticello and the University.

BOOKS

Of the many works and articles consulted in writing this book, the following were the most useful. None of them was written especially for young people, but they would find some very much worth looking into.

On Thomas Jefferson

BOWERS, CLAUDE G.—*Jefferson and Hamilton; the Struggle for Democracy in America*. By the Ambassador to Spain. A full and fascinating account of the conflict that was to decide whether America should be democratic or aristocratic.

CHINARD, GILBERT—*Thomas Jefferson, the Apostle of Americanism*. Very scholarly, especially on Jefferson's ideas.

COOKE, J. E.—*The Youth of Thomas Jefferson; or A Chronicle of College Scrapes at Williamsburg*. A work of fiction based on Jefferson's early letters to John Page.

DODD, WILLIAM EDWARD—*Statesmen of the Old South*. By the Ambassador to Germany. The essay on Jefferson, despite its brevity, is one of the most successful works on Jefferson as an actual human personality.

JEFFERSON, THOMAS—*Writings and Autobiography*. Jefferson's autobiography is very dry and brief. The letters and papers fill 20 volumes in the Monticello Edition, edited by Andrew A. Lipscomb.

KIMBALL, SIDNEY FISKE—*Thomas Jefferson, Architect*. The original architectural drawings made by Jefferson.

PIERSON, HAMILTON WILCOX—*Jefferson at Monticello*. This account is written from interviews with Edmund Bacon, Jefferson's chief overseer. It gives a picture of Jefferson as an agriculturist and in his old age, and a good description of his plantations.

RANDALL, HENRY STEPHENS—*The Life of Thomas Jefferson*. 3 volumes. Written when many people who knew Jefferson were still alive, these volumes give the most complete details of his life, but they make dull reading nowadays.

347

RANDOLPH, (MRS.) SARAH NICHOLAS—*The Domestic Life of Thomas Jefferson*. Compiled from family letters and reminiscences. Jefferson's family life and his neighborliness.

SCHOULER, JAMES—*Thomas Jefferson*. A good short life.

WILSTACH, PAUL—*Jefferson and Monticello*. The complete story of Monticello.

Background

ANBURY, MAJOR THOMAS—*Travels through Interior Parts of America in a Series of Letters*. Major Anbury was a British officer who, after being captured at Saratoga, was paroled and wrote letters home on his impressions of revolutionary Virginia.

BEARD, CHARLES A. AND MARY R.—*The Rise of American Civilization*. One of the finest American histories written. Chapters IV to IX deal with matters covered in this book.

BURNABY, REV. ANDREW—*Travels through the Middle Settlements in North America in the Years 1759 and 1760*.

BYRD, WILLIAM—*The Writings of Colonel William Byrd of Westover in Virginia, Esq.* Col. Byrd laid down the boundary line between Virginia and North Carolina, and his clever writings describe frontier and Indian life before Jefferson was born.

EARLE, ALICE MORSE—*Child Life in Colonial Days*.

FAY, BERNARD—*Revolutionary Spirit in France and America*.

FITHIAN, PHILIP VICKERS—*Journal and Letters 1767–1774*. Fithian was a young university graduate who was tutor to the children of a very wealthy Virginia planter during the years 1773–1774. His diary and letters give an interesting account of life in a manorial estate which is of special interest because of the school and social life of the children and young people.

JEFFERSON, THOMAS—*Notes on the State of Virginia*. Even today this first American geography is quite readable.

RAWLINGS, MARY—*The Albemarle of Other Days*.

SMITH, MRS. MARGARET (BAYARD)—*The First Forty Years of Washington Society*. Contains an account of Jefferson in the White House.

TYLER, LYON GARDINER—*Williamsburg, Old Colonial Capitol*.

WERTENBAKER, THOMAS J.—*Patrician and Plebeian in Virginia*.

INDEX

A

ADAMS, Abigail—Jefferson shops for, 176; letter concerning Polly Jefferson, 190; describes city of Washington, 281-2; writes letter of sympathy to Jefferson, 299

Adams, John—outlawed, 83; meets Jefferson, 89; on committee to answer Lord North's proposals, 91; and Declaration, 94, 96; rank in Harvard, 107; in Paris, 160, 163; minister to England, 167, 168; Jefferson sends him wine recipes, 175; weakness for pomp, 203-5, 231-2, 262; on British government, 210; quarrel with Jefferson over *Rights of Man*, 233; elected President, 250; keeps Washington's Cabinet, 251; confers with Jefferson on minister to France, 255-6; sets a day of fast, 258; and Matthew Lyon, 262; Hamilton's intrigues against, 265-6, 276; on unpopularity of army, 267; reconsiders XYZ affair, 269-70; defeated for re-election, 276; his "midnight judges," 279-80; flees Washington, 281; birthday celebrated, 285; Jefferson on his salary, 290; reconciliation with Jefferson, 310; letters to Jefferson, 311, 338; death, 343

Adams, Samuel—creates Committee of Correspondence, 75; outlawed, 83; asked by Jefferson for blessing on new government, 283

Agassiz, Louis (naturalist), 308

Age of Reason (Paine), 284

Alberti, Domenico (musician), 68

Alien Bill, 261-2, 264, 271; annulled, 283

Allen, Ethan, 89, 262

Ambler, Jacquelin—marries Rebecca Burwell, 49-50

American Philosophical Society, 251, 293

Anson's *Voyage around the World*, 22, 30-1

Arnold, Benedict, 136, 137, 138

Aurora (Republican newspaper), 258, 266

Austen (Vermont Republican), 263

B

BACHE, Benjamin Franklin (Republican editor), 258

Bacon, Edmund (Jefferson's overseer), 312, 313, 328, 338

Bacon, William (Jefferson's overseer), 313

Baptists, persecution of, 113-4

Barbary, *see* Pirates

Barbé-Marbois (French consul), 151

Beckwith, Colonel George (English agent), 229

Belinda, *see* Rebecca Burwell

Bellini, Professor Charles, 133, 177

Boston Tea Party, 79-80

Botetourt, Lord (Royal Governor of Virginia), 58

Breckenridge, John, 264

Brehan, Mme. de—visits America, 172-3

Brown—and the *Gaspee* incident, 74

Bryant, William Cullen, 297

Buffon, G. L. L. de, 180

Burke, Edmund, 83, 231, 232

Burr, Aaron—suggested for command, 266; tied with Jefferson for president, 276-7; duel with Hamilton, 300

Burwell, Fanny—cousin to Rebecca, 33; married to John Page, 50, 201

Burwell (Jefferson's servant), 342, 343

Burwell, Rebecca—and Jefferson, 33, 34, 39-40, 42, 48, 49; marries, 49

C

D

E

F

G

ence with, 33, 38-42, 48-9, 65, 67, 72, 132, 299; marries Fanny Burwell, 50; receives copy of Declaration, 98; runs for Governor against Jefferson, 130; in New York, second marriage, 201; begs Jefferson not to resign, 239

Paine, Thomas—writes *Common Sense*, 93; hero of Inner Revolution, 101; writes *The Rights of Man*, 232; invited by Jefferson to America, 284

Palladio, Andrea—his textbook on architecture, 64, 65, 328-9

Pendleton, Edmund—conflict with radicals, 109-10; aids in rewriting laws of Virginia, 124-6; summarizes Gerry's report, 268, 271

Petit (Jefferson's French steward), 174, 190, 289

Petit Démocrate, Le (French privateer), 246, 247

Phi Beta Kappa—founding of, 47

Pickering, Timothy, Secretary of State, 265

Pike, Lieutenant Zebulon (explorer), 297

Pinckney, General C. C.—minister to France, 254, 256-7, 267; Hamilton preferred to, 266; defeated for Presidency, 276, 300

Pinckney, Thomas (Federalist Presidential candidate), 250

Pirates, Barbary—rumor of Franklin's capture by, 164; description of, 165-7; account by Martha, 186; American tribute to, 256; Jefferson sends expedition against, 290

Pocahontas, 25, 189

Poe, Edgar Allan—student at University of Virginia, 335

Priestley, Joseph (scientist)—persecuted in America, 283, 327

Q

QUAKERS, persecution of, 112, 113; French admiration, 170

R

RALEIGH TAVERN, 8, 28, 34, 35, 48, 61, 69, 75, 87

Ramsay, Captain—Polly in love with, 190

Randall (Ben, cabinet-maker), 88, 93

Randolph, Ann (granddaughter of Jefferson), 225, 335

Randolph, Benjamin Franklin (grandson of Jefferson), 335

Randolph, Cornelia (granddaughter of Jefferson), 329, 337, 338

Randolph, Edmund (Attorney General), 211, 239

Randolph, Ellen (granddaughter of Jefferson), 335, 338

Randolph, George Wythe (grandson of Jefferson), 335

Randolph, Isham (grandfather of Jefferson), 7, 8

Randolph, James Madison (grandson of Jefferson), 335

Randolph, Jane (mother of Jefferson), 7, 8, 12, 92

Randolph, John (cousin of Jefferson), 68-9, 91

Randolph, John (of Roanoke), 107, 110

Randolph, Mary (granddaughter of Jefferson), 335

Randolph, Meriwether Lewis (grandson of Jefferson), 335

Randolph, Peter (cousin of Jefferson), 56

Randolph, Peyton—and Patrick Henry, 52-3; receives *Summary View*, 81; president of Continental Congress, 87

Randolph, Septimia (granddaughter of Jefferson), 335

Randolph, Thomas Jefferson (grandson of Jefferson), 335, 336, 338, 343

Randolph, Thomas Mann (son-in-law of Jefferson), 192; marries Martha Jefferson, 200; Congressman, 299

Randolph, Virginia (granddaughter of Jefferson), 335, 338

Randolph, William (friend of Peter Jefferson), 6, 7, 10, 11, 12

Riedesel, Baron (Hessian general), 129, 131

Riedesel, Baroness, 128

Roosevelt, Mrs. Franklin D.—copies Jefferson's chair, 320

Rossi, Vicenzo (workman of Mazzei), 77-8

Rousseau, Jean Jacques, 170, 194

Rowan, Archibald Hamilton (Irish patriot), 261

tated by Pendleton, 109; rewrites laws of Virginia, 124-6; receives presents from Jefferson, 176; aids Jefferson in rules for Senate, 252-253; successful fight for separation of state and church, 275; wills library to Jefferson, 338

XYZ

XYZ AFFAIR, 256-7, 267